W9-CGV-475

INTRODUCTION TO HEBREW

MOSHE GREENBERG
Professor of Biblical Studies
University of Pennsylvania

Prentice-Hall, Inc.
Englewood Cliffs, New Jersey

PRENTICE-HALL INTERNATIONAL, INC. *London*
PRENTICE-HALL OF AUSTRALIA, PTY., LTD. *Sydney*
PRENTICE-HALL OF CANADA, LTD. *Toronto*
PRENTICE-HALL OF INDIA (PRIVATE) LTD. *New Delhi*
PRENTICE-HALL OF JAPAN, INC. *Tokyo*

Current printing (last digit):
12 11 10 9 8 7 6 5

© 1965 by PRENTICE-HALL, INC.
Englewood Cliffs, N.J.

All rights reserved. No part of this book may be reproduced in any form, by mimeograph or any other means, without permission in writing from the publisher.

Library of Congress Catalog Card No.: 64–10135

Printed in the United States of America
48446-C

ACKNOWLEDGMENTS

I am happy to acknowledge the generous attention of the following persons whose comment and criticism have done much to lessen the imperfections of this work.

Dr. Haim Blanc went over an earlier draft of the grammar with me; the benefit of his comments to that draft continues into the present revision.

My father, Dr. Simon Greenberg, criticized the work from a pedagogic viewpoint; whatever merit it possesses on that count derives largely from his criticism.

The Hebrew parts underwent the careful scrutiny of Dr. Svi Rin.

Drs. D. N. Freedman and E. A. Speiser were good enough to review the philological material and supply many helpful observations.

I am indebted to the Department of Oriental Studies of the University of Pennsylvania and its chairman, Dr. Speiser, for having enabled me to publish and teach from successive drafts of the work and thus to accumulate precious classroom experience that I trust has accrued to its advantage.

I have dedicated this work to my parents, who instilled in me the love of the Hebrew language and its literature.

MOSHE GREENBERG

ON THE USE OF THIS BOOK

The plan of the work

The aim of this book is to teach the fundamentals of Hebrew grammar and to enable one to acquire a mastery over a basic vocabulary of Biblical Hebrew. The grammatical material has been selected on the basis of frequency, less common phenomena being omitted. Vocabulary and readings are based on a self-contained part of the Joseph story in Genesis 37–45, and illustrations of the grammar and the material for the exercises are drawn almost exclusively from these readings. The last stage of the course is the study of five chapters of Genesis. The essentials of Biblical Hebrew grammar, and roughly a third of the words of highest frequency in Biblical Hebrew (fifty occurrences and more) are included.

The order of study

The grammar and readings have been interlaced so as to illustrate and reinforce one another. Grammar sections 1–8 are to be studied consecutively. Thereafter, two readings (pp. 139–169) are to be covered

before each grammar section, as indicated at the end of each grammar section and reading.

Sections 27–30 are for reference only and are not integrated with readings. Following section 26, then, reading — which has now reached Genesis 44:10 — may proceed uninterruptedly. A convenient division of the remaining material into units is Genesis 44:11–23, 24–34; 45:1–15, 16–28.

Just before beginning the study of the biblical text the Orientation in the Hebrew Bible (pp. 173–179) may be read. To aid the student during this study, Notes on the Hebrew Text of Genesis 37, 42–45 (pp. 180–192), and a Glossary (pp. 197–207) are supplied. As each chapter is finished, the Questions for Review pertaining to it (pp. 193–196) may be utilized. The Index (pp. 219–224) brings together all the topics and grammatical terms in the book.

Abbreviations and signs

abs	absolute
apoc	apocopated form
art	the article
B.C.E	before the Common Era
c	common gender
C.E	Common Era
coh	cohortative
cond	condition(al)
conj	conjunction
cs	construct form, state
di obj	direct object
du	dual
f	feminine
fs, fpl	feminine singular, feminine plural
impf	imperfect
impf cons	imperfect consecutive
imv	imperative
inf	infinitive
juss	jussive

m	masculine
ms, mpl	masculine singular, masculine plural
MH	Modern Hebrew (Israeli)
neg	negative
part	particle
pass	passive
pers	person
pf	perfect
pf cons	perfect consecutive
pl	plural
pron	pronoun
pt	participle
s	singular
suf	suffix
term	terminitive
w	with
1	first person
1cs, 1cpl	first person common gender singular, " " " " plural
2	second person
2m, etc.	second person masculine
3	third person
3m, etc.	third person masculine
*	hypothetical form
>	becomes, became
<	(is) derived from
§	section
_'	stressed syllable; used as a rule only when stress is not on the final syllable

CONTENTS

	Introduction: The Hebrew Language	*1*
§ 1.	The Alphabet	*10*
§ 2.	Vocalization	*17*
§ 3.	The Noun Sentence	*24*
§ 4.	On the Structure of the Noun	*26*
§ 5.	The Article and the Adjective	*30*
§ 6.	The Construct State	*34*
§ 7.	Pronouns and Demonstratives	*38*
§ 8.	The Verb	*41*
§ 9.	*Qal* Perfect	*45*
§ 10.	*Qal* Imperfect and Related Forms	*49*
§ 11.	*Qal* Infinitive and Participle	*54*
§ 12.	The *Pi'el*	*58*
§ 13.	The *Hif'il*	*61*
§ 14.	Pronominal Suffixes with Masculine Nouns	*64*
§ 15.	Pronominal Suffixes with Feminine Nouns and with Verbs	*69*
§ 16.	*Wâw*-Consecutive	*74*
§ 17.	Hollow Verbs	*78*
§ 18.	The *Nif'al* and *Hiṯpa'el*	*84*
§ 19.	Final ה Verbs	*88*
§ 20.	Initial י Verbs	*93*
§ 21.	Final א and Initial א Verbs	*98*
§ 22.	Initial נ Verbs	*103*
§ 23.	Initial Laryngal Verbs	*108*
§ 24.	Middle and Final Laryngal Verbs	*113*
§ 25.	Vowel Changes in Noun Inflection	*118*
§ 26.	Segolate Nouns	*124*

§27. Word Order *128*
§28. The Accents *132*
§29. Some Effects of the Stress *135*
§30. Geminate Verbs *137*
Readings *139*
Aids to Reading the Bible *171*

Orientation in the Hebrew Bible *173*
Notes on the Hebrew Text of Genesis 37, 42–45 *180*
Questions for Review *193*
Glossary *197*

Tables of Verb and Noun Inflection *209*
Index *221*

INTRODUCTION TO HEBREW

לאבא ולאמא

-- ישעיה נט, כא

INTRODUCTION: THE HEBREW LANGUAGE

The Semitic languages

Hebrew belongs to a family of languages whose speakers anciently inhabited the area of present-day Iraq, Syria, Lebanon, Israel, Jordan, and the Arabian peninsula. In the eastern part of this region — the territory of modern Iraq — lived the ancient peoples of Assyria and Babylonia, who spoke dialects of *Akkadian.*[1]

In the west, the area from Syria to Israel comprises roughly the original home of the *Aramaic* and *Canaanite* languages (one of the latter being Hebrew). To the south, in the Arabian peninsula, the *Arabic* dialects originated. A branch of South Arabic later crossed the water to Africa, where it developed into *Ethiopic.*

Most of the peoples who lived in this area in biblical times were believed by the Israelites to have descended from Noah's son Shem

---

1 The Babylonians' own name for their language. Akkad was the chief city of the first Semitic empire in Mesopotamia (about 2300 B.C.E.); it is mentioned in the Bible in Genesis 10:10.

(written Sem in Greek and Latin Bibles). Modern scholars have accordingly found it convenient to refer to the languages spoken by them as Semitic languages, though, to be sure, the notions of filiation held by the ancient ethnographer (see Genesis 10) do not always agree with those of the modern student of these languages.[2]

"*The language of Canaan*"

To the Israelite of the monarchic period (10th–6th centuries B.C.E.) the language he spoke was "the language of Canaan" (Isaiah 19:18), which his ancestors had adopted from the natives of old Palestine (at that time called Canaan) well before it was conquered by Israel in the 13th century B.C.E. The language of the Bible is, in fact, a dialect of Canaanite, differing little from the languages spoken by Israel's neighbors–the Phoenicians, the Moabites, and the Edomites. Modern discoveries have furnished us with specimens of the languages of Canaan from as early as the 15th century B.C.E., in Palestinian forms, which are close to biblical Hebrew,[3] as well as in Syrian form, which is somewhat further removed.[4] In language, as in several aspects of their culture,

---

2 A striking example of disagreement concerns the filiation of Canaanite. According to Genesis 10:6, "Canaan," along with "Mizraim"(Egypt) and others, was a "son" of Ham. Yet we class Canaanite as a Semitic, not a Hamitic, language; i.e., Canaanite belongs rather with the languages spoken by the "sons of Shem" than with Egyptian and the other Hamitic tongues.

3 For example, Canaanite glosses in the Akkadian el-Amarna letters. These letters, discovered in Egypt in 1887, date from the 15th-14th centuries B.C.E.; they are directed to the Egyptian court from Egyptian officials and vassals in Canaan.

4 The reference is to Ugaritic, the language of a large treasure of documents unearthed at Ugarit, an ancient coastal city of Syria. The site, presently called Ras Shamra, has been yielding written documents since excavations began there in 1929.

the Israelites borrowed from their environment, though here, as in much else, the borrowed vessels were filled with new content.

The language of Canaan was the spoken and literary language of Israel to the end of the monarchy (6th century B.C.E.). The great bulk of biblical literature is composed in it, and a few contemporary extra-biblical inscriptions recovered by archaeologists in Palestine attest that the language of the Bible was really in current, vulgar use and is not an artificial literary creation. Traces remain of regional differences in the language, but these have been mostly effaced by the leveling process of later tradition.

Hebrew during the Second Temple period (5th century B.C.E.–1st century C.E.)

The Babylonian exile (586–538 B.C.E.) hastened a process that was already beginning during the last generations of Israelite independence: the coloring of Hebrew by Aramaic, the *lingua franca* of the Near East in the 6th century B.C.E. and for several centuries thereafter. We hear that the returning exiles — a minority in a non-Jewish milieu — were hard put to preserve their native language. Children of mixed marriages "spoke half in the language of Ashdod [probably a Canaanite or Aramaic dialect], and none of them could speak in the Jews' language [i.e., the language of the people of Judah], but according to the language of each people" (Nehemiah 13:24). From this time on the influence of Aramaic grew, especially in cosmopolitan Jerusalem and among the aristocratic and commercial classes.

Hebrew[5] continued as the vernacular of the rural population, which

---

5 The earliest datable use of "Hebrew" for the name of the language is found in a work of the 2nd century B.C.E. In the Bible, "Hebrew" is an ethnic appellation, infre-

comprised the bulk of the Jewish people. With the success of the Hasmonean revolt against Syrian–Greek domination and the subsequent regaining of Jewish independence under the Hasmonean dynasty (166-67 B.C.E.) Hebrew letters experienced a renascence. Court histories were composed in Hebrew, imitating biblical style, and official and administrative documents were issued in Hebrew, thus laying the groundwork for the legal language that was later to be fashioned into a fine tool in the rabbinical academies of Palestine.

At the end of the era Hebrew and Aramaic were both freely used in Jewish Palestine. It is a point of dispute among scholars as to which of the two was the original language of books written then that have survived only in non-Semitic translations (e.g., the Apocrypha). Even in the academies of Torah study both languages were employed, though the proceedings were summarized and transmitted almost exclusively in Hebrew.

Rabbinic Hebrew

After the Bible, the second great monument of the Hebrew language

---

quently used, and then chiefly to set off Israelites from other national groups. It first occurs in Genesis 14:13 in the phrase "Abram the Hebrew"; the later Jewish usage of "Hebrew" as the name of the language is based on the ethnic connotation of the word and on the idea that it was the language spoken by Abram "the Hebrew" and his descendants. Jewish etymologies carry the word back either to Eber, the ancestor of all the "Eberites" (Hebrews) of whom Abraham was a descendant (Genesis 10:21 and 11:14-26), or to a like-sounding Hebrew word meaning "the other side (namely, of the Euphrates River)," whence Abraham came (Joshua 24:3). The derivation of the word is still obscure; a connection with a flotsam element of the Near Eastern population of the 2nd millennium B.C.E. called "Hapiru" in cuneiform and "'Apiru" in Egyptian and Ugaritic sources has been widely accepted.

is Tannaitic literature — the product of scholars of the 1st century B.C.E. to the 3rd century C.E. whose commentaries upon and enlargement of the laws of the Bible crystallized in the great compendia of the Mishnah, the Tosefta, and the early Midrashim.[6] The Hebrew of the Tannaim, usually termed Mishnaic Hebrew but preferably Rabbinic Hebrew, represents a marked change from Biblical Hebrew. Its vocabulary is many times greater, doubtless including many words that accidentally failed to be recorded in the Bible, and in addition it borrowed freely from Aramaic, Greek, and Latin. Its structure is quite Aramaized; its capacity for precision remarkably augmented. Presumably originating in Hasmonean times, this Hebrew is the final stage reached in the organic growth of the ancient "language of Canaan" on Jewish soil. It represents the vernacular of the centuries just before and after the turn of the era, preserving the spiritedness and vigor of an earthy folk, but distilled and refined by scholars.

The natural base of the Hebrew language — the rural peasantry — was destroyed by the terrible bloodlettings that accompanied the two Jewish revolts against Rome (66-70, 132-135 C.E.). The second (Bar-Kochba) rebellion particulary ravaged Judaea; its population was slaughtered or deported into slavery by the hundreds of thousands. The center of Jewish life moved north into Galilee, a region of mixed population where Aramaic and Greek were the prevailing tongues. From the 3rd century even the rabbinical academies in which the study of the Mishnah was pursued adopted Aramaic as the medium of

---

6 The Mishnah and its supplement, the Tosefta, are two parallel systematizations of Jewish law. The Midrashim (pl of Midrash) are homiletic and legal commentaries to the Torah and various other biblical books. The period in question is called Tannaitic after the title of its scholars — Tanna ("reciter, teacher"), pl Tannaim.

discourse. Hebrew continued as the language of spiritual life — the synagogal liturgy and liturgical poetry, the study of Scripture and its traditional midrashic commentaries — and efforts were made to keep it up as a vernacular in some circles. But the organic life of the language as the vernacular of the Jewish people had come to an end. All further creativity in Hebrew — and there was a great deal of it — was based on a language learned from books and in schools. Rabbinic Hebrew continues even today as a literary medium for traditional scholars. Its bearers are fully capable of carrying on epistolary, and even conversational, intercourse in this medium, and in that sense Rabbinic Hebrew has never been a dead language. The point being made here is that it was a language lacking a natural linguistic habitat; it was not acquired by children as the spoken idiom of the community in which they grew up.

During the Middle Ages

The persistence of Hebrew as a vehicle of Jewish culture provided the foundation for the rise of varieties of the language during the Middle Ages, each adapted for special use. Under the influence of Islamic culture, the Jews of the Iberian peninsula developed a remarkable Hebrew literature during the 10th to 13th centuries. Poets and thinkers reflected the fulness of the Judaeo-Moslem civilization of the times, its secular as well as its religious sides in a rich and multifaceted creativity. In the hands of the best writers of the age Hebrew was as pliable an instrument as it had been in the hands of the psalmists; the latter do not eclipse the former in felicity of expression and boldness of invention.

Islamic culture also stimulated the rise of science among the Jews: it was the milieu in which Jewish philosophy, medicine, and grammar flourished. Accordingly, we find a distinct scientific-philosophic idiom

developing from about the 10th to the 15th centuries. The character of this idiom was determined by the fact that its classic, early representatives were translations from the Arabic (for the classic Jewish philosophers and scientists wrote in the language of their environment: it was chiefly for the edification of Jews living outside the Moslem world — notably in Christian Europe — that their works were translated into Hebrew). Scientific-philosophic Hebrew of medieval times has, therefore, a very marked Arabic flavor in its vocabulary, word structure, and syntax.

The modern Hebrew renascence

The renascence of Hebrew as a modern language took its rise in the 18th-century movement of enlightenment; its first object was the westernization and acculturation of the Jews of the European ghetto. The leaders of the enlightenment disdained the Yiddish vernacular of the masses, the Judaeo-German "jargon" as they contemptuously called it, and preferred to employ Hebrew as a medium of instruction and propaganda. The style they chose reflected their break with tradition; not the Rabbinic Hebrew of the religious authorities of the ghetto, but the old Biblical Hebrew — inadequate as it was for their purpose — was called into service. Thus the very language bespoke the ideal of the enlightenment: a return to the pristine source of inspiration — the pure, rational religion of the prophets (for so it was believed to have been).

The movement arose in central Europe, where it resulted in a significant literary and journalistic productivity in Hebrew. In eastern Europe the enlightenment prepared the ground for the birth, in the 19th century, of a vigorous nationalistic movement. While here, too, the linguistic

situation reflected a rejection of tradition in the tendency to prefer Biblical to Rabbinic Hebrew, east European Jewry's deeper roots in tradition showed themselves in the richer blend of all styles and epochs in the language they employed. It was in eastern Europe that the first classics of modern Hebrew literature were produced in the last years of the 19th and the first of the 20th centuries.

The revival of Hebrew as a spoken language is connected with the Zionist colonization of Palestine that began in the last decades of the 19th century. The prophet of the revival was Eliezer Ben Yehuda (1858–1922), whose tireless advocacy of resuscitation of Hebrew as a vernacular and whose monumental assemblage of the resources of the language in a *Complete Dictionary of Ancient and Modern Hebrew*[7] entitle him to be called the father of Modern Hebrew. The necessity for a common language to unify the diverse elements of the Jewish immigration helped Ben Yehuda and his colleagues persuade the leaders of the Palestinian community of the rightness of their cause. After a critical "war of languages" in 1913-14 the primacy of Hebrew in Jewish Palestine was firmly established. By the time the British Mandate was instituted Hebrew had come along far enough to be recognized, alongside Arabic and English, as one of the official languages of the Government (1922).

Thus, well before the State of Israel came into being in 1948, Hebrew had proved capable of serving as the vehicle of a modern culture as well as of a modern state. Cultivated lovingly by scholars and adopted by a dedicated population, the language had, in the course of but a half-century, spanned the gulf between medieval and modern times with astonishing success. To be sure, it is a far cry from Modern Hebrew to "the language of Canaan." Not only is the vocabulary of Modern

---

7 Completed in 16 volumes after Ben Yehuda's death.

Hebrew greatly augmented, not only does it throw together all historical varieties of Hebrew in bewildering juxtaposition, but its entire idiom and structure has undergone a radical Europeanization — inevitable, due to the European origin of most of its creators. But the chief agent of change has been the restoration of the language into the mouths of children. Hebrew has lost the timeless stability of a book language as it has re-entered the living organism of a community of generations. It is again transmitted from mouth to ear and has thus become subject to all the vicissitudes of organic life. The unpredictability of the course that Modern Hebrew has embarked upon is the sure sign that Hebrew has been reborn.

§ 1

THE ALPHABET

1.1 The Hebrew alphabet consists of 22 letters, all consonants.

Letter	*Name*		*Transcription*	*Remarks*
א	אלף	*'ȧlɛf*[1]	'	§1.3
ב	בית	*beṯ*	*b v*	§1.5
ג	גמל	*gi̇mɛl*	*g ḡ*	§1.5
ד	דלת	*dȧlɛṯ*	*d ḏ*	§1.5
ה	הא	*he*	*h*	
ו	וו	*wȧw* (MH *vȧv*)	*w* (MH *v*)	
ז	זין	*zȧ̇yin*	*z*	
ח	חית	*ḥeṯ*	*ḥ*	§1.3
ט	טית	*ṭeṯ*	*ṭ*	§1.4
י	יוד	*yoḏ*	*y*	
ך כ	כף	*kaf*	*k ḵ*	§1.5
ל	למד	*lȧ̇mɛḏ*	*l*	
ם מ	מם	*mem*	*m*	
ן נ	נון	*nun*	*n*	

1 Vowels are to be pronounced as in Spanish, Italian, or German; *ɛ* is the *e* in *set*, *ȧ* is the *a* in arm or the *o* in soft; see § 2.5.

Letter	*Name*		*Transcription*	*Remarks*
ס	סמך	*såmek̲*	*s*	
ע	עין	*ʿåyin*	ʿ	§1.3
פ ף	פא	*pe*	*p f*	§1.5
צ ץ	צדי	*ṣåd̲e*	*ṣ*	§1.4
ק	קוף	*qof*	*q*	§1.4
ר	ריש	*reš*	*r*	trill or flip of tongue-point against back of upper gums, or of uvula [cf. §1.4 (ק)] against raised back of tongue
שׂ	שׂין	*sin*	*ś*	=s
שׁ	שׁין	*šin*	*š*	*sh* as in *shoe*
ת	תו	*tåw* (MH *tåv*)	*t t̲*	§1.5

1.2 Hebrew is written from right to left, hence the predominantly leftward orientation of the letters.

Final forms are employed for the letters כ, מ, נ, פ, צ when they stand at the end of a word. In the case of כ, נ, פ, צ the downstroke is carried beneath the line (ך, ן, ף, ץ) instead of terminating in a leftward horizontal leading into the next letter of the word. The two forms of *mem* are variant developments of the earliest form (see §1.7).

The laryngals

1.3 The consonants א, ה, ח, ע are produced in the larynx and are therefore called laryngals.

The *larynx* is the "voice box" visible externally as the Adam's apple.

א is a glottal stop, produced by closing the glottis momentarily and then letting it spring open under the pressure of the breath.

The *glottis* is the opening between the vocal cords. Its extreme positions are: wide open during ordinary breathing, firmly closed when one holds one's breath with the mouth open.

ה, like English *h*, is made by narrowing the glottis so as to make the outgoing breath produce a friction noise.

ח is a very strongly whispered ה produced by tightening the throat muscles.

ע is a voiced ח.

A *voiced* sound is one in which the vocal chords are set vibrating by the outgoing breath, producing the musical sound which we call the voice.

Nonoriental speakers of MH do not usually distinguish ח from spirantized כ (see § 1.5), or ע from א.

The emphatics

1.4 The emphatics, ק, צ, ט, are produced further back in the mouth than are their nonemphatic correspondents. Precisely how they were sounded in antiquity is not certain; speakers of MH who pronounce emphatics distinctively sound them like their Arabic correspondents.

ט is a nonaspirate *t* sound produced with the back of the tongue approaching the soft palate.

An *aspirate* is a sound followed by a puff of breath. The *t* of *top* is an aspirate; the *t* of *stop* is not.

צ is an *s* sound produced with the back of the tongue raised toward the soft palate, the tip of the tongue not quite touching the back of the upper gums.

ק is a nonaspirate *k* sound produced with the back of the tongue touching the uvula.

The *uvula* is the fleshy lobe that hangs down in the center of the mouth at the back end of the soft palate.

Nonoriental speakers of MH do not usually distinguish ט from ת, or ק from כ. צ is sounded as *ts* in *pits*.

The letters begaḏ kefaṯ

1.5 The letters ת, פ, כ, ד, ג, ב (mnemonic: *begaḏ kefaṯ*[2]) each represent two sounds, a stop and a spirant.

A *stop* is produced when the outgoing breath is stopped momentarily by a closure of some part of the vocal organs. If the closure is effected by pressing the back of the tongue against the soft palate, the resultant stops are *k* or hard *g*; if by pressing the tip of the tongue against the back of the upper gums, the resultant stops are *t* or *d*; if by the closure of the lips, *p* or *b*. The first of each of these pairs (namely, *k*, *t*, *p*) are unvoiced stops; the second (namely, hard *g*, *d*, *b*) are voiced.

If, instead of completely stopping the exit of breath, the tongue and the lips leave it a very narrow passage, the outgoing breath produces a friction noise. This sound is called a *spirant*. Spirantized *t*, for example, is like the *th* of *thin*; spirantized *d*, like the *th* of *then*.

In writing, the stop sound is indicated by placing a dot, called in Hebrew *dâgeš qal* "gentle dagesh," within the letter: בּ *b*, גּ (hard) *g*, דּ *d*, כּ *k*, פּ *p*, תּ *t*. To indicate the spirant, the dagesh is left out: ב *v*, ג *g* (unrolled French *r*), ד *ḏ* (*th* as in *then*), כ *ḵ* (German *ch* as in *ach*), פ *f*, ת *ṯ* (*th* as in *thin*).

Begaḏ kefaṯ are primarily stops; they become spirants after a vowel [except when they are long consonants (§ 2.11)] or mobile *šewå*, a slurred vowel [§ 2.7 (b)]. Spirantization is the effect of the open position of the vocal organs in the pronunciation of the vowel being carried into the pronunciation of *begaḏ kefaṯ*. Thus פ is a stop in the name of the letter פא *pe*, but it is spirantized in אלף *ʾalɛ̆f*, since here it follows upon a vowel.

In the pronunciation of MH ג, ד, ת are never spirantized, but are always pronounced as the stops (hard) *g*, *d*, *t*.

2 A raised e indicates a hurried vowel, like the *e* of *stupefy*.

The development of the alphabet

1.6 The Hebrew alphabet, like the language, is Canaanite. It represents the crowning achievement of a long history of writing in the ancient Near East; the traces that remain of its development suggest that its Syro-Palestinian inventors were inspired by both Egyptian and Mesopotamian methods of writing.

Writing began in the 4th millennium B.C.E. both in Egypt and in Sumer. In both lands, pictographs gradually gave way to syllabic and logographic symbols that were numbered in the hundreds at any given time and so demanded long training to master. Some time in the first part of the 2nd millennium B.C.E., an anonymous genius living in Syria-Palestine — the crossroads of Egypt and Mesopotamia — hit upon the idea of reducing the number of symbols to the number of consonants in his language. The idea may have been stimulated by the development in Egyptian hieroglyphics of signs used purely as consonants, though in Egypt itself this never led to alphabetization.

Starting from the first half of the 2nd millennium, the glimmerings of alphabetic writing appear in Palestine in short inscriptions on tablets, potsherds, and household objects. Related to these are other inscriptions found at ancient Egyptian copper mines in the Sinai peninsula, dating from the 16th–14th centuries B.C.E. and commonly believed to be Canaanite.

Solid evidence for the achievement of an alphabet are the alphabetic texts from the ancient Syrian town of Ugarit (modern Ras Shamra) from the 15th-14th centuries B.C.E. Here in a simplified cuneiform script (showing Mesopotamian influence) the Canaanite dialect of Ugaritic is represented in hundreds of literary, religious and administrative texts. Even the present order of the letters was known at Ugarit — and all

signs point to the fact that the Ugaritic alphabet was not an original invention. By the 15th century, then, the Canaanites had already a long history of alphabetic experimentation behind them.

1.7 The direct ancestor of the Hebrew alphabet is the Phoenician, used by the Canaanites, the Israelites, and such neighbors of Israel as the Arameans and Moabites. This script, along with the Canaanite names and order of the letters, passed to the Greeks, probably through the agency of traders, in about the 9th century B.C.E.

As time went on the Phoenician script was gradually modified by the Arameans in the direction of simplicity and greater cursiveness. By the 6th century it had assumed a shape in which the present Hebrew letters can easily be recognized. During the 6th-4th centuries Hebrew scribes adopted the Aramaic "square letters," as they are called, abandoning the old Phoenician script for good [save in the case of some sectaries and for sporadic nationalistic purposes (e.g., for inscriptions on Jewish coins)].

The following specimens show the relationship of these scripts to one another.

Phoenician—Old Hebrew	*Greek*	*Aramaic*	*Hebrew*
𐤀	A	𐡀	א
𐤃	Δ	𐡃	ד
𐤄	E	𐡄	ה
𐤇	Θ	𐡇	ח
𐤊	K	𐡊	כ
𐤌	M	𐡌	מ
𐤎	Σ	𐡎	ס
𐤕	T	𐡕	ת

Assignment:

1. Learn the names of the letters in their proper order. Know how to read and write the names in Hebrew.

2. For each occurrence of the *begad kefat* letters in the names, determine why it is a stop or spirant, as the case may be.

§ 2
VOCALIZATION

2.1 The chief bearers of meaning in Hebrew, as in the other Semitic languages, are the consonants; the vowels serve merely to specify more particularly the meaning conveyed by the consonants. For example, the consonant group אכל carries the general sense of *eating*. Vowels particularize the meaning as follows: *'ôḵɛl* "food," *'åḵal* "he ate." *'aḵilå* "eating." Because of this the inventors of the alphabet ignored the vowels, relying on the native reader of the language to determine from the context which of these possibilities best fit the situation.

The vowel letters

2.2 To keep the possibilities within a reasonable range, however, it was desirable to limit their number as far as possible. If, in addition to the three words above, *'åḵelå* "she ate," *'åḵelu* "they ate," *'iḵli* "eat!" (fs), *'oḵel* "eater" are also candidates for the proper reading of the group אכל, the variables become too many to be handled with ease. Some method for indicating vowels — at least the major, long vowels — was early felt to be needed. From the 9th century B.C.E., Hebrew writing began to indicate final long vowels by the signs for consonants which

were formed with the same vocal organs as the vowel sound: י for final *i* (and later *e*), ו for final *u* (and later *o*), and ה for final *å* and other vowels. This usage soon became consistent and standard.

Some centuries later the use of vowel letters to indicate long vowels within the body of a word came into vogue: י stood for *i* and certain *e*'s, ו for *u* and certain *o*'s. This stage is reflected in biblical spelling, but while the usage of vowel letters to indicate final vowels was standardized early, there is no consistency in the use of internal vowel letters in the Bible.

The abovementioned forms of אכל appear in biblical spelling as follows:

1.	*'ōḵɛl* "food"	אכל	4.	*'åḵᵉlå* "she ate"	אכלה
2.	*'åḵal* "he ate"	אכל	5.	*'åḵᵉlu* "they ate"	אכלו
3.	*'ᵃḵilå* "eating"	אכלה or אכילה	6.	*'iḵli* "eat!" (fs)	אכלי
			7.	*'oḵel* "eater"	אכל or אוכל

2.3 Where the vowel letters appear, the writing is said to be *full*. When the vowel letters are absent in words in which they may be expected to appear, the writing is said to be *defective*. In the above words, the alternative spellings of 3 and 7 are defective.

As a rule, the later a text the fuller the spelling. In Rabbinic Hebrew texts vowel letters are often used even for short vowels.

Systems of vocalization

2.4 Needless to say, the use of vowel letters was not a final answer to the problem of representing the vowels. The ambiguity of each vowel letter, the frequency of defective spelling, and the complete lack of representation of the short vowels made it desirable to invent another,

more exact method of vocalization. The need became acute after Hebrew ceased as a vernacular and the tradition of the correct pronunciation of the sacred text of the Bible became more and more removed from life.

Several systems of diacritical marks were gradually developed to indicate the vowels with greater exactitude. Three main systems are known, of which the Tiberian — developed by the 10th century in the city of Tiberias in Palestine — finally prevailed, to become the standard vocalization of Hebrew.

The vocalization marks do not replace the old vowel letters, which had been fixed in the biblical text centuries before and were regarded as sacrosanct by the vocalizers. They merely add precision to them. Accordingly, the vocalizers never changed the spelling of any word, but rather added their diacritical marks above, below, and inside of the letters. Thus the present biblical text displays two systems of vocalization: the primitive vowel letters (normally representing only long vowels), and the new, Tiberian vocalization marks superimposed upon them.

The Tiberian vocalization

2.5 The Tiberian vocalization consists of the following signs:

Sign	*Name*[1]	*Transcription*	*Quality*
ָ	קָמֵץ *qåmeṣ*	*å*	*a* as in *arm*
ָ	קָמֵץ חָטוּף *qåmeṣ ḥåṭuf*[2]	*ŏ*	*o* as in *soft*

The *Ashkenazic* (central and east European) pronunciation of both *qåmeṣ*'s is as *o* in *soft*. That the Tiberian vocalizers also pronounced both alike is indicated by their failure to distinguish them graphically. Their pronunciation was probably similar to the Ashkenazic.

---

1 Variant pronunciations of each of these names exist; e.g., *qåmeṣ, qåmåṣ ; s*ᵉ*gol ; ḥiriq.*

2 Called also קָמֵץ קָטָן *qåmeṣ qåṭån.*

The *Sephardic* (Spanish-Portuguese) pronunciation of *qåmeṣ* differs from that of *qåmeṣ ḥåṭuf* as indicated above. MH pronunciation is in this case patterned after the Sephardic, and thus does not distinguish *qåmeṣ* from *påṯaḥ* (see the next sign).

Qåmeṣ ḥåṭuf is a phonetic variant of *qibbuṣ* (see below). As distinguished from *qåmeṣ*, it occurs only in syllables that are closed [§ 2.7 (a), § 25.2 (b)] and unstressed; e.g., אָזְנַיִם *'öz-nåyim*. (See further § 28.2[2].)

Sign	*Name*		*Transcription*	*Quality*
ַ	פַּתַח	*påṯaḥ*	*a*	*a* as in *arm*
ֶ	סֶגוֹל	*segol*	*ɛ*	*e* as in *set*
ֵ	צֵרֵי	*ṣere*	*e*	*e* as in *grey* (MH *ṣere* often = *segol*)
ִ	חִירֶק	*ḥireq*	*i*	*i* as in *siesta*
ֹ	חוֹלֶם	*ḥolem*	*o*	*o* as in *mold*
וּ	שׁוּרֶק	*šureq*	*u*	*u* as in *rule*
ֻ	קִבּוּץ	*qibbuṣ*	*u*	*u* as in *rule*

(a) All the vowel signs, except *ḥolem* and *šureq*, are sublinear. *Ḥolem* is placed above and to the left of its consonant, as in כֹּל *kol* "all," or directly over an already present vowel letter ו, as in חוֹלֶם. *Šureq* is a dot placed within an already present vowel letter ו to designate it as *u*, as in שׁוּרֶק.

Vowels are pronounced after the consonant beneath which (in the case of *ḥolem*, above which) they are written; see the names of the vowels for examples.

(b) The laryngals ע ,ח ,ה when they are final[3] cannot be preceded by any but an *a* vowel. Should another vowel precede them, a brief *a* sound glides in between the laryngal and that vowel. This *a* is indicated by *påṯaḥ* written beneath, but pronounced before, the laryngal; e.g., רוּחַ

[3] When final ה is consonantal it is marked with a dot called מַפִּיק *mappiq* to distinguish it from final ה as a vowel letter: תָּמַהּ *åmah* "he was astonished."

rûaḥ "spirit," שׁוֹמֵעַ *šomêa'* "(one who) hears." Such a *pa̱ṯaḥ* is called a "furtive *pa̱ṯaḥ*."

2.6 The vowel signs were designed to indicate the quality (sound) of the vowels, not their quantity (the length of time taken to utter the sound). Most of the signs are, in fact, ambiguous as to quantity, representing sounds that are now long, now short. The determinants of the quantity of vowels will be discussed later (§25). For the present it may be noted that ָ, ֵ, and ֹ represent vowels that are often a lengthened modification of short *a*, *i*, *u* (represented by ַ, ִ, ֻ), respectively.

Distinctions of length are not observed in the pronunciation of MH, but they are significant for understanding various grammatical phenomena.

The šewå

2.7 To mark a consonant that has no full vowel the Tiberian system uses a special sign ְ called שְׁוָא *šewå*.

(a) The *šewå* indicating complete vowellessness is called *quiescent šewå*. It occurs at the end of a syllable and closes the syllable; e.g., שִׁמְעוֹן *šim-'on* "Simeon," יִשְׁמֹר *yiš-mor* "he will guard."

(b) The *šewå* pronounced as a slurred vowel — like the *e* of English *stupefy* — is called *mobile šewå*. Mobile *šewå* derives from a full vowel that has become slurred owing to a shift in the word stress. For example, the feminine of גָּדוֹל *gåḏol* "big" is גְּדוֹלָה *geḏolå*, in which the mobile *šewå* represents a slurred *a*-vowel. Again, the plural of שָׁמַר *šåmar* "he guarded" is שָׁמְרוּ *šåmeru* (syllabified: *šå-meru*) "they guarded," in which the mobile *šewå* represents the slurred *pa̱ṯaḥ*. Every *šewå* at the beginning of a word (or a syllable) is a mobile *šewå*.

(c) Mobile *šewå* retains enough of the force of its original vowel to cause a following *begaḏ kefaṯ* to be spirantized. Thus, for example, when the particle לְ־ *le* "to" is prefixed to בֵּן *ben* "son," the result is לְבֵן *leven* "to a son."

The distinction between quiescent and mobile *šewå* is fundamental for understanding the vocalization. In the pronunciation of MH, however, mobile *šewå* tends to be elided; the two examples of (b) are normally sounded as *gdolå*, *šåmru*.

2.8 Vowellessness at the end of a word is not marked by a *šewå*; thus בַּיִת *baʿyiṯ* "house." Chief exceptions to this rule are (a) final *kaf*, which, when vowelless, bears in it a *šewå* in order to distinguish it from final *nun*; thus הָלַךְ *hålaḵ* "he went"; and (b) final *tåw* of 2 fs pronominal elements; e.g., אַתְּ *'att* "you" (fs), שָׁמַרְתְּ *šåmart* "you (fs) guarded."

2.9 With the laryngals (א, ה, ח, ע), and occasionally with other consonants, *šewå* may be combined with *paṯaḥ*, *segol*, or *qåmeṣ ḥåṭuf* to form the composites חֲטָף פַּתַח *ḥaṭåf paṯaḥ*, חֲטָף סֶגוֹל *ḥaṭåf segol*, and חֲטָף קָמֵץ *ḥaṭåf qåmeṣ*. The purpose of the *ḥaṭåf*s is chiefly to facilitate the articulation of the laryngals: יַעֲקֹב *Ya'aqov* "Jacob," אֱלֹהִים *'elohim* "God," צָהֳרַיִם *ṣōhŏraʿyim* "noon."

The dåḡeš

2.10 To mark certain peculiarities in consonants, the Tiberian vocalization places a dot, called דָּגֵשׁ *dåḡeš*, inside the letters.

(a) To indicate that *begaḏ kefaṯ* are to be pronounced as stops, a dot called דָּגֵשׁ קַל *dåḡeš qal*, "gentle *dåḡeš*," is placed within them (§ 1.5).

(b) Long (doubled) consonants are indicated by a dot called דָּגֵשׁ חָזָק *dåḡeš ḥåzåq* "strong *dåḡeš*." Consonants are long:

1. as a result of the juncture of two identical consonants, the

first of which ends its syllable; the two are fused into one long consonant: נָתַנְנוּ* > נָתַנּוּ *nåṯannu* "we gave";

2. as a result of the assimilation of one consonant to another: מִן זֶה *min zɛ* "from this" combines as מִזֶּה *mizzɛ*, with *nun* having assimilated to *záyin*, and *záyin*, therefore, long;

3. as a characteristic of the form: the article הַ־ *ha-* "the" requires that the following consonant be long: הַבֵּן *habben* "the son."

2.11 When *begaḏ kefaṯ* are long (i.e., bear within them a strong *dåges̱*), they are pronounced as stops even though they follow a vowel (as in the case of הַבֵּן). The strong *dåges̱* thus serves the function of the gentle *dåges̱* when it appears in *begaḏ kefaṯ*.

Assignment

Learn the names of the vowels and other diacritical marks. Know their functions.

§ 3

THE NOUN SENTENCE

3.1 A sentence (or clause) in which the subject is a noun and the predicate is a noun or adjective is called a noun sentence (or clause). Its simplest form consists of two nouns, or a noun and an adjective, juxtaposed. The tense of a noun sentence is determined by its context; when there is no context, the present tense is understood.

Examples, using יוֹסֵף "Joseph," גָּדוֹל "big," נַעַר "(a)[1] lad": יוֹסֵף גָּדוֹל "Joseph is big"; יוֹסֵף נַעַר "Joseph is a lad."

3.2 The normal order is subject—predicate. If the predicate is to be emphasized, it is placed first; e.g., נַעַר יוֹסֵף "Joseph is (only) a lad."

* * * * * * *

big	גָּדוֹל	Joseph	יוֹסֵף
small	קָטֹן	lad	נַעַר
brother	אָח	Benjamin	בִּנְיָמִין

1 Hebrew has no element equivalent to the English indefinite article ("a[n]").

what?	מַה[2]	Jacob	יַעֲקֹב
who?	מִי	man	אִישׁ

Read and translate :

1. יוֹסֵף נַעַר. 2. בִּנְיָמִין נַעַר. 3. יוֹסֵף גָּדוֹל. 4. בִּנְיָמִין קָטֹן.
5. בִּנְיָמִין אָח. 6. יוֹסֵף אָח. 7. יַעֲקֹב אִישׁ. 8. יַעֲקֹב גָּדוֹל.
9. קָטֹן בִּנְיָמִין. 10. אִישׁ יַעֲקֹב.

Render your translation back into Hebrew, without referring to the above. Answer in Hebrew :

1. מַה יוֹסֵף? 2. מַה בִּנְיָמִין? 3. מִי נַעַר? 4. מִי גָּדוֹל? 5. מִי קָטֹן? 6. מִי אָח? 7. מִי אִישׁ? 8. מַה יַעֲקֹב?

---

2 See § 5.3 for vocalization of מה.

§ 4

ON THE STRUCTURE OF THE NOUN

4.1 Hebrew recognizes two genders: masculine and feminine, and all nouns are either the one or the other according to their form. The masculine has no distinguishing sign; the feminine is distinguished by the ending ־ָה or ־ת. Thus נַעַר "lad," אָח "brother," and אִישׁ "man" are masculine; פָּרָה "cow," אִשָּׁה "woman," כֻּתֹּנֶת "tunic" are feminine.

Some nouns are feminine though they lack the characteristic feminine ending. Among these are אֶרֶץ "land," עִיר "city," פַּעַם "a time"; paired organs of the body, such as יָד "hand," עַיִן "eye," אֹזֶן "ear," רֶגֶל "foot"; and words denoting females, such as אֵם "mother," אָתוֹן "she-donkey."

4.2 The regular plural ending of masculines is ־ִים; e.g., נְעָרִים "lads," אַחִים "brothers"

The regular plural ending of feminines is ־וֹת; e.g., פָּרוֹת "cows."

But the plural form is not always indicative of the gender of a word. The plural of אָב "father" is אָבוֹת, of אִשָּׁה "woman" is נָשִׁים. Hence the singular

is a better guide to gender — but see §4.1. The only sure index of gender, when it is available, is the form of an associated adjective or verb, which must agree with the noun in gender.

4.3 Hebrew also has a dual number, indicated by the termination ־ַיִם, which serves to indicate two-ness in certain nouns; e.g., expressions of time: פַּעַם "one time," פַּעֲמַיִם "twice." In objects that come normally in pairs, the dual termination is used for the plural: יָדַיִם "hands," אָזְנַיִם (*'ŏz-*) "ears," רַגְלַיִם "feet," עֵינַיִם "eyes."

Thus "seven eyes" is שֶׁבַע עֵינַיִם (this does *not* mean "seven pairs of eyes"). To say "two eyes," the word for "two" must be used: שְׁתֵּי עֵינַיִם.

4.4 The main stress generally falls on the final syllable; e.g., יוֹסֵף *Yosêf*, נְעָרִים *ne'ârîm*.

In certain vowel patterns, however, the stress always falls on the first of a pair of vowels, resulting in penultimate (next-to-last-syllable) stress. Such vowel patterns are ־ָ־ְ (רֶגֶל), ־ֶ־ (כֶּתֹנֶת, אֹזֶן), ־ַ־ (פַּעַם, נַעַר), ־ִ־ (עַיִן, and in the dual termination; e.g., יָדַיִם). There are other exceptions to the rule of final stress; they will be marked with ־ as they occur.

4.5 When a noun is inflected in the plural or dual, or an adjective receives the feminine ־ָה, these plural, dual, and feminine terminations attract the stress to themselves, away from the beginning of the word. Consequently, the beginning of the word is pronounced hurriedly, with the result that vowels there may be shortened or slurred, or such sequences as *-ayi-* contracted into single vowels. For example: the *ḥôlem* of אֹזֶן is shortened to *qâmeṣ ḥâṭuf* in the dual אָזְנַיִם (*'ŏz-*); the *qâmeṣ* of גָּדוֹל is slurred to mobile *šewâ* in the feminine גְּדוֹלָה and the plural גְּדוֹלִים, גְּדוֹלוֹת; the sequence *-ayi-* in עַיִן contracts to *e* in the dual עֵינַיִם.

These vowel changes due to the shift in the place of the stress follow regular rules, but discussion of them must be deferred till later. For the present it is enough to note that when in the course of inflection the stress of a word shifts forward (to the end), vowel changes — shortening or slurring — may be expected to occur at the beginning of the word.

* * * * * * *

The words of the previous lesson are inflected thus:

big	fpl גְּדוֹלוֹת, mpl גְּדוֹלִים, f גְּדוֹלָה, גָּדוֹל		lad	pl נְעָרִים, נַעַר	
small	fpl קְטַנּוֹת, mpl קְטַנִּים, f קְטַנָּה[1], קָטֹן		brother	pl אַחִים, אָח	
			man	pl אֲנָשִׁים, אִישׁ	

New words:

Leah	לֵאָה	and (*see below for vocalization*)	וְ־
to, for (*see below for vocalization*)	לְ־	Reuben	רְאוּבֵן
hand	f (du יָדַיִם) יָד	Rachel	רָחֵל
eye	f (du עֵינַיִם) עַיִן	woman, wife	(pl נָשִׁים) אִשָּׁה

Vocalization of וְ: Normally וְ; וּ before labials (ב, מ, פ) and *šewå* (e.g., וּרְאוּבֵן, וּבִנְיָמִין); before *ḥaṭåf*s, vocalized with the vowel component of the *ḥaṭåf* (e.g., וַאֲנָשִׁים).

Vocalization of לְ: Normally לְ; לִ before *šewå* (e.g., לִרְאוּבֵן); before *ḥaṭåf*s, vocalized with the vowel component of the *ḥaṭåf* (e.g., לַאֲנָשִׁים).

"Have" is expressed thus: לְיוֹסֵף אָח "Joseph has a brother" (lit., "to Joseph [is] a brother"). (אָח לְיוֹסֵף can mean the same, but when the phrase is in the predicate it means only "a brother to/of Joseph"; e.g., בִּנְיָמִין אָח לְיוֹסֵף "Benjamin is a brother to/of Joseph)."

---

1 This and the following forms are based on an alternative base קָטָן

Read and translate:

1. בִּנְיָמִין וְיוֹסֵף נְעָרִים. 2. יוֹסֵף וּבִנְיָמִין קְטַנִּים. 3. רְאוּבֵן אָח. 4. יוֹסֵף וּבִנְיָמִין וּרְאוּבֵן אַחִים. 5. יוֹסֵף וּבִנְיָמִין קְטַנִּים וּרְאוּבֵן גָּדוֹל. 6. רְאוּבֵן אִישׁ וְיַעֲקֹב אִישׁ. 7. יַעֲקֹב וּרְאוּבֵן אֲנָשִׁים. 8. יַעֲקֹב וּרְאוּבֵן גְּדוֹלִים. 9. רָחֵל אִשָּׁה וְלֵאָה אִשָּׁה. 10. רָחֵל וְלֵאָה נָשִׁים. 11. רָחֵל גְּדוֹלָה וְלֵאָה גְּדוֹלָה. 12. רָחֵל וְלֵאָה גְּדוֹלוֹת. 13. לְיַעֲקֹב נָשִׁים. 14. רָחֵל וְלֵאָה נָשִׁים לְיַעֲקֹב. 15. יָד גְּדוֹלָה. 16. יָדַיִם גְּדוֹלוֹת. 17. עַיִן קְטַנָּה. 18. עֵינַיִם קְטַנּוֹת. 19. לַאֲנָשִׁים יָדַיִם וְעֵינַיִם. 20. לְמִי עֵינַיִם? לְאִישׁ עֵינַיִם. 21. לְמִי יָד? לְאִשָּׁה יָד. 22. לַאֲנָשִׁים וּלְנָשִׁים יָדַיִם וְעֵינַיִם.

Answer in Hebrew:

1. מִי נְעָרִים? 2. מִי קְטַנִּים? 3. מִי גְּדוֹלִים? 4. מִי אַחִים? 5. מִי אֲנָשִׁים? 6. מִי אִשָּׁה? 7. מִי נָשִׁים? 8. מִי גְּדוֹלָה? 9. מִי גְּדוֹלוֹת? 10. לְמִי נָשִׁים? 11. מִי נָשִׁים לְיַעֲקֹב? 12. לְמִי יָדַיִם? 13. לְמִי עֵינַיִם? 14. מַה קְטַנָּה?

§ 5

THE ARTICLE AND THE ADJECTIVE

The article

5.1 The article is ·הַ־; i.e., prepositive הַ followed by a long consonant (one bearing within it a strong *dåg̲eš*): הַנַּעַר "the lad."

5.2 Laryngals (א, ה, ח, ע) and ר are not normally susceptible to lengthening and hence do not normally bear strong *dåg̲eš* in them. When the article is prefixed to a word beginning with a laryngal it is vocalized thus:

(a) If the initial consonant is א or ר, the ַ of the article is lengthened to ָ (§ 2.6) by way of compensation: הָאִישׁ "the man," הָרֶגֶל "the foot." This usually occurs with initial ע as well: הָעַיִן "the eye."

(b) If the initial consonant is ה or ח, the article remains הַ, though the laryngal does not take *dåg̲eš*: thus הַחַיָּה "the animal."

(c) But if the initial consonant is חָ or unstressed הָ or עָ, the article is vocalized הֶ: הֶעָרִים "the cities," הֶחָכָם "the wise man."

5.3 The vocalization of מה "what?" is similar. Generally מה is closely attached to the following word and is vocalized ·מַה; e.g., מַה זֹּאת "What

is this (f)?" (In the biblical text a hyphen connects מַה with the next word, making the two words a single grammatical unit.)

When the initial consonant of the following word is a laryngal or ר:

(a) If it is א or ר, the *pa̱ṯaḥ* of מה is lengthened to *qāmeṣ*; e.g., מָה רָאָה "what did he see?"

(b) If it is עָ, חָ, הָ, the vocalization is מֶה; e.g., מֶה הָיָה "what was...?"

(c) If it is ע, ח, ה with other vowels, the vocalization varies, except that before the article it is regularly מָה.

5.4 When the article is preceded by the prepositions ל־ "to, for," ב־ "in," כ־ "like," the ה is elided and its vowel is thrown back to the preposition; thus לַנַּעַר (<לְ+הַנַּעַר) "to the lad," כָּאִישׁ (<כְּ+הָאִישׁ) "like the man," בֶּעָרִים (<בְּ+הֶעָרִים) "in the cities."

The adjective

5.5 In Hebrew, attributive adjectives follow their noun and agree with it in number and gender; moreover, if the noun has the article, the attributive must have it too.

An attributive adjective is one that, in English, stands before the noun it qualifies to denote the qualification as assumed rather than predicated. In *the big man* the adjective *big* is an attributive, as distinguished from *the man is big*, where it is a predicate adjective.

Examples of the attributive:

"a big woman"	אִשָּׁה גְּדוֹלָה	"a big man"	אִישׁ גָּדוֹל
"the big woman"	הָאִשָּׁה הַגְּדוֹלָה	"the big man"	הָאִישׁ הַגָּדוֹל
"big women"	נָשִׁים גְּדוֹלוֹת	"big men"	אֲנָשִׁים גְּדוֹלִים
"the big women"	הַנָּשִׁים הַגְּדוֹלוֹת	"the big men"	הָאֲנָשִׁים הַגְּדוֹלִים

The explanation for this thoroughgoing agreement is that the attributive adjective is really in apposition to its noun. The adjective is actually a substantive (a noun equivalent), and the phrase אִישׁ גָּדוֹל is thus literally "a man, a big one," while הָאִישׁ הַגָּדוֹל is literally "the man, the big one."

5.6 Predicate adjectives also agree with their nouns in number and gender, but they do not take the article (except where they would in English).

Examples of the predicate adjective:

"the woman is big" הָאִשָּׁה גְּדוֹלָה	"the man is big" הָאִישׁ גָּדוֹל
"the women are big" הַנָּשִׁים גְּדוֹלוֹת	"the men are big" הָאֲנָשִׁים גְּדוֹלִים

[but רְאוּבֵן הַגָּדוֹל "(it is) Reuben (who) is the big one"]

Ambiguities do remain. By itself אִישׁ גָּדוֹל can mean both "a big man" and "a man is big"; and while הָאִישׁ הַגָּדוֹל would normally be taken as "the big man," it may also mean "(it is) the man (who) is the big one." Such theoretical ambiguities are almost always resolved by the context.

* * * * * * *

house(hold) m (pl בָּתִּים)	בַּיִת	cow	פָּרָה (pl פָּרוֹת)
field m (pl שָׂדוֹת)	שָׂדֶה	good	טוֹב
father	אָב	shepherd	רוֹעֶה (pl רוֹעִים)
is not m	אֵינֶנּוּ	beau- (fpl יָפוֹת, mpl יָפִים)	יָפֶה (f יָפָה)
where?	אֵיפֹה	tiful, handsome	
		in	בְּ־

Read and translate:

1. הָאָח קָטֹן. 2. הָאַחִים הַקְּטַנִּים. 3. הַפָּרָה טוֹבָה. 4. הָרוֹעֶה טוֹב. 5. הָאִשָּׁה יָפָה. 6. הַנָּשִׁים הַיָּפוֹת בַּבַּיִת. 7. הַשָּׂדֶה הַגָּדוֹל יָפֶה. 8. הַפָּרָה בַּשָּׂדֶה. 9. הָאָב הַטּוֹב בַּבַּיִת. 10. הַשָּׂדֶה הַיָּפֶה לְיַעֲקֹב. 11. לָרוֹעִים בָּתִּים. 12. יַעֲקֹב הָאָב. 13. יַעֲקֹב אָב טוֹב. 14. הָאַחִים רוֹעִים. 15. הָרוֹעִים הַטּוֹבִים בַּשָּׂדֶה. 16. הַפָּרוֹת בַּשָּׂדֶה. 17. בִּנְיָמִין נַעַר קָטֹן וְיוֹסֵף נַעַר גָּדוֹל. 18. בִּנְיָמִין אֵינֶנּוּ בַּשָּׂדֶה וְיַעֲקֹב אֵינֶנּוּ בַּשָּׂדֶה.

19. בִּנְיָמִין וְיַעֲקֹב וְהַנָּשִׁים בַּבַּיִת. 20. הָאַחִים הַגְּדוֹלִים רוֹעִים בַּשָּׂדֶה הַיָּפֶה. 21. הָאָב יַעֲקֹב אֵינֶנּוּ רוֹעֶה.

Answer in Hebrew :

1. מִי רוֹעִים? 2. מִי אֵינֶנּוּ רוֹעֶה? 3. מִי בַּשָּׂדֶה? 4. מִי בַּבַּיִת? 5. מִי גָּדוֹל וּמִי קָטֹן? 6. אֵיפֹה הַנָּשִׁים? 7. לְמִי הַנָּשִׁים? 8. אֵיפֹה יַעֲקֹב? 9. אֵיפֹה יוֹסֵף? 10. אֵיפֹה בִּנְיָמִין? 11. מָה הָאַחִים? 12. לְמִי הַבַּיִת? 13. לְמִי בָּתִּים? 14. לְמִי הַשָּׂדֶה?

Translate :

1. The good shepherd is in a field. 2. Jacob has a beautiful house. 3. In the big house are a man and a woman. 4. The wife is good to Jacob. 5. The big man is a shepherd. 6. The small brother is good. 7. The handsome lad is in the house. 8. The shepherd has a beautiful wife.

Rewrite the preceding exercise, pluralizing all nouns and adjectives.

§ 6

THE CONSTRUCT STATE

6.1 Two nouns may be combined so that the second defines or otherwise particularizes the first (e.g., through indicating its possessor). Thus יָד "hand" may be defined by הַנַּעַר "the lad" in the combination יַד הַנַּעַר "the lad's hand." The first noun, יַד, is said to govern the second, and to be in *construction* (i.e., combination; Lat. *construere* "bring together") with it. Phonetically the two are considered one word: the first, or governing, noun loses its main stress (retaining, at best, a secondary stress), which now falls on the second, or governed, noun. Consequently, the governing noun often undergoes vowel reduction or loss. Note how the *qâmeṣ* of יָד shortens to *paṯaḥ* in construction. Again, when בַּיִת is in construction with, say, הָאִישׁ, as in בֵּית הָאִישׁ "the man's house," the sequence *ayi* contracts to *e* due to the shift of stress.

6.2 The governing noun, which often undergoes change, is said to be in the *construct state*; the governed noun, unchanged, is said to be in the *absolute state*. The various internal vowel changes that nouns in the

construct state undergo will be treated later; here we shall note certain regular changes that occur at the end of such nouns.

(a) The feminine termination הָ־ becomes תַ־. Example: פָּרָה "cow," פָּרַת יַעֲקֹב "Jacob's cow."

The explanation of this change is as follows: The feminine termination was originally *-aṯ*. When in final position, the *ṯ* dropped off, and the vowel was compensatorily lengthened to *å*. This final, long *å* was represented by the vowel-letter ה, later by the preceding *qåmeṣ*. Thus פָּרָה < **påraṯ*. Now, the condition of the loss of the *ṯ* was that it be the final consonant. When *påraṯ* was in the construct state, it was the first part of a compound word; the *ṯ*, now internal, was not dropped, and thus the original *-aṯ* termination reappears in the feminine singular construct state.

(b) The dual ַ־ַיִם and the — usually masculine — plural ִ־ים terminations become ֵי־. Examples: עֵינַיִם "eyes," עֵינֵי הָאִישׁ "the man's eyes"; אַחִים "brothers," אֲחֵי יוֹסֵף "Joseph's brothers."

No change occurs in the termination of masculine singular and the— usually feminine — plural termination וֹת־.

6.3 A noun in the construct state does not take the definite article, because it is already defined by the noun it governs. The governed noun, on the other hand, may take the article. These, then, are the possibilities: בֵּית אִישׁ "a man's house"; בֵּית הָאִישׁ "the man's house" ("the house of the man," but also "a house of the man").

* * * * * * *

Henceforth, for nouns in which there is some irregularity, the following data will be given in parentheses and in this order: singular construct state, plural, plural construct state. Construct state forms will be followed by a hyphen.

Irregular forms of some nouns so far met with:

man	אִישׁ (אִישׁ־, אֲנָשִׁים, אַנְשֵׁי־)	father	אָב (אֲבִי־, אָבוֹת, אֲבוֹת־)
woman	אִשָּׁה (אֵשֶׁת־, נָשִׁים, נְשֵׁי־)	brother	אָח (אֲחִי־, אַחִים, אֲחֵי־)

בַּיִת (בֵּית־, בָּתִּים, בָּתֵּי־) house(hold)

New words

land	f (w art אֶרֶץ (הָאָרֶץ	these	אֵלֶּה
Canaan	כְּנַעַן	son	בֵּן (בֶּן־, בָּנִים, בְּנֵי־)
Judah	יְהוּדָה	he	הוּא
sheep (more exactly: small cattle — sheep, goats)	f צֹאן	they	m הֵם

The 3 pers pronoun is frequently used as a binder between the subject and predicate of a noun sentence; e.g., יַעֲקֹב הוּא אִישׁ "Jacob is a man."

Read and translate:

1. יַעֲקֹב הוּא אֲבִי יוֹסֵף וַאֲבִי רְאוּבֵן. 2. אֵלֶּה בְּנֵי יַעֲקֹב: רְאוּבֵן וִיהוּדָה[1] וְיוֹסֵף וּבִנְיָמִין. 3. בְּנֵי יַעֲקֹב הֵם אֲחֵי יוֹסֵף. 4. רְאוּבֵן הוּא בֶּן יַעֲקֹב. 5. הוּא רוֹעֵה צֹאן.[2] 6. בְּנֵי יַעֲקֹב הֵם רוֹעֵי צֹאן. 7. רָחֵל אֵשֶׁת יַעֲקֹב. 8. עֵינֵי רָחֵל יָפוֹת. 9. נְשֵׁי יַעֲקֹב טוֹבוֹת. 10. נְשֵׁי יַעֲקֹב בְּבֵית יַעֲקֹב. 11. בֵּית יַעֲקֹב בְּאֶרֶץ כְּנַעַן. 12. הָאָרֶץ אֶרֶץ יָפָה. 13. אֲחֵי יוֹסֵף רוֹעֵי צֹאן בְּאֶרֶץ כְּנַעַן הַיָּפָה. 14. בִּנְיָמִין אֲחִי יוֹסֵף הַקָּטֹן אֵינֶנּוּ רוֹעֶה. 15. בִּנְיָמִין הַקָּטֹן וּנְשֵׁי יַעֲקֹב בַּבַּיִת. 16. לַאֲחֵי יוֹסֵף בָּתִּים. 17. בְּבָתֵּי הָאַחִים נָשִׁים. 18. אֵשֶׁת רְאוּבֵן טוֹבָה. 19. אֵלֶּה נְשֵׁי יַעֲקֹב: רָחֵל וְלֵאָה. 20. פָּרַת אֵשֶׁת יַעֲקֹב גְּדוֹלָה. 21. פָּרוֹת הַנָּשִׁים בַּשָּׂדֶה. 22. הַצֹּאן בַּשָּׂדֶה וְהַשָּׂדֶה בָּאָרֶץ.

---

1 Note that וִי־ > וְיִ־.

2 Not a tautology. רוֹעֶה (cs רוֹעֵה) means "one who pastures" ("pastor" in the original sense); standing alone it is understood to refer to צֹאן, but the full expression is רוֹעֵה צֹאן.

Answer in Hebrew :

1. אַבִי מִי יַעֲקֹב? 2. מִי בְּנֵי יַעֲקֹב? 3. מִי אֲחֵי יוֹסֵף? 4. מִי רוֹעֵי צֹאן? 5. מִי נְשֵׁי יַעֲקֹב? 6. לְמִי עֵינַיִם יָפוֹת? 7. אֵיפֹה נְשֵׁי יַעֲקֹב? 8. אֵיפֹה בֵּית יַעֲקֹב? 9. אֵיפֹה רוֹעֵי הַצֹּאן? 10. מִי אֵינֶנּוּ רוֹעֶה? 11. מִי בַּבַּיִת? 12. מִי בְּבָתֵּי הָאַחִים? 13. אֵיפֹה פָּרוֹת הַנָּשִׁים? 14. אֵיפֹה הַצֹּאן? 15. אֵיפֹה הַשָּׂדֶה?

Translate :

1. Who is he? He is Joseph's father. 2. Who are they? They are Joseph's big brothers. 3. The beautiful land is the land of Canaan. 4. Judah's wife has small sons. 5. These are men of Canaan. 6. Jacob's wives have sheep. 7. The sheep of Judah's son are in the field. 8. Jacob's sons have good wives.

§ 7

PRONOUNS AND DEMONSTRATIVES

7.1 The independent personal pronouns are:

plural			*singular*		
we	אֲנַחְנוּ, נַחְנוּ (אָנוּ)	1c	I	אֲנִי, אָנֹכִי	1c
you	אַתֶּם	2m	thou	אַתָּה	2m
you	אַתֵּן (אַתֶּן), אַתֵּנָה	2f	thou	אַתְּ	2f
they	הֵם, הֵמָּה	3m	he	הוּא	3m
they	הֵנָּה (הֵן)	3f	she	הִיא	3f

הִיא is written הוּא throughout the Pentateuch in all but eleven occurrences; the reason for this is uncertain.

Forms in parentheses are found in Postbiblical Hebrew.

The independent pronouns may be used only as subjects (or in agreement with subjects); they cannot be used as objects or with prepositions.

7.2 In addition to the independent pronouns there are pronominal suffixes, which may be attached to nouns to indicate possession or to

prepositions or verbs to indicate their object. For example, the 3ms suffix ־וֹ may be attached to nouns, as in צֹאנוֹ "his sheep"; to prepositions, as in לוֹ "to him," or to verbs, as in שְׁמָרוֹ "he guarded (שָׁמַר) him."

The pronominal suffixes will be set forth in detail later.

7.3 The demonstratives are:

plural		*singular*	
these	אֵלֶּה c	this	זֶה m
			זֹאת f

The demonstratives for far objects — "that," "those" — are the 3 pers independent pronouns: הוּא, הִיא, הֵם, הֵנָּה.

The demonstratives may be used as pronouns or as adjectives.

(a) As pronouns: זֶה אִישׁ "this is a man," זֹאת אִשָּׁה "this is a woman," אֵלֶּה אֲנָשִׁים "these are men," הוּא הָאִישׁ "that is the man."

(b) As adjectives: הָאִישׁ הַזֶּה "this man," הָאִישׁ הַהוּא "that man," הָאֲנָשִׁים הָהֵם "those men" (note the *qâmeṣ* of הָהֵם). The demonstrative, as well as the noun, takes the article.

7.4 When a noun is qualified both by an attributive and a demonstrative adjective, the order is attributive–demonstrative; e.g., הָאִישׁ הַגָּדוֹל הַזֶּה "this great man."

* * * * * * *

Read and translate :

1. מִי אַתָּה? אֲנִי יַעֲקֹב אֲבִי יוֹסֵף. 2. מִי אַתֶּם? אֲנַחְנוּ בְּנֵי יַעֲקֹב. 3. מִי אַתְּ? אֲנִי אִשֶּׁת יַעֲקֹב. 4. וּמִי אַתֶּן? אֲנַחְנוּ נְשֵׁי רְאוּבֵן. 5. מִי זֶה? זֶה בִּנְיָמִין אֲחִי יוֹסֵף הַקָּטָן. 6. מִי זֹאת? זֹאת אִשֶּׁת רְאוּבֵן הַטּוֹבָה. 7. מִי

אֵלֶּה? אֵלֶּה צֹאן יַעֲקֹב. 8. הַבָּנִים הָאֵלֶּה בְּנֵי יַעֲקֹב הֵם. 9. מִי הַנְּעָרִים הַקְּטַנִּים הָהֵם? הֵם רוֹעֵי צֹאן יַעֲקֹב. 10. הַבָּתִּים הָאֵלֶּה וְהַשָּׂדֶה הַהוּא לִרְאוּבֵן. 11. לְמִי הַפָּרָה הַהִיא? הִיא לִבְנֵי יַעֲקֹב. 12. אַנְשֵׁי הַבַּיִת הַזֶּה גְּדוֹלִים הֵם וְטוֹבִים. 13. הָאָרֶץ הַיָּפָה הַזֹּאת אֶרֶץ כְּנַעַן הִיא.

Translate:

1. What are you? I am a shepherd. 2. Whose son is that? That is Jacob's son. 3. Reuben's beautiful wife is in this house. 4. The houses of the sons are in this land. 5. Those are the hands of a man, and these are the eyes of a woman. 6. Reuben has a large hand. 7. This house is not small. 8. Those sheep belong to those men. 9. That field is good for the cows. 10. Those cows have big eyes. 11. Whose cow is this? She belongs to Jacob's men.

§ 8

THE VERB

Roots

8.1 One of the chief characteristics of the Semitic languages is that roots of three consonants, expressing some general idea, are the basis of most words. By means of fixed vowel patterns and formative elements the root is embodied in words particularizing aspects and nuances of the root idea. (In the language itself of course we meet only the words from which the root is a grammatical abstraction.)

Thus the root פתח "opening" is embodied in the words פָּתַח "he opened," נִפְתַּח "he (it) was opened," פֶּתַח "doorway."

The root שקל "weight" is embodied in the words שָׁקַל "he weighed," נִשְׁקַל "he was weighed," שֶׁקֶל "a *shekel* weight," מִשְׁקָל "weight."

The root שמר "guarding" is embodied in the words שָׁמַר "he guarded," נִשְׁמַר "he was guarded, he guarded himself," מִשְׁמָר "guardhouse, jail."

8.2 There is also a large number of biconsonantal roots, from which are derived the "hollow" verbs (§ 17) — verbs having a long vowel between their two root consonants. These roots exhibit the same patterning; e.g.,

from קוּם "standing, arising" are derived קָם "he stood, arose," מָקוֹם "place" (lit., "where one stands"); from בּוֹא "coming" are derived בָּא "he came," מָבוֹא "entrance."

Verb patterns

8.3 The first word of each series in §8.1 — פָּתַח, שָׁקַל, שָׁמַר — illustrates one verb pattern, active in meaning. The second word of each series — נִפְתַּח, נִשְׁקַל, נִשְׁמַר — illustrates another, passive (and, in the case of נִשְׁמַר, reflexive) in meaning. Note that besides the internal vowel difference the passive pattern augments the root with a preformative נ.

Other verb patterns are seen in סִפֵּר "he recounted, told" and its passive סֻפַּר "(it) was recounted." These patterns have an internal augment in the lengthening of the middle root consonant (indicated by the *dâgeš*). The pattern of הִתְאַפֵּק "he restrained himself" — reflexive in meaning — shows the same internal augment and a preformative הִתְ besides. The patterns of הִזְכִּיר "he reminded" and its passive הָזְכַּר (*hŏzkar*) "he was reminded" have a preformative ה as an augment.

These patterns may be grouped according to their form and interrelationship thus:

III	II	I	
הִזְכִּיר	סִפֵּר	שָׁמַר	active
הָזְכַּר	סֻפַּר	נִשְׁמַר	passive
	הִתְאַפֵּק	נִשְׁמַר	reflexive

For convenience the patterns have been given names: The שָׁמַר pattern, since it is wholly unaugmented, is called קַל *qal* "light" (i.e., "unencumbered"). For the rest, the model root פעל ("acting") is articulated with the vowels and augments of each pattern, the resulting forms being the names of the patterns. Thus נִשְׁמַר belongs to the נִפְעַל

nif'al pattern, סִפֵּר to the פִּעֵל *pi'el*,[1] הִזְכִּיר to the הִפְעִיל *hif'il*, and so on. The system of Hebrew verb patterns is, then, as follows:

hif'il group	*pi'el* group	*qal* group	
הִפְעִיל (הִזְכִּיר)	פִּעֵל (סִפֵּר)	קַל (שָׁמַר)	active
הָפְעַל (הָזְכַּר)	פֻּעַל (סֻפַּר)	נִפְעַל[2] (נִשְׁמַר)	passive
	הִתְפַּעֵל (הִתְאַפֵּק)	נִפְעַל (נִשְׁמַר)	reflexive

Very few verbal roots actually appear in all patterns.

The interrelation of members within each group is clear; it remains only to indicate the relation of *pi'el* and *hif'il* to *qal*.

8.4 Roughly speaking the relation is this: In the *pi'el*, the verbal idea of the *qal* is made more complex or given a special nuance; *qal* סָפַר "he counted," *pi'el* סִפֵּר "he recounted, told" [compare early English "tell" = count (as in "teller"), modern English "tell" = recount].

The *hif'il* is commonly causative: the subject makes the object do the action or be in the state expressed by the *qal* verb; *qal* זָכַר "he remembered," *hif'il* הִזְכִּיר "he reminded" (lit., "made remember").

Comparable in English are "lie" (שָׁכַב), "lay" (הִשְׁכִּיב); "fall" (נָפַל), "fell" (הִפִּיל < הִנְפִּיל*).

8.5 Other, less common, patterns exist, of which the by-forms of the *pi'el* group appearing with biconsonantal and otherwise irregular roots are the most important. כִּלְכֵּל "he sustained" (root כול) illustrates the *pilpel* pattern, a by-form of *pi'el* found with some hollow verbs. הִתְגּוֹלֵל "he found a pretext" (root גלל) illustrates the *hiṯpolel* pattern, a by-form of *hiṯpa'el* found with some geminate (§30) and hollow verbs.

---

1 Since the laryngal ע is not susceptible to lengthening (cf. § 5.2), the lengthened middle root consonant of *pi'el* cannot be indicated in the name.

2 Originally the passive of *qal* was expressed by a *pu'al* form (presumably distinguished from the *pu'al* passive of *pi'el* by its short middle consonant); thus שֻׁמַר* "he was guarded," נִשְׁמַר "he guarded himself." This *qal* passive survives only rudimentarily in Biblical Hebrew, and in most cases is vocalized as the passive of *pi'el*.

* * * * * * *

Identify the root and verb pattern of the following verbs:

1. הָלַךְ 2. נִבְהַל 3. הִשְׁלִיךְ 4. חִפֵּשׂ 5. נִכְמַר 6. גָּנַב 7. בִּקֵּשׁ 8. אָהַב
9. הִפְשִׁיט 10. סִפֵּר 11. יָדַע 12. הִתְחַנֵּן 13. הִרְחִיק 14. דִּבֵּר
15. הִתְאַבֵּל 16. לָקַח 17. נִשְׁאַר 18. מִלֵּא 19. הִתְנַפֵּל 20. הִשְׁבִּיר.

In the following verbs there are some irregularities, owing to the presence of a laryngal or a weak consonant (א, ה)*; identify the verb pattern:*

1. מָצָא 2. נִמְצָא 3. נִחֵשׁ 4. שִׁלַּח 5. נֶאֱמַן 6. הֶאֱמִין 7. הֶחֱיָה 8. עָלָה
9. כִּלָּה 10. הִתְנַחֵם 11. מֵאֵן 12. הִתְרָאָה 13. נֶאֱסַר 14. חָטָא
15. עָשָׂה 16. הִתְוַדַּע.

Supply the meaning:

שָׁמַע	he heard	:	נִשְׁמַע	————
"	he heard	:	הִשְׁמִיעַ	————
פָּשַׁט	he undressed (intr.)	:	הִפְשִׁיט	————
מָכַר	he sold	:	נִמְכַּר	————
מָלַךְ	he was king	:	הִמְלִיךְ	————
בִּקֵּשׁ	he sought	:	בֻּקַּשׁ	————
יָרַד	he went down	:	הוֹרִיד (*hif'il*)	————
בָּחַן	he tested	:	נִבְחַן	————
הִשְׁלִיךְ	he threw	:	הָשְׁלַךְ	————
סִפֵּר	he narrated	:	סֻפַּר	————
נִחַם	he consoled	:	הִתְנַחֵם	————
מִלֵּא	he filled	:	הִתְמַלֵּא	————
בָּא[3] (*qal*)	he came	:	הֵבִיא (*hif'il*)	————
מֵת (*qal*)	he died	:	הֵמִית (*hif'il*)	————
שָׁב (*qal*)	he came back	:	הֵשִׁיב (*hif'il*)	————

(*To be followed by Reading 1, p. 139.*)

3 This and the following two verbs derive from hollow roots (§ 8.2).

§ 9

QAL PERFECT

Active and stative roots

9.1 The *qal* expresses the verbal idea of the root in its simplest sense; thus from יֹשֵׁב "sitting," יָשַׁב "he sat"; from אהב "loving," אָהַב "he loved"; and from שׁמר "guarding," שָׁמַר "he guarded."

9.2 These roots all convey the idea of some activity. There are, however, roots denoting quality or state. Verbs derived from such roots are *stative*, as opposed to *active* verbs derived from active roots. So, for example, from זקן "agedness," זָקֵן "he was/became aged"; from כבד "heaviness," כָּבֵד "he was/became heavy"; from קטן "smallness," קָטֹן "he was/became small." Stative verbs are in reality nothing but adjectives inflected verbally.

The perfect

9.3 Each verb pattern has two aspects: a *perfect* and an *imperfect.*[1] The perfect (used in the sense of Lat. *perfectus*, "carried through to the

---

1 These are commonly called "tenses"; but "tense" is here a misnomer, since the perfect and imperfect do not denote *time* of action or state so much as *type* of action or state. See ahead in the text and §10.1.

end, finished") denotes action that is completed and over with, or a state achieved and complete. It generally corresponds to English past tenses and is conventionally rendered by the English past, though the precise nuance depends on the context.

Often, especially with statives, the perfect denotes the English present perfect or the present; i.e., it is expressive of an accomplished act or state whose effect is presently felt or apparent. Thus כָּבֵד may also be rendered "he has become/is heavy."

9.4 The *qal* perfect has an active form — שָׁמַר "he guarded," with *pàṯaḥ* as the second vowel — and two stative forms — כָּבֵד "he was heavy" and קָטֹן "he was small," with *ṣére* and *ḥôlem*, respectively, as second vowel. This, the 3ms, is called the *groundform*. The inflectional elements are affixed to the end of the groundform; they are *afformatives*.

The *qal* perfect:

	plural				*singular*		
1c	שָׁמַרְנוּ	כָּבַדְנוּ	קָטַנּוּ(=קָטֹנְנוּ*)		שָׁמַרְתִּי	כָּבַדְתִּי	קָטֹנְתִּי
2m	שְׁמַרְתֶּם	כְּבַדְתֶּם	קְטַנְתֶּם (-*ṭŏn*-)		שָׁמַרְתָּ	כָּבַדְתָּ	קָטֹנְתָּ
2f	שְׁמַרְתֶּן	כְּבַדְתֶּן	קְטַנְתֶּן (-*ṭŏn*-)		שָׁמַרְתְּ	כָּבַדְתְּ	קָטֹנְתְּ
3c	שָׁמְרוּ	כָּבְדוּ	קָטְנוּ		שָׁמַר	כָּבֵד	קָטֹן
					שָׁמְרָה	כָּבְדָה	קָטְנָה

(a) Note that the *ṣére*-stative is identical with the active except in the groundform. The *ḥôlem*-stative, on the other hand, retains its characteristic vowel throughout the 1 and 2 pers.

(b) Afformatives made up of one consonant are not stressed; the stress remains on the second syllable, as in the groundform. But the "heavy," biconsonantal afformatives of 2mpl and 2fpl (־תֶן, ־תֶם) are stressed. Consequently, in these forms the *qâmeṣ* of the first syllable is slurred to mobile *šewâ*. Moreover, in the *ḥôlem*-stative, the now unstressed *ḥôlem* is shortened to *qâmeṣ ḥâṭuf*.

(c) The afformatives of the 1cpl ־נוּ, 2ms ־תָּ, 2fs ־תְּ, 2mpl ־תֶּם, and 2fpl ־תֶּן are identical with the terminations of the corresponding independent pronouns. The afformative of the 1cs ־תִּי may be derived from the *-ki* of אָנֹכִי with $k > t$ under the influence of the 2 pers afformatives. The 3 pers afformatives are noun terminations: ־ָה for fs, and ־וּ for the pl (an old plural termination of nouns).

* * * * * * *

Conjugate :

יָשַׁב, זָקֵן, יָכֹל "be able."

Complete with the correct perfect form of the indicated verb :

שָׁמַר: 1. אַתֶּם _____ אֶת הַצֹּאן. 2. רָחֵל וְלֵאָה _____ אֶת הַנְּעָרִים. 3. אֲנַחְנוּ _____ אֹתוֹ.

יָשַׁב: 4. אַתְּ _____ בַּבַּיִת. 5. רָחֵל _____ בְּבֵית יַעֲקֹב. 6. יַעֲקֹב וּבִנְיָמִין _____ בַּבַּיִת.

אָהַב: 7. אֲנִי _____ אֶת הַבֵּן. 8. אַתָּה _____ אֶת הַדָּבָר. 9. אֲנַחְנוּ _____ אֶת הָאָרֶץ.

שָׂנֵא: 10. הִיא _____ כָּל רָע. 11. אֲחֵי יוֹסֵף _____ אֹתוֹ.

זָקֵן: 12. אַתֶּם _____. 13. לֵאָה _____. 14. אֲנַחְנוּ _____.

כָּבֵד: 15. הָאִישׁ _____ מִן הָאִשָּׁה. 16. הַנָּשִׁים _____. 17. יַד הָאָב _____ עַל הַבֵּן.

Change the number of the subjects in the preceding exercise and complete again.

Vocalize and translate :

1. הנשים ישבו בבית כי זקנו. 2. שמרתם את הצאן מכל רע. 3. אהבנו את הארץ. 4. יְדי האיש כבדו כי זקן. 5. הדבר קטן בעיני

האיש. 6. לאה, עם מי ישבת? 7. ישבה אשת הרועה ושמרה את כל בניו. 8. שנאו את הדבר הרע ההוא. 9. לא הגיד לו איפה ישב כי שנא אתו.

(*To be followed by Reading 3, p. 141.*)

§ 10

QAL IMPERFECT AND RELATED FORMS

10.1 The imperfect aspect expresses action or state as unaccomplished, continuing, or customary. It corresponds generally to English present and future: יִשְׁמֹר "he guards, will guard." When expressing continuity or custom (e.g., Genesis 44:5 זֶה אֲשֶׁר יִשְׁתֶּה אֲדֹנִי בּוֹ "this is (the very one) from which my lord *always drinks*"), it may refer to the past as well (e.g., Judges 21:25 אִישׁ הַיָּשָׁר בְּעֵינָיו יַעֲשֶׂה "every man *used to do* as he pleased").

10.2 Occasionally (especially in poetry) the imperfect is used as a simple past tense, like the perfect. In all likelihood this is due to the coalescence with the imperfect of a distinct preterit form found in Akkadian. A far more important survival of this preterit is the so-called *imperfect consecutive* (see §16).

10.3 The imperfect also expresses that which may, could, should, is wished, or is supposed to be. For example: Genesis 37:8 הֲ... תִּמְלֹךְ עָלֵינוּ "Do... *you mean to be king* over us?"; 37:10 הֲ... נָבוֹא "*Are...*

we supposed to come?"; 43:7 הֲ... נֵדַע כִּי יֹאמַר "*Could... we have known* that he would say"; 44:8 וְאֵיךְ נִגְנֹב "How, then, *could we steal?*"

10.4 The inflectional elements of the imperfect are attached to the beginning (*preformatives*) and the end (*afformatives*) of the verb form.

The imperfect of active verbs has *ḥôlεm* as its second, thematic vowel (יִשְׁמֹר "he will guard"). The thematic vowel of both statives is *pa̰ṯaḥ* (יִכְבַּד "he will be heavy," יִקְטַן "he will be small").

The *qal* imperfect:

	singular			*plural*		
1c	אֶשְׁמֹר	אֶכְבַּד	אֶקְטַן	נִשְׁמֹר	נִכְבַּד	נִקְטַן
2m	תִּשְׁמֹר	תִּכְבַּד	תִּקְטַן	תִּשְׁמְרוּ	תִּכְבְּדוּ	תִּקְטְנוּ
2f	תִּשְׁמְרִי	תִּכְבְּדִי	תִּקְטְנִי	תִּשְׁמֹרְנָה	תִּכְבַּדְנָה	תִּקְטַנְּה (=תִּקְטַנֶּנָה)[1]
3m	יִשְׁמֹר	יִכְבַּד	יִקְטַן	יִשְׁמְרוּ	יִכְבְּדוּ	יִקְטְנוּ
3f	תִּשְׁמֹר	תִּכְבַּד	תִּקְטַן	תִּשְׁמֹרְנָה	תִּכְבַּדְנָה	תִּקְטַנְּה

(a) The preformatives of the 1 and 2 pers are either the initial (א־) or characteristic consonant (נ־, ת־) of the corresponding independent pronouns. The preformative of 3m (י־) is of uncertain origin. That of 3f is probably the same as the *t* of the original feminine noun termination [§ 6.2(a)].

(b) To distinguish 2fs from 2ms, an old feminine termination ־ִי [which appeared also in the original form of the 2fs independent pronoun אתי* (*'atti*) as in the written text of II Kings 4:16, 23] is employed. The 2 and 3mpl are distinguished from their respective singulars by the old plural noun termination ־וּ, which also appears in the pf 3cpl. The 2 and 3fpl are distinguished from their respective singulars by the afformative ־נָה, found also in the corresponding independent pronouns אַתֵּנָה, הֵנָּה.

---

1 Cf. § 2.10(b)1.

The cohortative, the jussive, and negative commands

10.5 The *cohortative* expresses volition on the part of the 1 pers: אֶשְׁמְרָה "let me guard!" "I would (fain) guard," נִשְׁמְרָה "let's guard!" Its form is the impf 1 pers with *paragogic* (i.e., protracting) הָ־.

Thus:

plural			*singular*		
נִקְטְנָה	נִכְבְּדָה	נִשְׁמְרָה	אֶקְטְנָה	אֶכְבְּדָה	אֶשְׁמְרָה

10.6 The *jussive* expresses volition concerning the 2 or 3 pers: תִּשְׁמֹר "may you (ms) guard!" יִשְׁמֹר "may he (let him) guard." In *qal* of the regular verb the jussive forms are identical with the impf 2 and 3 pers.

10.7 Negative commands are expressed by אַל with the jussive: אַל תִּשְׁמֹר "don't guard!" אַל יִשְׁמֹר "may he (let him) not guard!"

The imperative

10.8 Positive commands are expressed by the imperative. The imv ms is generally identical with the base to which the preformatives of the imperfect are attached, and may be derived by removing the תִּ־ preformative of the 2ms, thus שְׁמֹר(תִּ). The rest of the forms follow closely the impf 2 pers.

	plural			*singular*	
m	שִׁמְרוּ	כִּבְדוּ	m	שְׁמֹר	כְּבַד
f	שְׁמֹרְנָה	כִּבַּדְנָה	f	שִׁמְרִי	כִּבְדִי

Imperatives do not occur for קָטֹן-type statives.

10.9 The imv ms is often found with paragogic הָ־; e.g., שְׁלֻחָה, lengthened from שְׁלַח "send!" Originally the lengthened form expressed emphasis or urgency, but this is no longer evident in many cases.

* * * * * * *

Conjugate in the qal *imperfect and imperative :*

זָקֵן, מָלַךְ.

Complete with the imperfect of the indicated verbs :

שָׁמַר: 1. הַבֵּן _____ אֶת הָאֲלֻמּוֹת. 2. אַתָּה _____ אֶת הָאַחִים.
3. הָאִשָּׁה _____ אֶת הַדָּבָר.
מָלַךְ: 4. יוֹסֵף _____ עַל אֶחָיו. 5. אַל _____ אִשָּׁה עַל הָאָרֶץ!
6. אֲנִי _____ עַל כָּל הָאֲנָשִׁים.
זָקֵן: 7. הָאֵם _____. 8. הָאָב _____. 9. אַתְּ _____.
כָּבֵד: 10. יַד הַזָּקֵן _____. 11. הָאִישׁ _____ מִן הָאִשָּׁה.
12. אַתָּה _____.

Change subjects and verbs of the above to plural and complete again (*pl of* אֵם *is* אִמּוֹת).

Vocalize and translate :

1. חלמתי חלום על השמש. 2. אמך מלכה עלינו. 3. הנה הנער אשר שמר את הצאן. 4. אחיך שמרו את הבתים. 5. את שמרת את בניו מכל רע. 6. זקנו עוד. 7. יד האיש אשר מלך כבדה עלינו. 8. לא שמרתם את השדה.

Change above verbs to imperfect.

Change the following negative commands to positive ones (*i.e., imperatives*) *:*

1. אַל תִּשְׁמֹר![2] 2. אַל תִּמְלְכִי! 3. אַל תִּכְבְּדוּ! 4. אַל תִּמְלֹךְ! 5. אַל

---

2 Hereafter in the Hebrew exercises imperatives (positive and negative) will be indicated by an exclamation mark.

תִּזְקַן! 6. אַל תִּזְקְנוּ! 7. אַל תִּשְׁמֹרְנָה! 8. אַל תִּשְׁמְרִי! 9. אַל תִּכְבַּדְנָה! 10. אַל תִּכְבְּדִי! 11. אַל תִּמְלְכוּ! 12. אַל תִּשְׁמְרוּ!

(*To be followed by Reading 5, p. 144.*)

§ 11

QAL INFINITIVE AND PARTICIPLE

The infinitive absolute

11.1 There are two infinitives, an absolute and a construct. The infinitive absolute takes the form שָׁמוֹר[1]; it is commonly used to add some sort of emphasis to the finite verb, which immediately follows it. For example, in Genesis 37:8 הֲמָלֹךְ תִּמְלֹךְ עָלֵינוּ אִם מָשׁוֹל תִּמְשֹׁל בָּנוּ "Do you *really* mean to be king over us? Do you *really* mean to rule us?" The two infinitives absolute express the indignation of the brothers over Joseph's pretentious dreams. Similarly 37:10 הֲבוֹא נָבוֹא "Are we *actually* supposed to come?...." Other kinds of emphasis: 43:7 שָׁאוֹל שָׁאַל הָאִישׁ "The man inquired *closely*"; הֲיָדוֹעַ נֵדַע "Could we *possibly* have known"; 37:33 טָרֹף טֹרַף[2] יוֹסֵף "Joseph *must* have been torn to pieces."

---

1 Often written defectively (i.e., without the vowel letter, see § 2.3) as in some of the following examples. (The infinitive absolute of the biconsonantal roots is like בּוֹא.)

2 A rare example of old passive *qal* (§ 8.3, note 2).

The infinitive construct

11.2 Whereas the infinitive absolute is not inflected or commonly brought into grammatical construction with other words in the sentence,[3] the infinitive construct is. It is a verbal noun, the name of the action or state expressed by the verb, having the form שְׁמֹר "(the act of) guarding" in the *qal* regular verb. [Statives, too, generally have *ḥôlem* in the infinitive construct, notwithstanding their *a*-vowel in the imperfect; e.g., שְׂנֹא "(the state/act of) hating" from שָׂנֵא–יִשְׂנָא.] Like all nouns, the infinitive construct may govern another noun (שְׁמֹר הָאִישׁ "the man's guarding," בּוֹא יוֹסֵף "Joseph's coming") and take pronominal suffixes (שָׁמְרוֹ "his guarding," בּוֹאִי "my coming") and prepositions (כְּבוֹאִי "at my coming" = "when I come"). Most commonly it appears with לְ־ in the form לִשְׁמֹר, employed just like the English infinitive "to guard."

The participles

11.3 The active participle has the form שׁוֹמֵר "(one) guarding"; the statives, כָּבֵד "heavy" and יָכֹל "able." Stative participles are pure adjectives.

The participle inflects like any noun or adjective:

	plural				*singular*		
m	שׁוֹמְרִים	כְּבֵדִים	יְכֹלִים	m	שׁוֹמֵר	כָּבֵד	יָכֹל[4]
f	שׁוֹמְרוֹת	כְּבֵדוֹת	יְכֹלוֹת	f	שׁוֹמֶרֶת (שׁוֹמְרָה)	כְּבֵדָה	יְכֹלָה

---

3 With some exceptions; e.g., when it is used as an imperative: שָׁמוֹר אֶת יוֹם הַשַּׁבָּת (Deuteronomy 5:12) "Keep the Sabbath day."

4 Since קָטֹן does not inflect regularly it is here replaced by יָכֹל.

11.4 Being a verbal adjective, the active participle has the qualities both of a verb and of an adjective. Like an adjective, it may be used as an attributive or in the predicate; e.g., הָאִישׁ הַשּׁוֹמֵר "the guarding man" ("the man who is guarding"); הָאִישׁ שׁוֹמֵר "the man is guarding." And just as an adjective may be used substantivally (הַגָּדוֹל "the big one"), so may a participle: הַשּׁוֹמֵר "the guard" (lit., "the guarding one"). As a substantive, it may be in construct with a following noun, שׁוֹמֵר הָאִישׁ "the man's guard" ("the one guarding the man"), or take pronominal suffixes, שׁוֹמְרוֹ "his guard."

Like a verb, the participle may govern an object; e.g., יוֹסֵף שׁוֹמֵר אֶת הַצֹּאן "Joseph is guarding the sheep."

The use of רוֹעֶה illustrates the substantival and verbal sides of the participle: in יוֹסֵף רוֹעֶה "Joseph is a shepherd," the substantival; in יוֹסֵף רוֹעֶה אֶת הַצֹּאן "Joseph is tending the sheep," the verbal.

11.5 Active verbs have a passive participle, which inflects thus: ms שָׁמוּר "guarded," fs שְׁמוּרָה, mpl שְׁמוּרִים, fpl שְׁמוּרוֹת.

* * * * * * *

Complete with active or stative participle of indicated verb :

מָצָא: 1. יוֹסֵף _____ אֶת אֶחָיו. 2. הָרוֹעִים _____ אֶת הַצֹּאן.
3. הַנָּשִׁים _____ אֶת בְּנוֹ.

הָלַךְ: 4. אִשֶּׁת יַעֲקֹב _____ אֶל הַבַּיִת. 5. הֵן _____ אֶל הַשָּׂדֶה.
6. בְּנֵי יַעֲקֹב _____ שְׁכֶמָה.

אָהַב: 7. טוֹב הָאִישׁ הָ_____ שָׁלוֹם. 8. טוֹבָה הָאִשָּׁה הָ_____ אֶת הָאִישׁ הַהוּא.

זָקֵן: 9. הָאִשָּׁה _____. 10. הַנָּשִׁים הַ_____ בַּבַּיִת. 11. אַחַי _____.

מָלַךְ: 12. נְעָרִים _____ עָלֵינוּ. 13. הָאִשָּׁה הַ_____ טוֹבָה. 14. רַע הָאִישׁ הַ_____ עַל הָאָרֶץ.

Complete with passive participle of verb in the first clause :

1. הוּא שׂוֹנֵא[5] אֶת הָאִישׁ; הָאִישׁ _____. 2. לוֹקְחִים אֶת הָאִשָּׁה; הָאִשָּׁה _____. 3. שׁוֹמְרִים אֶת הַדָּבָר; הַדָּבָר _____. 4. הָאֵם שׁוֹמֶרֶת אֶת בָּנָיו; בָּנָיו _____. 5. לוֹקְחִים אֶת הַפָּרוֹת; הַפָּרוֹת _____.

In the preceding exercise change the number of the object of the first clause and complete again.

Vocalize and translate :

1. אני הולך למצא את אחי. 2. אמרנו לך לשאל אתו. 3. שמענו אתו אומר: אני הולך אל ביתו. 4. כאשר ראו היושבים את הזקן בא, קמו מעל הארץ. 5. שומעים אנחנו כי (that) תמלך עלינו. 6. אני אוהבת לשאל. 7. החולם חלומות כל היום איננו אהוב. 8. תמצאו את בעל הבית בשדה עם אחיו. 9. האיש המבקש שלום הוא המוצא אתו. 10. טוב לשנא את הרע. 11. אחד מבניו בקש למלך. 12. הצאן הולכות משדה אל שדה. 13. הם לוקחים בית בעמק היפה ההוא.

(*To be followed by Reading 7, p. 146.*)

5 Although שָׂנֵא–יִשְׂנָא is a stative, like other statives expressing a relational (transitive) state ("be hostile toward") it is often construed actively (הוּא שָׂנֵא אוֹתוֹ "he hated him"), and its participle takes the active form שׂוֹנֵא.

§ 12

THE PI'EL

12.1 The *pi'el* serves to modify the meaning of *qal* in a number of ways, the precise modification in any given case being unpredictable. The *pi'el* meaning may be more complex or somehow more intensive than that of *qal* (hence the usual styling of *pi'el* as the "intensive" stem); e.g., *qal* סָפַר "he counted," *pi'el* סִפֵּר "he recounted, narrated"; *qal* שָׁלַח "he sent," *pi'el* שִׁלַּח "he let go, released."

Frequently *pi'el* has a causative sense, especially with stative roots; e.g., *qal* מָלֵא "he was full," *pi'el* מִלֵּא "he filled"; *qal* כָּלָה "he came to an end," *pi'el* כִּלָּה "he finished, made an end of"; *qal* שָׁכֹל "he was bereaved," *pi'el* שִׁכֵּל "he bereaved."

Pi'el is the favored stem for denominative verbs (i.e., verbs made out of nouns); e.g., אִלֵּם "he made a sheaf" (אֲלֻמָּה); נִחֵשׁ "he practiced divination" (נַחַשׁ).

Some *pi'el* verbs have no *qal* to which they stand in relation; e.g., בִּקֵּשׁ "he sought," צִוָּה "he ordered."

12.2 The formal characteristic of the *pi'el* (and the rest of its group) is the lengthening of the second root consonant (indicated by strong *dågeš*).

The *pi'el* סִפֵּר "he recounted":

INFINITIVE ABSOLUTE	COHORTATIVE[1]	IMPERFECT	PERFECT
סַפֵּר, סַפֹּר	אֲסַפְּרָה s	אֲסַפֵּר 1cs	סִפַּרְתִּי 1cs
	נְסַפְּרָה pl	תְּסַפֵּר 2m	סִפַּרְתָּ 2m
INFINITIVE CONSTRUCT		תְּסַפְּרִי 2f	סִפַּרְתְּ 2f
(לְ)סַפֵּר	IMPERATIVE	יְסַפֵּר 3m	סִפֵּר 3m
	סַפֵּר ms	תְּסַפֵּר 3f	סִפְּרָה 3f
PARTICIPLE	סַפְּרִי f	נְסַפֵּר 1cpl	סִפַּרְנוּ 1cpl
מְסַפֵּר ms	סַפְּרוּ mpl	תְּסַפְּרוּ 2m	סִפַּרְתֶּם 2m
מְסַפֶּרֶת f	סַפֵּרְנָה f	תְּסַפֵּרְנָה 2f	סִפַּרְתֶּן 2f
מְסַפְּרִים mpl		יְסַפְּרוּ 3m	סִפְּרוּ 3c
מְסַפְּרוֹת f		תְּסַפֵּרְנָה 3f	

The pf 3ms often has ־ for its second vowel, e.g., שִׁלֵּם "he repaid," נִחֵם "he consoled, comforted." The *segol* of דִּבֶּר "he spoke" is anomalous [דִּבֵּר only in pause; see § 29.1(e)].

12.3 The passive of *pi'el* is *pu'al*, the skeleton paradigm of which is: pf 3ms סֻפַּר; impf 3ms יְסֻפַּר; pt ms מְסֻפָּר.

* * * * * * *

Conjugate :

בִּקֵּשׁ, נִחַם.

When the second root consonant is a laryngal it does not receive a *dāgeš*. If it is ח, as in נִחַם, usually no change in the preceding vowel takes place. In forms in which the second consonant would normally take *šewā*, the laryngal takes *ḥaṭāf paṯaḥ*; e.g., pf 3cpl נִחֲמוּ, impf 3mpl יְנַחֲמוּ.

---

1 Jussive forms are the same as the impf 2 and 3 pers.

Fill in the perfect, imperfect, and participle of the indicated verbs :

סִפֵּר: 1. הַבָּנוֹת _____ לוֹ אֶת הַחֲלוֹם. 2. אַתֶּם _____ אֶת כָּל אֲשֶׁר עָשָׂה.

בִּקֵּשׁ: 3. אֲנַחְנוּ _____ אֶת אָחִינוּ. 4. הֵם _____ לִמְכֹּר אֶת הַשָּׂעִיר.

נִחֵם: 5. בְּנוֹת הַזָּקֵן _____ אֹתוֹ. 6. אַתֶּן _____ אֹתָהּ יָמִים רַבִּים.

Change verbs and subjects in the preceding exercise to singular.

Translate :

1. Seek (fs) the valley and you will find it. 2. If we relate the dream, will you (mpl) listen or not? 3. Don't sell a slaughtered he-goat. 4. Relate (fpl) to me what you heard when you sat inside the house. 5. If you love (pt ms) her, comfort her. 6. When you (mpl) asked her why she did not go, what did the daughter say?

Vocalize and translate :

1. כאשר לא היה מה לאכל נתנו את השעיר לשוחט לשחט. 2. יבקשו את הדם ולא ימצאו אתו. 3. אנשים רעים השליכו את הפרה בבור; אנשים טובים העלו אתה משם. 4. השוחט את פרתו לא ימכר אתה. 5. לא שמעתי מה שאל האיש. 6. באו ימים טובים והיה שלום לכל יושבי הארץ. 7. לא הכיר הזקן את בניו. 8. שאלנו את האב השבו בנותיו אם לא.

(*To be followed by Reading 9, p. 148.*)

§ 13
THE HIF'IL

13.1 The *hif'il* serves, in the first place, as the causative of *qal*. Thus: *qal* פָּשַׁט "he took off (his garment)," *hif'il* הִפְשִׁיט "he stripped (someone else of his garment)," lit., "made (him) take off"; מָלַךְ "he was king," הִמְלִיךְ "he made king"; בָּא "he came," הֵבִיא "he brought," lit., "made come"; שָׁב "he came back," הֵשִׁיב "he brought/gave back"; מֵת "he died," הֵמִית "he put to death."

Hif'il verbs derived from statives have an elative meaning: רָחַק "he went far," הִרְחִיק "he went very far."

Related to the causative meaning of *hif'il* is the estimative or declarative: אָמֵן "he was true, firm," הֶאֱמִין "he considered true, believed."

Some *hif'il* verbs have no *qal* to which they stand in relation; e.g., הִשְׁלִיךְ "he threw."

13.2 The prepositive ה, which is the characteristic of *hif'il*, appears in the perfect, imperative, and infinitives. In the imperfect and participle it is elided after the preformatives: יַשְׁלִיךְ < *יְהַשְׁלִיךְ; מַשְׁלִיךְ < *מְהַשְׁלִיךְ.

The *hif'il* הִשְׁלִיךְ "he threw":

INFINITIVE ABSOLUTE	COHORTATIVE	IMPERFECT	PERFECT
הַשְׁלֵךְ	אַשְׁלִיכָה s	אַשְׁלִיךְ 1cs	הִשְׁלַכְתִּי 1cs
	נַשְׁלִיכָה pl	תַּשְׁלִיךְ 2m	הִשְׁלַכְתָּ 2m
INFINITIVE CONSTRUCT		תַּשְׁלִיכִי 2f	הִשְׁלַכְתְּ 2f
(לְ)הַשְׁלִיךְ	JUSSIVE	יַשְׁלִיךְ 3m	הִשְׁלִיךְ 3m
	יַשְׁלֵךְ 3ms	תַּשְׁלִיךְ 3f	הִשְׁלִיכָה 3f
PARTICIPLE		נַשְׁלִיךְ 1cpl	הִשְׁלַכְנוּ 1cpl
מַשְׁלִיךְ ms	IMPERATIVE	תַּשְׁלִיכוּ 2m	הִשְׁלַכְתֶּם 2m
מַשְׁלֶכֶת f	הַשְׁלֵךְ ms	תַּשְׁלֵכְנָה 2f	הִשְׁלַכְתֶּן 2f
מַשְׁלִיכִים mpl	הַשְׁלִיכִי f	יַשְׁלִיכוּ 3m	הִשְׁלִיכוּ 3c
מַשְׁלִיכוֹת f	הַשְׁלִיכוּ mpl	תַּשְׁלֵכְנָה 3f	
	הַשְׁלֵכְנָה f		

13.3 The passive of *hif'il* is *hŏf'al* (*huf'al*), the skeleton paradigm of which is: pf 3ms הָשְׁלַךְ; impf 3ms יֻשְׁלַךְ; pt מֻשְׁלָךְ.

The first vowel varies between (the original) *u* and its phonetic variant *ŏ*. In the participle it is usually *u*.

* * * * * * *

Conjugate :

הִכִּיר, הִגִּיד, הִפְשִׁיט.

The last two verbs are derived from נגד and נכר, respectively. In *hif'il* the נ assimilates to the following consonant, which is, consequently, lengthened [§ 2.10(b)2]. The vowel pattern remains unchanged.

Complete with perfect, imperfect, and participle of the indicated verbs :

הִמְלִיךְ: 1. הַמִּצְרִים _____ אֶת פַּרְעֹה. 2. אַתֶּם _____ אֶת הַשָּׂר.

הִכִּיר: 3. אֲנַחְנוּ _____ אֶת הַמָּקוֹם. 4. הֵנָּה _____ אֶת פְּנֵי הָעֶבֶד.

הִגִּיד: 5. הַבָּנוֹת _____ אֶת הַדָּבָר. 6. הַשָּׂרִים _____ לַמֶּלֶךְ.

Change verbs and subjects of the preceding exercise into the singular.

Translate:

1. Don't tell (ms) the king what you know (pt) about that place. 2. You (mpl) won't recognize him at night. 3. The wicked king will throw many officers into the pit. 4. Just as you (fs) told me, so it was. 5. In the morning you (fs) will recognize the face of the mother. 6. Tell (ms) me, what will you seek there? 7. I shall seek to become familiar with (recognize) the houses of the place. 8. We told them that we recognized the blood that was on the ground. 9. How did you (fpl) throw the lad into the pit?

Vocalize and translate:

1. אחר הלילה בא הבקר. 2. המלך השליך את השרים אשר חטאו לו אל הבור. 3. אין הרועים יודעים אנה הלכו הצאן. 4. לא ידעתי אם שב עוד אל מקומו. 5. הגידי לי, הישיב לי את הפרה ביום אם בלילה? 6. חרה אף המלך ברועה כי לא הביא לו שעיר טוב לאכל. 7. המלך ימית את אשר לקח את ביתו.

(*To be followed by Reading 11, p. 151.*)

§ 14

PRONOMINAL SUFFIXES WITH MASCULINE NOUNS

14.1 Pronominal suffixes are attached to nouns to express possession: חֲמוֹר "donkey," חֲמוֹרִי "my donkey." Prolongation of the noun by the suffix causes the stress to move forward (as in the construct state, §6.1)

Hence it is that when the construct form of a noun differs from its absolute form, it is to the construct form (or a modification of it) that suffixes are attached; e.g., בַּיִת, בֵּית־, with suffix בֵּיתִי; שָׁלוֹם, שְׁלוֹם־, with suffix שְׁלוֹמִי.

14.2 The pronominal suffixes, as attached to חֲמוֹר, are:

plural suffixes		*singular suffixes*		
our d.	חֲמוֹרֵנוּ	my d.	חֲמוֹרִי	1c
your (m) d.	חֲמוֹרְכֶם	thy (m) d.	חֲמוֹרְךָ	2m
your (f) d.	חֲמוֹרְכֶן	thy (f) d.	חֲמוֹרֵךְ	2f
their (m) d.	חֲמוֹרָם	his d.	חֲמוֹרוֹ	3m
their (f) d.	חֲמוֹרָן	her d.	חֲמוֹרָהּ	3f

14.3 Attached to the plural — more exactly, to the construct plural חֲמוֹרֵי־ — the suffixes are:

plural suffixes		*singular suffixes*	
our dd.	חֲמוֹרֵינוּ	my dd.	חֲמוֹרַי 1c
your (m) dd.	חֲמוֹרֵיכֶם	thy (m) dd.	חֲמוֹרֶיךָ 2m
your (f) dd.	חֲמוֹרֵיכֶן	thy (f) dd.	חֲמוֹרַיִךְ 2f
their (m) dd.	חֲמוֹרֵיהֶם	his dd.	חֲמוֹרָיו 3m
their (f) dd.	חֲמוֹרֵיהֶן	her dd.	חֲמוֹרֶיהָ 3f

Note that the י is pronounced only in חֲמוֹרַי and חֲמוֹרַיִךְ. In the other forms it is written but not pronounced. It derives from *-ay*, the original dual and plural construct termination, which in most forms has contracted to ־ֵי or ־ֶי, the י quiescing.

Note also that the "heavy," biconsonantal suffixes ־כֶם, ־כֶן, ־הֶם, ־הֶן attract the stress to themselves.

14.4 The pronominal possessive suffixes as attached to regular nouns may be tabulated as follows:

plural suffixes		*singular suffixes*	
with pl nouns	*with s nouns*	*with pl nouns*	*with s nouns*
־ֵינוּ	־ֵנוּ	־ַי	־ִי 1c
־ֵיכֶם	־ְכֶם	־ֶיךָ	־ְךָ 2m
־ֵיכֶן	־ְכֶן	־ַיִךְ	־ֵךְ 2f
־ֵיהֶם	־ָם	־יו	־וֹ 3m
־ֵיהֶן	־ָן	־ֶיהָ	־ָהּ 3f

(a) The 1 and 2 pers suffixes are like the endings of the corresponding independent pronouns — the ת element of the 2 pers being replaced throughout by כ.

(b) The 3m suffix was originally *hu* (still seen with certain noun forms ending in a vowel: אָבִיהוּ "his father," פִּיהוּ "his mouth," alternating with the commoner contracted forms אָבִיו, פִּיו). Affixed with a connecting

vowel *a* to the singular (e.g., **ḥamor-a-hu*) it contracted to *aw* > *o*. Affixed to the plural (**ḥamoray-hu*) *ayhu* > *ayw*, and then, with the quiescing of the *yod*, יָו־.

(c) The 3f suffix was originally *ha* (appearing still in אָבִיהָ "her father," פִּיהָ "her mouth"). Affixed to the singular, *-a-ha* > הָ־; to the plural, *-ay-ha* contracted to יָהָ־.

14.5 Here are some irregular inflections:

"father"	"brother"	"son"
אָב אֲבִי־:	אָח, אֲחִי־:	בֵּן, בֶּן־:
אָבִי	אָחִי	בְּנִי
אָבִיךָ	אָחִיךָ	בִּנְךָ
אָבִיךְ	אָחִיךְ	בִּנֵּךְ
אָבִיו	אָחִיו	בְּנוֹ
אָבִיהָ	אָחִיהָ	בִּנָּהּ
אָבִינוּ	אָחִינוּ	בְּנֵנוּ
אֲבִיכֶם־ן	אַחִיכֶם־ן	בִּנְכֶם־ן
אֲבִיהֶם־ן	אַחִיהֶם־ן	בִּנָּם־ן
אָבוֹת, אֲבוֹת־:	אַחִים, אֲחֵי־:	בָּנִים, בְּנֵי־:
אֲבוֹתַי...	אַחַי	בָּנַי
	אַחֶיךָ	בָּנֶיךָ
	אַחַיִךְ	בָּנַיִךְ
	אֶחָיו	בָּנָיו
	אַחֶיהָ	בָּנֶיהָ
	אַחֵינוּ	בָּנֵינוּ
	אַחֵיכֶם־ן	בְּנֵיכֶם־ן
	אַחֵיהֶם־ן	בְּנֵיהֶם־ן

(similarly פָּנִים, נָשִׁים)

14.6 Some common prepositions and particles:

direct object sign	"to"	"in"
אֵת, אֶת־:	לְ:	בְּ:
אֹתִי	לִי	בִּי
אֹתְךָ	לְךָ	בְּךָ
אֹתָךְ	לָךְ	בָּךְ
אֹתוֹ	לוֹ	בּוֹ
אֹתָהּ	לָהּ	בָּהּ
אֹתָנוּ	לָנוּ	בָּנוּ
אֶתְכֶם־ן	לָכֶם־ן	בָּכֶם־ן
אֹתָם־ן	לָהֶם־ן	בָּהֶם/בָּם
		בָּהֶן

"with"	"with"
עִם:	אֵת, אֶת־:
עִמִּי	אִתִּי
עִמְּךָ	אִתְּךָ
עִמָּךְ	אִתָּךְ
עִמּוֹ	אִתּוֹ
עִמָּהּ	אִתָּהּ
עִמָּנוּ	אִתָּנוּ
עִמָּכֶם־ן	אִתְּכֶם־ן
עִמָּהֶם־ן	אִתָּם־ן

Note that in all the above forms the connecting vowel before the 2fs and 1cpl suffixes is ָ (לָךְ, אִתָּךְ; לָנוּ, אִתָּנוּ, etc.) instead of ִ which is normal with nouns.

* * * * * * *

Inflect with pronominal suffixes :

פִּתְרוֹן, תּוֹךְ־, צֹאן, אִישׁ, אֱלֹהִים, פָּנִים, פִּתְרוֹנִים, שְׂעִירִים

Translate :

1. אָסַפְתָּ אֶת צֹאנְךָ מִן הַשָּׂדֶה. 2. אֵין נוֹתְנִים לָאֲסוּרִים אֹכֶל כִּי חָטְאוּ לַמֶּלֶךְ וְחָרָה אַפּוֹ בָּהֶם. 3. עִמְּדוּ עִמָּהּ! 4. אִם יְכַלֶּה הָרָעָב אֶת כָּל הָאֹכֶל אֲשֶׁר בְּבָתֵּיהֶם יָמוּתוּ. 5. אֶרֶץ מִצְרַיִם קְרוֹבָה אֶל אַרְצֵנוּ. 6. חַכְמֵיהֶם פָּתְרוּ לוֹ אֶת חֲלוֹמוֹ. 7. חָטָא פַּרְעֹה לֵאלֹהִים כִּי הִשְׁלִיךְ אֶת בָּנֵינוּ לְתוֹךְ הַיְאוֹר. 8. יִתֵּן אֱלֹהִים שָׁלוֹם לְעַמּוֹ. 9. בָּנֶיהָ יָדְעוּ כִּי אָהַבָה אֶת אִישָׁהּ. 10. אֵין עוֹד מָקוֹם בְּבֵיתְכֶם כִּי אֲסַפְתֶּם לְתוֹכוֹ אֹכֶל רַב. 11. חֲכָמָה הָאִשָּׁה כִּי רוּחַ אֱלֹהִים בָּהּ.

Translate :

1. Thy (m) son restored (returned) my spirit to me. 2. Your (m) wise brother knew (how) to speak with him. 3. Our God and the God of our fathers is king over us. 4. Her sons gave her food many days. 5. They will not recognize thy (f) son. 6. You (m) asked her and her brother where her father stood on that day, but they did not answer you. 7. We took their sons and went with them to their fathers' houses. 8. Their (m) house was in the valley in which their sheep pastured. 9. Your (m) son is a prisoner with us, and we will sell him as a slave if you tell the king.

(*To be followed by Reading 13, p. 153.*)

§ 15

PRONOMINAL SUFFIXES WITH FEMININE NOUNS AND WITH VERBS

15.1 Since suffixes are attached to the construct form of nouns (§14.1), feminine nouns ending in ־ָה recover their original ־ת ending [§6.2(a)] before suffixes: פָּרָה "cow," פָּרַת־, פָּרָתִי "my cow." The full inflection is:

plural suffixes		*singular suffixes*	
our c.	פָּרָתֵנוּ	my c.	פָּרָתִי 1c
your (m) c.	פָּרַתְכֶם	thy (m) c.	פָּרָתְךָ 2m
your (f) c.	פָּרַתְכֶן	thy (f) c.	פָּרָתֵךְ 2f
their (m) c.	פָּרָתָם	his c.	פָּרָתוֹ 3m
their (f) c.	פָּרָתָן	her c.	פָּרָתָהּ 3f

Note that the vowel preceding the ת is *qāmeṣ*, except with the heavy suffixes ־כֶם ־ן, where it is *pāṯaḥ* (as in the construct form).

15.2 The plural, פָּרוֹת "cows," inflects thus:

plural suffixes		*singular suffixes*		
our cc.	פָּרוֹתֵינוּ	my cc.	פָּרוֹתַי	1c
your (m) cc.	פָּרוֹתֵיכֶם	thy (m) cc.	פָּרוֹתֶיךָ	2m
your (f) cc.	פָּרוֹתֵיכֶן	thy (f) cc.	פָּרוֹתַיִךְ	2f
their (m) cc.	פָּרוֹתֵיהֶם	his cc.	פָּרוֹתָיו	3m
their (f) cc.	פָּרוֹתֵיהֶן	her cc.	פָּרוֹתֶיהָ	3f

Note that the suffixes are the same as those attached to the plural masculine nouns: פָּרוֹתַי like חֲמוֹרַי, פָּרוֹתֶיךָ like חֲמוֹרֶיךָ, etc. The –י– element in –ֶיךָ, –ַיִךְ, –ָיו, etc. — properly a plural termination of masculine nouns (§14.3) — has through analogy been retained with the feminine.

15.3 Some irregular feminines:

אִשָּׁה, אֵשֶׁת־ : אִשְׁתִּי... ; נָשִׁים, נְשֵׁי... "woman" (like בָּנִים, §14.5)

בַּת, בַּת־ : בִּתִּי... ; בָּנוֹת, בְּנוֹת־ : בְּנוֹתַי... "daughter"

15.4 אֶל "to" and עַל "on" inflect as masculine plurals:

אֶל :	עַל :
אֵלַי	עָלַי
אֵלֶיךָ	עָלֶיךָ
אֵלַיִךְ	עָלַיִךְ
אֵלָיו	עָלָיו
אֵלֶיהָ	עָלֶיהָ
אֵלֵינוּ	עָלֵינוּ
אֲלֵיכֶם־ן	עֲלֵיכֶם־ן
אֲלֵיהֶם־ן	עֲלֵיהֶם־ן

Verbal suffixes

15.5 The direct object pronoun is expressed either by inflected אֶת־ (§14.6) or by pronominal suffixes attached to the verb.[1]

Suffixes are attached to the perfect שָׁמַר "he guarded" thus:

he g. us	שְׁמָרָנוּ	he g. him	שְׁמָרוֹ	he g. me	שְׁמָרַנִי
he g. you	שְׁמַרְכֶם־ן	(it befell him	קָרָהוּ)	he g. thee (m)	שְׁמָרְךָ
he g. them	שְׁמָרָם־ן	he g. her	שְׁמָרָהּ	he g. thee (f)	שְׁמָרֵךְ

(a) Note that the connecting vowel between the pf 3ms and the suffix (when there is one) is *a/å* (־ַ/־ָ), except in שְׁמָרֵךְ.

(b) Contrast the verbal suffix for 1cs ־נִי with the nominal ־ִי.

(c) The 3ms suffix ־הוּ usually is attached to forms ending in a vowel. Exception: שְׁמָרַתְהוּ "she g. him."

15.6 Suffixes are attached to the imperfect יִשְׁמֹר "he will guard" thus:

he w.g. us	יִשְׁמְרֵנוּ	he w.g. him	יִשְׁמְרֵנּוּ	he w.g. me	יִשְׁמְרֵנִי
he w.g. you	יִשְׁמָרְכֶם־ן		יִשְׁמְרֵהוּ	he w.g. thee (m)	יִשְׁמָרְךָ
he w.g. them	יִשְׁמְרֵם־ן	he w.g. her	יִשְׁמְרֶנָּה		
			יִשְׁמְרָהָ(־רָה)	he w.g. thee (f)	יִשְׁמָרֵךְ

(a) Note that the connecting vowel between the imperfect and the suffix (when there is one) is *ε/e* (־ֶ/־ֵ).

(b) The suffixes of the 3s have two forms: the primary m ־ֵהוּ, f ־ֶהָ and one augmented with נ: m ־ֶנּוּ < הוּ + ־ֶנ, f ־ֶנָּה < הָ + ־ֶנ. The augmented forms occur with the ordinary imperfect; the primary, with the jussive and *wåw*-consecutive (§16).

(c) The imperfect theme vowel *o* becomes ־ִ before suffixes, but the *a* theme is retained as *qåmeṣ* before suffixes: יִשְׁלַח, יִשְׁלָחֵנִי "he will send me"; יִמְצָא, יִמְצָאֵם "he will find them."

---

1 Occasionally a verbal suffix stands for an indirect object.

15.7 Other verb forms also receive suffixes:

(a) the imperative שְׁמֹר : שָׁמְרֵהוּ (*šŏm-*) "guard him!"

(b) the infinitive לִשְׁמֹר : (לְ)שָׁמְרוֹ (*šŏm-*) "to guard him"

(c) the participle שׁוֹמֵר : שׁוֹמְרוֹ "his guard, the one guarding him."

15.8 The inflections of אֵין־, עוֹד, and מִן employ the verbal suffixes.

"from me," etc.	"I am still," etc.	"I am not," etc.
מִמֶּנִּי	עוֹדֶנִּי, עוֹדִי	אֵינֶנִּי
מִמְּךָ	עוֹדְךָ	אֵינְךָ
מִמֵּךְ	עוֹדָךְ	אֵינֵךְ
מִמֶּנּוּ	עוֹדֶנּוּ	אֵינֶנּוּ
מִמֶּנָּה	עוֹדֶנָּה	אֵינֶנָּה
מִמֶּנּוּ	עוֹדֵנוּ	אֵינֶנּוּ
מִכֶּם־ן	עוֹדְכֶם־ן	אֵינְכֶם־ן
מֵהֶם־ן	עוֹדָם־ן	אֵינָם־ן

* * * * * * *

Inflect with suffixes:

אָבוֹת, חֲלוֹמוֹת, חַיּוֹת, חַיָּה, אֲלֻמָּה.

Translate:

1. He is still gathering his sheaves. 2. She does not sit in her house during the day. 3. When Pharaoh's seven daughters came down to the river, his ten servants came up from it. 4. Do you (ms) remember if you sent him much food? 5. They said to her father: She is not coming today because her sons and daughters have not yet returned. 6. His wife recognized that he was wiser than she (from her). 7. How

can I remember which of you (who from you) spoke with me that day? 8. They did not speak the truth about you (fpl). 9. The land upon which we stand (pt) belongs to the Egyptians. 10. Send (mpl) twelve of them (from them) to seek the place in which the king is imprisoned.

Translate :

1. בִּתּוֹ יָרְדָה עִם פָּרוֹתָיו לְתוֹךְ שְׂדֵה הָעִיר וְעוֹדֶנָּה שָׁם. 2. הָעִיר הַהִיא אֵינֶנָּה קְרוֹבָה אֵלֵינוּ. 3. שָׁלַחְנוּ אֵלָיו שֶׁבַע פָּרוֹת. 4. נָשִׂינוּ עָלוּ מִמִּצְרַיִם עִמָּנוּ. 5. שִׁלְחוּ מִכֶּם אֶחָד וִיבַקֵּשׁ אֹכֶל, וְלֹא תָמוּתוּ בָּרָעָב! 6. נַעַר חָכָם אֵינֶנּוּ מְדַבֵּר לִפְנֵי אִישׁ חָכָם מִמֶּנּוּ וְגָדוֹל מִמֶּנּוּ בַּשָּׁנִים. 7. בִּתָּהּ נָתְנָה לְפָנֶיהָ לֶחֶם.

Rewrite, replacing the verbal suffix with a corresponding form of אֶת־:

1. שְׁלָחַנִי אֱלֹהִים לִפְנֵיכֶם. 2. קָמוּ כָּל בְּנוֹתָיו לְנַחֲמוֹ. 3. מִיָּדִי תְּבַקְשֶׁנּוּ. 4. חַיָּה רָעָה אֲכָלַתְהוּ. 5. הֵם לֹא הִכִּירוּהוּ. 6. אֶשְׁלָחֵךְ[2] אֶל אַחֶיךָ. 7. נְתָנַנִי אֱלֹהִים אָדוֹן עַל כָּל אֶרֶץ מִצְרַיִם. 8. הַשְׁלִיכֵהוּ אֶל הַבּוֹר! 9. נִמְכְּרֶנּוּ לַיִּשְׁמְעֵאלִים. 10. רָאָם וְלֹא הִכִּירָם. 11. יִמְצָאֲכֶם בַּשָּׂדֶה. 12. לֹא יַכִּירוּךָ אוֹהֲבֶיךָ. 13. אֶזְכְּרֶנּוּ עוֹד. 14. לְקַחְתִּיהָ. 15. בַּקֵּשׁ לִרְאוֹתוֹ.

(*To be followed by Reading 15, p. 156.*)

---

2 Cf. §15.6(c).

§ 16

WÂW-CONSECUTIVE

16.1 In the narratives, the two aspects of Biblical Hebrew are employed in the following sequence: If past events are being narrated, the first verb is normally in the perfect, but the consecutive verbs in the line of the narration — each standing at the head of a clause and linked by וְ to the preceding clause — appear in the so-called *imperfect with wâw-consecutive*, or *imperfect consecutive*. For example, the report that Joseph's brothers made to Jacob upon their return from Egypt as it appears in Reading 16 runs:

דִּבֶּר הָאִישׁ... אִתָּנוּ קָשׁוֹת, וְנָתַן אֹתָנוּ כִּמְרַגְּלִים. אָמַרְנוּ אֵלָיו: לֹא הָיִינוּ מְרַגְּלִים... אָמַר אֵלֵינוּ הָאִישׁ...

But in the original of Genesis 42:30-33 the sequence of tenses is:

דִּבֶּר הָאִישׁ... אִתָּנוּ קָשׁוֹת, וַיִּתֵּן אֹתָנוּ כִּמְרַגְּלִים... וַנֹּאמֶר אֵלָיו: לֹא הָיִינוּ מְרַגְּלִים... וַיֹּאמֶר אֵלֵינוּ הָאִישׁ...

The first verb, דִּבֶּר, is in the perfect; the subsequent verbs in the line of the narrative (וַיֹּאמֶר, וַנֹּאמֶר, וַיִּתֵּן) each stand at the head of their clause and are in the imperfect consecutive (הָיִינוּ is in a quotation). The imperfect consecutive is rendered in English as a past.

This apparently inverted imperfect is in all likelihood a survival of an early preterit tense which later coalesced in form with the imperfect; see § 10.2.

16.2 A verb expressing an action or circumstance that is not consequent upon the preceding verb is thrown back into its normal aspect. The interruption of a line of imperfect consecutives by a perfect often indicates an action or circumstance simultaneous with, or prior to, what came before:

(a) Simultaneity: וַיִּפֹּל עַל צַוְּארֵי[1] בִנְיָמִין אָחִיו וַיֵּבְךְּ וּבִנְיָמִין בָּכָה עַל צַוָּארָיו[2] (45:14) "then he fell on his brother Benjamin's neck and wept, while Benjamin wept on his neck."

(b) Priority: וַיֵּבְךְּ אֹתוֹ אָבִיו. וְהַמִּדְיָנִים מָכְרוּ אֹתוֹ (37:35 f.) "...so his father bewailed him. Meanwhile, the Midianites had sold him..."

Note the distinctive, invariable word order of such nonconsecutive clauses: the subject precedes the verb.

16.3 *Wåw*-consecutive is vocalized. ·וַ; i.e., וַ followed by a long consonant (one bearing a strong *dågeš*; see the above examples). Before א it is וָ: וָאֶשְׁמֹר [ַ is lengthened to ָ because the laryngal א cannot be lengthened; cf. the vocalization of the article ה, § 5.1, 2(a)].

יְ following a *wåw*-consecutive is not lengthened; e.g., וַיְדַבֵּר.

16.4 When a shortening of the imperfect form is possible, *wåw*-consecutive is usually attached to the shortened form. In the sound (regular) verbs — verbs from triconsonantal roots in which there are no weak consonants (א, ה, ו, י) — the imperfect form is not susceptible to shortening. The one exception is the *hif'il* jussive יַשְׁלֵךְ (compare the imperfect יַשְׁלִיךְ); accordingly the imperfect consecutive is וַיַּשְׁלֵךְ.

---

1 Read *ṣawwᵉre* (MH *ṣavvᵉre*); the dot in the וּ is a strong *dågeš*. Thus every וּ with a vowel sign is a long (doubled) *wåw*.

2 Read *ṣawwåråw* (MH *ṣavvåråv*).

But in "hollow" verbs (§8.2) such as שׁוּב, or in verbs one or more of whose consonants are weak, shortening of the imperfect form can occur. The more important cases are:

(a) When the imperfect has an open penult (next-to-last syllable). A syllable is open when it ends in a vowel; the penults of the following verbs are open: יֵשֵׁב, יֵלֵךְ, יָשׁוּב, יָשִׂים, יֹאמַר.

In the imperfect consecutive the stress recedes to the penult and the final vowel is, consequently, shortened: וַיֵּשֶׁב, וַיֵּלֶךְ, (-*šŏv*) וַיָּשָׁב, וַיָּשֶׂם, וַיֹּאמֶר.

There are many exceptions to this rule. It is not operative, for example, in 1cs; hence וָאֵלֵךְ, וָאָשׁוּב, וָאָשִׂים.

(b) When the imperfect ends in ־ֶה. The ־ֶה is dropped and the resultant short forms are variously vocalized; e.g.:

imperfect	*imperfect consecutive*	
יִהְיֶה	וַיְהִי	he/it was
יַעֲשֶׂה	וַיַּעַשׂ	he did, made
יִרְאֶה	וַיַּרְא	he saw
יְצַוֶּה	וַיְצַו	he ordered

16.5 Corresponding to the imperfect consecutive, which occurs in narration of past events, is the *perfect consecutive*, which occurs in narration of future events. The narration opens with a verb in the imperfect, imperative, or another form implying a future; it is then carried on by a chain of perfect consecutives.

For example, Genesis 45:9-11:

רְדָה אֵלַי אַל תַּעֲמֹד׃ וְיָשַׁבְתָּ בְּאֶרֶץ גֹּשֶׁן[3] וְהָיִיתָ קָרוֹב אֵלַי...

[3] In most printings of vocalized Hebrew, when *ḥôlem* precedes שׂ the characteristic dot over the right prong of the *šin* does duty for the *ḥôlem* as well — as in גֹּשֶׁן.

וְכִלְכַּלְתִּי אֹתְךָ. "Come down to me without delay! You shall live in the land of Goshen and be near to me... and I shall sustain you."

16.6 *Wåw*-consecutive with the perfect is vocalized like the copula וְ "and" (see p. 28). The stress moves forward to the end in the 1cs and 2ms forms of the perfect consecutive (וְכִלְכַּלְתִּי, וְיָשַׁבְתָּ); in 1cpl and many forms of final ה verbs (e.g., הָיָה) this stress shift does not occur (וְהָיִיתָ, וְשָׁמַרְנוּ).

* * * * * * *

Translate, then convert imperfect consecutives into perfects, perfect consecutives into imperfects; change object suffixes into אֶת־ *forms:*

1. וַיֵּשֶׁב יַעֲקֹב בְּאֶרֶץ כְּנָעַן. 2. וַיַּגֵּד לְאֶחָיו. 3. וַיֵּלְכוּ לִרְעוֹת אֶת הַצֹּאן.
4. וַיִּמְצָאֵהוּ אִישׁ בַּשָּׂדֶה. 5. וַיַּפְשִׁיטוּ אֶת יוֹסֵף אֶת כֻּתָּנְתּוֹ. 6. וַיְסַפֵּר
אֶל אָבִיו. 7. וַיִּקָּחוּהוּ וַיַּשְׁלִיכוּהוּ הַבּוֹרָה. 8. וַיִּמְכְּרוּ אֶת יוֹסֵף.
9. וַיָּבוֹאוּ אֶל יוֹסֵף. 10. וַיָּשָׁב רְאוּבֵן אֶל הַבּוֹר. 11. וַיַּכִּירָהּ וַיֹּאמֶר:
כְּתֹנֶת בְּנִי! 12. וַיְשַׁלְּחוּ אֶת כְּתֹנֶת הַפַּסִּים. 13. וַיֵּרֶד יְהוּדָה לִפְנֵיהֶם.
14. וַיָּבֹא אֲלֵיהֶם בַּבֹּקֶר וַיַּרְא אוֹתָם. 15. הִנֵּה שֶׁבַע שָׁנִים בָּאוֹת –
שָׂבָע גָּדוֹל בְּכָל הָאָרֶץ; וְקָמוּ אַחֲרֵיהֶן שֶׁבַע שְׁנֵי רָעָב וְכִלָּה הָרָעָב
אֶת הָאָרֶץ. 16. וַיַּכִּירֵם וַיְדַבֵּר אֲלֵיהֶם קָשׁוֹת. 17. וַיַּעַשׂ לָהֶם כֵּן.
18. וַיַּעַן רְאוּבֵן אֹתָם. 19. וַיִּקַּח מֵאִתָּם אֶת שִׁמְעוֹן וַיֶּאֱסֹר אוֹתוֹ.
20. וַנְּסַפֵּר לוֹ וַיִּפְתֹּר לָנוּ אֶת חֲלוֹמוֹתֵינוּ. 21. וַיְהִי יוֹסֵף אָדוֹן לְכָל
אֶרֶץ מִצְרַיִם. 22. וַיִּקָּחֵהוּ וַיִּתְּנֵהוּ בְּבֵית הָאֲסוּרִים.

(*To be followed by Reading 17, p. 158.*)

§ 17
HOLLOW VERBS

17.1 Hollow verbs derive from biconsonantal roots. In many forms a characteristic long vowel appears between the two consonants, hence the term "hollow," adopted here from Arabic grammar. Examples: שׁוּב "return," שִׂים "put," בּוֹא "come," מוּת "die."[1]

These forms are infinitive construct, the form by which hollow verbs are referred to since their pf 3ms does not show the characteristic long vowel.

This long vowel appears in the *qal* imperfect and related forms and in the infinitive. In the perfect and participle, where it does not appear, hollow verbs all inflect alike (except insofar as statives differ from actives; see the paradigm).

---

[1] These verbs are commonly referred to as middle-*wâw* or middle-*yod* verbs, reflecting the theory that the characteristic middle vowel was originally a consonantal *wâw* or *yod*. Some evidence can be mustered for this view (e.g., the consonantal *wâw* in מָוֶת "death" from the root מוּת); however the difficulties it puts in the way of deriving the verbal forms make it preferable to adopt the view set forth above and to assume that the consonantal *wâw* in such words as מָוֶת arose secondarily.

17.2 The *qal*:

PERFECT

stative	*active*			
מַתִּי	בָּאתִי	שַׂמְתִּי	שַׁבְתִּי	1cs
מַתָּ	בָּאתָ	שַׂמְתָּ	שַׁבְתָּ	2m
מַתְּ	בָּאת	שַׂמְתְּ	שַׁבְתְּ	2f
מֵת	בָּא	שָׂם	שָׁב	3m
מֵתָה	בָּאָה	שָׂמָה	שָׁבָה	3f
מַתְנוּ	בָּאנוּ	שַׂמְנוּ	שַׁבְנוּ	1cpl
מַתֶּם	בָּאתֶם	שַׂמְתֶּם	שַׁבְתֶּם	2m
מַתֶּן	בָּאתֶן	שַׂמְתֶּן	שַׁבְתֶּן	2f
מֵתוּ	בָּאוּ	שָׂמוּ	שָׁבוּ	3c

IMPERFECT

אָמוּת	אָבוֹא	אָשִׂים	אָשׁוּב	1cs
תָּמוּת	תָּבוֹא	תָּשִׂים	תָּשׁוּב	2m
תָּמוּתִי	תָּבוֹאִי	תָּשִׂימִי	תָּשׁוּבִי	2f
יָמוּת	יָבוֹא	יָשִׂים	יָשׁוּב	3m
תָּמוּת	תָּבוֹא	תָּשִׂים	תָּשׁוּב	3f
נָמוּת	נָבוֹא	נָשִׂים	נָשׁוּב	1cpl
תָּמוּתוּ	תָּבוֹאוּ	תָּשִׂימוּ	תָּשׁוּבוּ	2m
תְּמוּתֶינָה	תְּבוֹאֶינָה	תְּשִׂימֶינָה	תְּשׁוּבֶינָה	2&3f
תָּמֹתְנָה	תָּבֹאנָה	תָּשֵׂמְנָה	תָּשֹׁבְנָה	
יָמוּתוּ	יָבוֹאוּ	יָשִׂימוּ	יָשׁוּבוּ	3m

COHORTATIVE

אָמוּתָה	אָבוֹאָה	אָשִׂימָה	אָשׁוּבָה
נָמוּתָה	נָבוֹאָה	נָשִׂימָה	נָשׁוּבָה

JUSSIVE & IMPERFECT CONSECUTIVE

יָמֹת	יָבוֹא	יָשֵׂם	יָשֹׁב
וַיָּמָת	וַיָּבוֹא	וַיָּשֶׂם	וַיָּשָׁב

IMPERATIVE

מוּת	בּוֹא	שִׂים	שׁוּב	ms
מֻתִּי	בֹּאִי	שִׂימִי	שׁוּבִי	f
מֻתוּ	בֹּאוּ	שִׂימוּ	שׁוּבוּ	mpl
מֻתְנָה	בֹּאנָה	שֵׂמְנָה	שֹׁבְנָה	f

INFINITIVE ABSOLUTE & CONSTRUCT

מוֹת	בּוֹא	שׂוֹם	שׁוֹב
(לָ)מוּת	(לָ)בוֹא	(לָ)שִׂים	(לָ)שׁוּב
		(לָ)שׂוּם	

PARTICIPLE

מֵת	בָּא	שָׂם	שָׁב	ms
מֵתָה	בָּאָה	שָׂמָה	שָׁבָה	f
מֵתִים	בָּאִים	שָׂמִים	שָׁבִים	mpl
מֵתוֹת	בָּאוֹת	שָׂמוֹת	שָׁבוֹת	f

(a) In the perfect of בּוֹא the א quiesces and the preceding ◌ֵ>◌ָ by way of compensation (§21.1).

(b) The impf 2 and 3fpl have two forms: the longer, commoner one keeps the original long vowel and inserts a vowel ◌ֶ before the ◌נָה termination; the spelling ◌ֶי shows the influence of the final ה verb form תִּבְכֶּינָה (§19). In the shorter form וֹ>◌ֹ, ◌ִי>◌ֵ, as in the jussive. ◌ֹ and ◌ֵ are in turn shortened to ◌ָ (*ŏ*) and ◌ֶ, respectively, in the imperfect consecutive [see §16.4(a)]. The long וֹ of בּוֹא remains unchanged throughout.

(c) The pt ms is identical with the pf 3ms. The stress position of the pt fs (קָמָה) distinguishes it from the pf 3fs (קָמָה).

17.3 The *hif'il*:

COHORTATIVE

אָשִׁיבָה

נָשִׁיבָה

JUSSIVE & IMPERFECT CONSECUTIVE

יָשֵׁב

וַיָּשֶׁב

IMPERATIVE

הָשֵׁב ms

הָשִׁיבִי f

הָשִׁיבוּ mpl

הָשֵׁבְנָה f

INFINITIVE ABSOLUTE & CONSTRUCT

הָשֵׁב

(לְ)הָשִׁיב

PARTICIPLE

מֵשִׁיב ms

מְשִׁיבָה f

מְשִׁיבִים mpl

מְשִׁיבוֹת f

PERFECT

	type a	*type b*	
1cs	הֶשִׁיבוֹתִי	הֶשַׁבְתִּי	הֵבֵאתִי
2m	הֶשִׁיבוֹתָ (הֶ־ ־שֵׁ־)	הֶשַׁבְתָּ	הֵבֵאתָ
2f	הֶשִׁיבוֹת	הֶשַׁבְתְּ	הֵבֵאת
3m	הֵשִׁיב	(*type a*)	הֵבִיא
3f	הֵשִׁיבָה	(*type a*)	הֵבִיאָה
1cpl	הֶשִׁיבוֹנוּ (הֶ־)	הֶשַׁבְנוּ	הֵבֵאנוּ
2m	הֶשִׁיבוֹתֶם (־שֵׁ־)	הֶשַׁבְתֶּם	הֵבֵאתֶם
2f	הֶשִׁיבוֹתֶן	הֶשַׁבְתֶּן	הֵבֵאתֶן
3c	הֵשִׁיבוּ	(*type a*)	הֵבִיאוּ

IMPERFECT

אָשִׁיב 1cs

תָּשִׁיב 2m

תָּשִׁיבִי 2f

יָשִׁיב 3m

תָּשִׁיב 3f

נָשִׁיב 1cpl

תָּשִׁיבוּ 2m

תָּשֵׁבְנָה 2f

יָשִׁיבוּ 3m

תָּשֵׁבְנָה 3f

(a) Perfect *type a* is the more common in Biblical Hebrew; *type b* (closer to the pattern of the sound verb, cf. הִשְׁלַכְתִּי) more common in Post-biblical. The paradigm shows the dominant pattern; the parentheses give divergences in attested forms of הֵשִׁיב.

17.4 The *hŏf'al*: pf 3ms הוּשַׁב, impf 3ms יוּשַׁב, pt ms מוּשָׁב.[2]

* * * * * * *

Conjugate in qal:

קום.

Conjugate in hif'il:

כון.

Supply correct form of indicated verb in perfect, imperfect, participle:

1. שָׂם: הָאִשָּׁה _____ אֶת הָאֹכֶל לִפְנֵי אִישָׁהּ. 2. בָּא: אֲנִי _____ עִמְּךָ. 3. הֵשִׁיב: אַתְּ _____ לִי אֶת חֲמוֹרִי. 4. הֵבִיא: אַתָּה _____ מַיִם.

Change the subjects and verbs of the preceding exercise to the plural.

Vocalize and translate:

1. הכן את הלחם והמים כי באים השרים לאכל אתנו! 2. אם תשובו, תשיבו לו את הכסף. 3. המיתו את העבד כי בקש להמית את המלך. 4. צרות גדולות תבואנה עליכם אם לא תכינו אכל לדרך. 5. זכרנו את רחמיך הרבים. 6. המים משיבים את הנפש. 7. באמת הדרך קשה, והיא תביא אתכם אל עירכם. 8. בתחלה ישימו מים לפניו, ואחר יביאו את הלחם. 9. אני מביאה את הילד אל אמו.

Translate:

1. Let him come (juss) into your (ms) house. 2. They will put the rations on their donkeys. 3. At noon she gave them money and

---

2 In Genesis 43:12 הַמּוּשַׁב occurs in close connection with the following word — a quasi-construct form.

returned them by the way in which they came. 4. They did not find the present that they had brought for the king. 5. Many men have feared to bring blood upon their hands. 6. Ten donkeys carrying food are coming down into the valley. 7. Who will tell us a good way to go back to our house? 8. Put (mpl) the sheaves there! 9. According to (עַל פִּי) the woman's words, she got up and returned to her father's house because her husband spoke to her harshly.

(*To be followed by Reading 19, p. 162.*)

§ 18

THE NIF'AL AND HIṮPA'EL

The nif'al

18.1 The *nif'al* is primarily the reflexive of *qal*, but serves often as its passive as well: נִשְׁמַר "he guarded himself," but also "he was guarded"; נִבְחַן "he was tested"; נִמְצָא "he was found."

Nif'al verbs frequently express a state or feeling that comes or acts upon the subject: נִכְמַר "he grew hot," נֶעֱצַב "he was grieved," נִבְהַל "he became terrified."

Sometimes *nif'al* is used as the passive of patterns other than *qal*; e.g., נֶאֱמַן "he was confirmed, verified, held true" (passive of *hif'il* הֶאֱמִין "hold true, believe").

18.2 The characteristic נ augment appears in the perfect, participle, and one form of the infinitive absolute. In the imperfect and related forms and in other forms of the infinitive — where it is preceded by preformatives — the נ is assimilated to the first root consonant, which is therefore lengthened: יִנְשָׁמֵר* > יִשָּׁמֵר.

The *nif'al* נִשְׁמַר "he guarded himself/was guarded":

INFINITIVE ABSOLUTE	COHORTATIVE	IMPERFECT	PERFECT
נִשְׁמֹר, הִשָּׁמֵר	אִשָּׁמְרָה s	אֶשָּׁמֵר 1cs	נִשְׁמַרְתִּי 1cs
	נִשָּׁמְרָה pl	תִּשָּׁמֵר 2m	נִשְׁמַרְתָּ 2m
INFINITIVE CONSTRUCT		תִּשָּׁמְרִי 2f	נִשְׁמַרְתְּ 2f
(לְ)הִשָּׁמֵר	IMPERATIVE	יִשָּׁמֵר 3m	נִשְׁמַר 3m
	הִשָּׁמֵר ms	תִּשָּׁמֵר 3f	נִשְׁמְרָה 3f
	הִשָּׁמְרִי f	נִשָּׁמֵר 1cpl	נִשְׁמַרְנוּ 1cpl
PARTICIPLE	הִשָּׁמְרוּ mpl	תִּשָּׁמְרוּ 2m	נִשְׁמַרְתֶּם 2m
נִשְׁמָר ms	הִשָּׁמַרְנָה f	תִּשָּׁמַרְנָה 2f	נִשְׁמַרְתֶּן 2f
נִשְׁמֶרֶת f		יִשָּׁמְרוּ 3m	נִשְׁמְרוּ 3c
נִשְׁמָרִים mpl		תִּשָּׁמַרְנָה 3f	
נִשְׁמָרוֹת f			

(a) The pf 3ms and the pt ms are alike save for the second vowel: in the perfect it is ַ; in the participle, which is a noun form, it is ָ [see §§ 11.3 and 25.8(a)].

(b) When the first root consonant is a laryngal or ר, in the imperfect, imperative, and infinitive construct the preformative vowel is always lengthened to ֵ in order to compensate for the lack of lengthening of the laryngal; e.g., יֵאָסֵר "he will be imprisoned"; יֵעָצֵב "he will be grieved."

The hiṯpa'el

18.3 The *hiṯpa'el* serves as the reflexive, less often as the passive, of *pi'el*: הִתְנַחֵם "he consoled himself, was consoled," הִתְוַדַּע "he made himself known." Frequently, however, no corresponding *pi'el* is attested, as in the case of הִתְאַפֵּק "he restrained himself," הִתְנַפֵּל "he fell upon, attacked."

In the plural, *hiṯpa'el* may have a reciprocal sense: הִתְרָאוּ "they stared at one another."

Sometimes it has the sense "to act as, play the part of": הִתְנַכֵּר "he acted as a stranger."

18.4 Like *pi'el*, *hiṯpa'el* has a long (*dâgeš*-bearing) middle root consonant. The prepositive הִתְ־ appears in the perfect, imperative, and infinitives; elsewhere the ה is elided after the preformatives.

The *hiṯpa'el* הִתְאַפֵּק "he restrained himself":

INFINITIVE ABSOLUTE	COHORTATIVE	IMPERFECT	PERFECT
הִתְאַפֵּק	אֶתְאַפְּקָה s	אֶתְאַפֵּק 1cs	הִתְאַפַּ֫קְתִּי 1cs
	נִתְאַפְּקָה pl	תִּתְאַפֵּק 2m	הִתְאַפַּ֫קְתָּ 2m
INFINITIVE CONSTRUCT		תִּתְאַפְּקִי 2f	הִתְאַפַּ֫קְתְּ 2f
(לְ)הִתְאַפֵּק	IMPERATIVE	יִתְאַפֵּק 3m	הִתְאַפֵּק 3m
	הִתְאַפֵּק ms	תִּתְאַפֵּק 3f	הִתְאַפְּקָה 3f
	הִתְאַפְּקִי f	נִתְאַפֵּק 1cpl	הִתְאַפַּ֫קְנוּ 1cpl
PARTICIPLE	הִתְאַפְּקוּ mpl	תִּתְאַפְּקוּ 2m	הִתְאַפַּ֫קְתֶּם 2m
מִתְאַפֵּק ms	הִתְאַפֵּ֫קְנָה f	תִּתְאַפֵּ֫קְנָה 2f	הִתְאַפַּ֫קְתֶּן 2f
מִתְאַפֶּ֫קֶת f		יִתְאַפְּקוּ 3m	הִתְאַפְּקוּ 3cpl
מִתְאַפְּקִים mpl		תִּתְאַפֵּ֫קְנָה 3f	
מִתְאַפְּקוֹת f			

18.5 When the first root consonant is a sibilant (a consonant pronounced with a hissing sound: ז, ס, צ, ש), in order to avoid the juncture of the sibilant and the ת of the prepositive הִתְ־, the two exchange places. Thus the *hiṯpa'el* of שמר is הִשְׁתַּמֵּר; the *hiṯpa'el* of שחוה is הִשְׁתַּחֲוָה (but see note, p. 141). This exchange is called metathesis.

When the sibilant is צ, after metathesis the ת becomes ט: the *hiṯpa'el* of צדק is הִצְטַדֵּק. The ת has been partially assimilated to the צ by being pronounced, like it, as an emphatic (see §1.4).

* * * * * * *

Conjugate in nif'al:

נִגְנַב, נִמְכַּר.

Conjugate in hiṯpa'el:

הִתְחַנֵּן, הִתְאַבֵּל.

Translate:

1. הֻחְמְרוּ אֲשֶׁר נִגְנְבוּ נִמְצְאוּ בְּבֵית הָעֶבֶד. 2. נִשְׁלַחְתֶּם לִרְדֹּף אַחַר הָעֶבֶד אֲשֶׁר יָצָא מִבֵּית אֲדוֹנָיו בַּלַּיְלָה וְלֹא הִשַּׂגְתֶּם אֹתוֹ. 3. הָאֲנָשִׁים יֵאָסְרוּ כִּי אֲשֵׁמִים הֵם. 4. הַשַּׁקִּים נִפְתְּחוּ, וְהַכֶּסֶף הַנִּמְצָא בְּתוֹכָם נִגְנַב. 5. בָּכוּ וְהִתְאַבְּלוּ וְלֹא הִתְנַחֲמוּ. 6. הַיּוֹם תֵּאָסַפְנָה הָאֲלֻמּוֹת הָעוֹמְדוֹת בַּשָּׂדֶה. 7. יִבָּחֲנוּ דְּבָרָיו וְיִמָּצְאוּ אֱמֶת. 8. אִם לֹא יִנָּתֵן לָאֲסוּרִים לֶחֶם לֶאֱכֹל וּמַיִם לִשְׁתּוֹת יָמוּתוּ בָּרָעָב. 9. הָאֲשֵׁמִים נִלְקְחוּ לְהִמָּכֵר לָעֲבָדִים. 10. גַּם אִם תִּתְחַנְּנוּ אֵלָיו לֹא יִשְׁמַע אֲלֵיכֶם.

Translate:

1. I was asked whether I recognized her face; after these many years I could not. 2. Bring her back to the land from which (that from there) she and her daughter were taken. 3. Ten men from your (mpl) midst will be taken and sent; they shall not return. 4. The words that come out of the mouth of the wise man are listened to (heard). 5. Will you (ms) mourn (over) your son all your days? 6. The slave came out of the city this morning, has been pursued all day, but they still haven't overtaken him. 7. We were consoled because we were not alone in our distress. 8. Don't (fs) plead with me; you will be put in prison today! 9. Will she be remembered when she is gone (is not)?

(*To be followed by Reading 21, p. 164.*)

§ 19

FINAL ה VERBS

19.1 The third root consonant of such verbs as בָּכָה "he wept," עָשָׂה "he made, did," עָלָה "he went up" was in most cases originally י. Except in the *qal* passive participle (e.g., עָשׂוּי "made, done"), this י has as a rule quiesced.

(a) When in final position, the quiescent י is replaced in writing by the vowel letter ה, which stands for the following vowels:

ָ־ in the pf 3ms: *qal* בָּכָה "he wept," *pi'el* צִוָּה "he ordered," *hif'il* הִרְבָּה "he did/made much."

ֶ־ in the impf and pt ms: יִבְכֶּה, בּוֹכֶה; יְצַוֶּה, מְצַוֶּה; יַרְבֶּה, מַרְבֶּה

ֵ־ in the imv: בְּכֵה, צַוֵּה, הַרְבֵּה

(b) Before consonantal afformatives the י is written as part of a long vowel, which is:

ֶ־י in the impf (and imv): תִּבְכֶּינָה, תְּצַוֶּינָה, תַּרְבֶּינָה

ִ־י or ֵ־י in the pf: בָּכִיתִי, צִוִּיתִי (צִוֵּיתִי), הִרְבֵּיתִי

ֶ־י/ה and ֵ־י/ה have contracted from an original *ay*: יִבְכֶּה from **yibkay* (after the stative pattern of יִכְבַּד), תִּבְכֶּינָה from **tibkayna*, הִרְבֵּיתִי from **hirbayti* (cf. the sound הִשְׁלַכְתִּי). [Compare the analogous contraction of the original plural construct termination *ay* in חֲמוֹרֵי־ (< **ḥamoray*), with suffix חֲמוֹרֶיךָ (< **ḥamorayka*), §14.3.] ִ־י is contracted from *iy*: בָּכִיתִי from **bakiyti* (after the stative pattern **kabidti* > כָּבַדְתִּי).

(c) Before vowel afformatives the י is dropped, hence בָּכוּ, תִּבְכִּי, בּוֹכָה. It is likewise dropped before the infinitive construct ending, which is uniformly ־וֹת: (לְ)בְכוֹת, (לְ)צַוּוֹת, (לְ)הַרְבּוֹת.

(d) The pf 3fs, בָּכְתָה, has a double feminine termination: **baka+t+å(h)*, bringing it into conformity with the pattern of the sound verb: שָׁמְרָה.

19.2 An apocopated ("clipped") form, in which the ־ֶה termination of the imperfect is dropped, serves for the jussive and imperfect consecutive; e.g., יִבְךְ (<יִבְכֶּה), יְצַו. In *qal* (and *hif'il*) apocopation results in the formation of a consonant cluster; e.g., **tirb* < תִּרְבֶּה (from רבה "be great"); **yiḥr* < יֶחֱרֶה (from חרה "burn"); **ya'n* < יַעֲנֶה (from ענה "answer"). The cluster is then often broken by the insertion of a helping vowel: ־ֶ as in תֵּרֶב, or, after laryngals, ־ַ as in יִחַר, יַעַן. For more apocopated forms see §16.4(b).

19.3 In the *qal* imperfect of verbs that have both final ה and initial ע (such as עָנָה, עָלָה, עָשָׂה) the preformative ־ִ vowel is replaced by ־ַ, in accordance with the tendency of laryngals to demand homorganic vowels before them: thus יַעֲלֶה (but אֶעֱלֶה). The apocopated form is יַעַל; the inf cs לַעֲלוֹת.

19.4 Exceptions to the rule that laryngals demand homorganic vowels before them are the verbs הָיָה and חָיָה. These inflect alike, except in the pt, which is rare for הָיָה.

impf: אֶהְיֶה, תִּהְיֶה, תִּהְיִי, יִהְיֶה, תִּהְיֶה, נִהְיֶה, תִּהְיוּ, תִּהְיֶינָה, יִהְיוּ, תִּהְיֶינָה

apoc: יְהִי

imv: הֱיֵה, הֲיִי, הֱיוּ, הֲיֶינָה

inf cs: הֱיוֹת, לִהְיוֹת

pt: (חָיָה): חַי, חַיָּה, חַיִּים, חַיּוֹת

19.5 Final ה verbs:

	QAL	PI'EL	HIF'IL
1cs pf	בָּכִיתִי	צִוִּיתִי (־וֵ־)	הִרְבֵּיתִי (־בֵּ־)
2m	בָּכִיתָ	צִוִּיתָ	הִרְבֵּיתָ (־בֵּ־)
2f	בָּכִית	צִוִּית	הִרְבֵּית (־בֵּ־)
3m	בָּכָה	צִוָּה	הִרְבָּה
3f	בָּכְתָה	צִוְּתָה	הִרְבְּתָה
1cpl	בָּכִינוּ	צִוִּינוּ	הִרְבִּינוּ
2m&f	בְּכִיתֶם–ן	צִוִּיתֶם–ן	הִרְבֵּיתֶם–ן (־בֵּ־)
3c	בָּכוּ	צִוּוּ	הִרְבּוּ
1cs impf	אֶבְכֶּה	אֲצַוֶּה	אַרְבֶּה
2m	תִּבְכֶּה	תְּצַוֶּה	תַּרְבֶּה
2f	תִּבְכִּי	תְּצַוִּי	תַּרְבִּי
3m	יִבְכֶּה	יְצַוֶּה	יַרְבֶּה
3f	תִּבְכֶּה	תְּצַוֶּה	תַּרְבֶּה
1cpl	נִבְכֶּה	נְצַוֶּה	נַרְבֶּה
2m	תִּבְכּוּ	תְּצַוּוּ	תַּרְבּוּ
2f	תִּבְכֶּינָה	תְּצַוֶּינָה	תַּרְבֶּינָה
3m	יִבְכּוּ	יְצַוּוּ	יַרְבּוּ
3f	תִּבְכֶּינָה	תְּצַוֶּינָה	תַּרְבֶּינָה
apoc	יֵבְךְ	יְצַו	יֶרֶב
ms imv	בְּכֵה	צַוֵּה	הַרְבֵּה
f	בְּכִי	צַוִּי	הַרְבִּי
mpl	בְּכוּ	צַוּוּ	הַרְבּוּ
f	בְּכֶינָה	צַוֶּינָה	הַרְבֶּינָה
inf abs	בָּכֹה	צַוֹּה, צַוֵּה	הַרְבֵּה (הַרְבָּה)
inf cs	בְּכוֹת, לִבְכּוֹת	(לְ)צַוּוֹת	(לְ)הַרְבּוֹת
ms pt	בּוֹכֶה	מְצַוֶּה	מַרְבֶּה
f	בּוֹכָה	מְצַוָּה	מַרְבָּה

	QAL	PI'EL	HIF'IL
mpl pt	בּוֹכִים	מְצַוִּים	מַרְבִּים
f	בּוֹכוֹת	מְצַוּוֹת	מַרְבּוֹת
pass pt	עָשׂוּי		

* * * * * * *

Conjugate in qal:

שתה, עשה, חיה.

Conjugate in pi'el:

כלה.

Conjugate in hif'il:

בכה.

Vocalize and translate:

1. עלינו למקומנו. 2. צוו להראות להם את הדם. 3. איפה רעית את צאנך בצהרים? 4. השיבותם לי רעה תחת הטובה אשר עשיתי לכם. 5. ראו כי נקרעו שמלותיו. 6. בכתה והתחננה אל המלך כי לא ימית אתה. 7. חפשו מים לשתות ולא מצאו בכל המקום ההוא. 8. הרעב כלה את הארץ. 9. כאשר עלתה השמש היינו בדרך. 10. השתחוו ארצה ובקשו רחמים לפני המלך. 11. ראיתם את אשר עשיתי. 12. שתית את כל המים אשר היו בבור. 13. כאשר כלתה לדבר איש לא ענה אתה.

Change above verbs to imperfects.

Replace the following imperfect consecutives with perfects :

1. וַיַּעַן אֹתָם רְאוּבֵן. 2. וַיֵּבְךְ אֹתוֹ אָבִיו. 3. וַיִּחַר אַף הַמֶּלֶךְ. 4. וַתְּחִי רוּחַ יַעֲקֹב. 5. וַיְכַל אֶת הָאֹכֶל. 6. וַיְצַו יוֹסֵף אֶת אֲשֶׁר עַל בֵּיתוֹ. 7. וַתֹּאכַל וַתֵּשְׁתְּ וַתָּקָם וַתֵּלֶךְ. 8. וַתְּמַהֵר וַתַּעַשׂ אֶת דְּבַר הַמֶּלֶךְ.

Translate :

1. Drink (mpl) from this water but don't finish it. 2. We shall see what will come of (be) his dreams. 3. You (fs) shall yet see what will befall them. 4. Pharaoh's cows will go up from the river after (that) they finish drinking (to drink). 5. They (fpl) are doing that which she ordered them to do. 6. He who orders the old man to return alone has no compassion. 7. Better to die in well-being than to live in misery (evil). 8. What shall I do if he does not answer? 9. She had not yet finished speaking (to speak) when (and) her young son came into the room crying.

(*To be followed by Reading 23, p. 167.*)

§ 20

INITIAL י VERBS

20.1 Initial י verbs comprise two classes: verbs originally initial ו and a much smaller number of verbs originally initial י.

20.2 Original ו > י wherever it was initial. Thus from ולד* "give birth" are derived *qal* יָלַד, *pi'el* יִלֵּד, *pu'al* יֻלַּד and, by analogy, *hitpa'el* הִתְיַלֵּד. The inflection of the entire *pi'el* group is regular, since the secondary י is maintained even after preformatives (e.g., *pi'el* impf יְיַלֵּד, pt מְיַלֵּד). In *qal* impf, etc., the initial root-consonant drops, as described below.

Original ו was maintained when preceded by the נ augment of *nif'al* (נוֹלַד, יִוָּלֵד) and the ה augment of *hif/hŏf'al* (הוֹלִיד, יוֹלִיד; הוּלַד).

(a) Maintained ו is consonantal when it begins the syllable: יִוָּלֵד < **yinwaled*.[1] At the syllable end, ו and the preceding vowel contract to וֹ, וּ: **hawlid* > הוֹלִיד, **huwlad* > הוּלַד

(b) Initial ו > י in nouns too: **wald* > **yald* > יֶלֶד "child"; but **mawladt* > מוֹלֶדֶת "family."

20.3 In *qal* impf, etc., initial ו verbs fall into two inflectional patterns, according as they are active or stative.

---

1 Cf. הִתְוַדַּע; הִתְיַלֵּד, cited above, follows the analogy of *pi'el*.

The actives — including the common verbs יָלַד, יָצָא, יָרַד, יָשַׁב — build their imperfect and imperative on a biconsonantal base consisting of only the last two root consonants vocalized with ־ְ; the preformatives of the imperfect are also vocalized with ־ְ: יֵלֵד, יֵצֵא, יֵרֵד, יֵשֵׁב; לֵד! שֵׁב! רֵד! צֵא! But יֵדַע דַּע!, the ־ַ due to the laryngal (§ 23.2).

The infinitive construct adds the feminine ת ending to this biconsonantal base: (לָ)דַעַת, (לָ)לֶדֶת, (לָ)צֵאת[1], (לָ)רֶדֶת, (לָ)שֶׁבֶת.

20.4 The imperfect and related forms and the infinitive construct of הָלַךְ inflect in the same pattern: יֵלֵךְ, לֵךְ! (לְכָה!), (לָ)לֶכֶת.

20.5 The stative initial ו verbs inflect after the pattern of יִכְבַּד. Thus יָרֵא "he was afraid": יִירָא, יָרֵא!, לִירֹא.

In the imperfect and imperative of יָרֵא, ־ֵ is lengthened to ־ָ to compensate for the quiescence of the א.

20.6 The verb יָכֹל has an anomalous imperfect, יוּכַל, which appears to be inflected according to the *hŏf'al* pattern.

20.7 Initial ו verbs:

QAL

stative		*active*		
אוּכַל	אִירָא	אֵדַע	אֵלֵד	1cs impf
תּוּכַל	תִּירָא	תֵּדַע	תֵּלֵד	2m
תּוּכְלִי	תִּירְאִי	תֵּדְעִי	תֵּלְדִי	2f
יוּכַל	יִירָא	יֵדַע	יֵלֵד	3m
תּוּכַל	תִּירָא	תֵּדַע	תֵּלֵד	3f
נוּכַל	נִירָא	נֵדַע	נֵלֵד	1cpl
תּוּכְלוּ	תִּירְאוּ	תֵּדְעוּ	תֵּלְדוּ	2m
תּוּכַלְנָה	תִּירֶאנָה	תֵּדַעְנָה	תֵּלַדְנָה תֵּצֶאנָה	2&3f
יוּכְלוּ	יִירְאוּ	יֵדְעוּ	יֵלְדוּ	3m

[1] צֵאת is contracted from צֶאֱת*.

	QAL *active*	QAL *stative*
juss	יֵלֵד (וַיֵּלֶד)	
ms imv	לֵד, רְדָה דַּע	יְרָא
f	לְדִי דְּעִי	יִרְאִי
mpl	לְדוּ דְּעוּ	יִרְאוּ
f	לֵדְנָה דַּעְנָה צְאֶנָה	יִרְאֶנָה
inf cs	(לָ)לֶדֶת (לָ)דַעַת (לָ)צֵאת	(לִ)יראֹ

	NIF'AL	HIF'IL
1cs pf	נוֹלַדְתִּי	הוֹלַדְתִּי
2m&f	נוֹלַדְתָּ–תְּ	הוֹלַדְתָּ–תְּ
3m	נוֹלַד	הוֹלִיד
3f	נוֹלְדָה	הוֹלִידָה
1cpl	נוֹלַדְנוּ	הוֹלַדְנוּ
2m&f	נוֹלַדְתֶּם–ן	הוֹלַדְתֶּם–ן
3c	נוֹלְדוּ	הוֹלִידוּ
1cs impf	אִוָּלֵד	אוֹלִיד
2m	תִּוָּלֵד	תּוֹלִיד
2f	תִּוָּלְדִי	תּוֹלִידִי
3m	יִוָּלֵד	יוֹלִיד
3f	תִּוָּלֵד	תּוֹלִיד
1cpl	נִוָּלֵד	נוֹלִיד
2m	תִּוָּלְדוּ	תּוֹלִידוּ
2&3f	תִּוָּלַדְנָה	תּוֹלַדְנָה
3m	יִוָּלְדוּ	יוֹלִידוּ
juss	יִוָּלֵד	יוֹלֵד (וַיּוֹלֶד)
imv	הִוָּלֵד	הוֹלֵד
inf cs	(לְ)הִוָּלֵד	(לְ)הוֹלִיד
pt	נוֹלָד	מוֹלִיד

20.8 The few originally initial י verbs inflect as statives; e.g., יטב "be good, pleasing," which occurs only in *qal* impf יִיטַב, וַיִּיטַב and *hif'il* pf הֵיטִיב, impf יֵיטִיב, pt מֵיטִיב.

* * * * * * *

Conjugate in qal *and* hif'il:

ירד, ישב.

Conjugate in nif'al:

יתר "be left, remaining."

Give corresponding forms:

in hif'il: יָדַעְתִּי, יָדְעוּ, תֵּדְעִי, יוֹדְעִים, לָדַעַת,
יָצְאָה, אֵצֵא, תֵּצְאוּ, צֵא! צְאֶנָּה! לָצֵאת.
in nif'al: יָדְעָה, יָדַעְתֶּם, תֵּדְעִי, דְּעוּ! יוֹדְעוֹת,
יָשְׁבוּ, אֵשֵׁב, תֵּשַׁבְנָה, לָשֶׁבֶת.

Vocalize and translate:

1. מכל בניו נותרו לו שנים. 2. לא תלכו עמנו. 3. אם ישימו לפניהם אכל רב לא יוכלו לאכל אתו כי קטנים הם. 4. בבקר הורדנו את הצאן אל העמק. 5. אחר אשר התודעו אלי הכרתי אתם. 6. לא נירא למות. 7. הם הולידו בנים רבים לפני שני הרעב. 8. טוב כי תצאו מן העיר בטרם יוציאו אתכם השומרים. 9. דעו לפני מי אתם עומדים! 10. אל תיראו לרדת מצרימה! 11. האנשים אוהבים כי נשיהם תלדנה בנים.

Change verbs of above paragraph to singular.

Convert imperfect consecutives to perfects :

1. וַיִּוָּתֵר יַעֲקֹב לְבַדּוֹ. 2. וַיִּוָּלְדוּ לוֹ בָנִים בְּחֶבְרוֹן. 3. וַתָּשָׁב אֶל אָבִיהָ וַתֵּשֶׁב לְפָנָיו וַתֵּבְךְ. 4. וַיּוֹלֶד בָּנִים וּבָנוֹת. 5. וַיֹּאכַל וַיִּשְׁתְּ וַיָּקָם וַיֵּלֶךְ. 6. וַגֵּרֶד מִצְרַיְמָה וַנֵּשֶׁב שָׁם.

Translate :

1. When they come down, we shall be able to go. 2. Can she rule this great land? 3. When they informed (caused to know) him that his brother reigned instead of his father, he raised his voice and wept. 4. How will one man be able to do that which many are not able to do? 5. If it pleases you, give him five wagons. 6. We shall prepare food for you (mpl) before the day is done (goes out). 7. His feelings were stirred toward the donkey, so he hastily took (down) the heavy saddlebag from off him. 8. May God take out his hard heart and put a good heart in its place. 9. Of all the goats that went out into the field not one remained, for the wild animals ate them.

(To be followed by Genesis 37:1–8, 9–17.)

§ 21

FINAL א AND INITIAL א VERBS

Final א *verbs*

21.1 When א stands at the end of a word and usually, also, when at the end of a syllable, it quiesces, and the preceding vowel is lengthened by way of compensation. Hence **måṣa'* > *måṣå* (מָצָא), **yimṣa'* > *yimṣå* (יִמְצָא).

21.2 This process results in some forms of final א verbs sounding like corresponding forms of final ה verbs; e.g., מָצָא like בָּכָה. Consequently a certain mixture of final א and final ה forms takes place, with final ה forms more often imposing themselves on the final א paradigm than vice versa, owing to their greater frequency. Thus the impf 2 and 3fpl are תִּמְצֶאנָה, like תִּבְכֶּינָה; and outside of *qal* the perfect inflects throughout with ־ִ before consonantal afformatives: מִלֵּאתִי like צִוִּיתִי; הִמְצֵאתִי like הִרְבֵּיתִי.

In Rabbinic Hebrew final א verbs assimilated to the final ה pattern prevailingly.

21.3 Final א verbs:

	QAL *active*	QAL *stative*	NIF'AL	PI'EL	HIF'IL
1cs pf	מָצָאתִי	שָׂנֵאתִי	נִמְצֵאתִי	מִלֵּאתִי	הִמְצֵאתִי
2m&f	מָצָאתָ־ת	שָׂנֵאתָ־ת	נִמְצֵאתָ־ת	מִלֵּאתָ־ת	הִמְצֵאתָ־ת
3m&f	מָצָא־צְאָה	שָׂנֵא־נְאָה	נִמְצָא־צְאָה	מִלֵּא־לְאָה[1]	הִמְצִיא־צִיאָה
1cpl	מָצָאנוּ	שָׂנֵאנוּ	נִמְצֵאנוּ	מִלֵּאנוּ	הִמְצֵאנוּ
2m&f	מְצָאתֶם־ן	שְׂנֵאתֶם־ן	נִמְצֵאתֶם־ן	מִלֵּאתֶם־ן	הִמְצֵאתֶם־ן
3c	מָצְאוּ	שָׂנְאוּ	נִמְצְאוּ	מִלְּאוּ[1]	הִמְצִיאוּ
1cs impf	אֶמְצָא		אֶמָּצֵא	אֲמַלֵּא	אַמְצִיא
2m&f	תִּמְצָא־צְאִי		etc.	etc.	etc.
3m&f	יִמְצָא, תִּ־				
1cpl	נִמְצָא				
2m	תִּמְצְאוּ				
2&3f	תִּמְצֶאנָה		תִּמָּצֶאנָה	תְּמַלֵּאנָה	תַּמְצֶאנָה
3m	יִמְצְאוּ				
ms imv	מְצָא fpl מְצֶאנָה		הִמָּצֶאנָה fpl	מַלֵּאנָה	הַמְצֶאנָה
inf cs	(לְ)מְצֹא				
ms pt	מוֹצֵא		נִמְצָא	מְמַלֵּא	מַמְצִיא
f	מוֹצֵאת		נִמְצֵאת	מְמַלֵּאת	מַמְצֵאת
m&fpl	מוֹצְאִים־אוֹת		נִמְצָאִים־אוֹת	מְמַלְּאִים־אוֹת[1]	מַמְצִיאִים־אוֹת

(a) Note that in *qal* stative the ־ֵ is retained throughout the perfect (contrast כָּבַדְתִּי, etc.).

(b) *Qal* imperfect inflects always on the יִכְבַּד pattern.

(c) Note that the pt fs replaces ־ָ ־ֶת with ־אֶת (שׁוֹמֶרֶת but מוֹצֵאת).

---

1 On the unlengthened לְ see p. 105, note 1.

Initial א *verbs*

21.4 In the *qal* imperfect, initial א verbs fall into two inflectional patterns:

(a) When the א does not quiesce, as in אָסַף "he gathered," the inflection is:

אֶאֱסֹף, תֶּאֱסֹף, תַּאַסְפִי, יֶאֱסֹף, תֶּאֱסֹף, נֶאֱסֹף, תַּאַסְפוּ, תֶּאֱסֹפְנָה, יַאַסְפוּ, תֶּאֱסֹפְנָה.

The preformative vowel is ־ֶ, except in forms having vowel afformatives, in which case it is ־ַ. In the latter case the vowel under the א is a full vowel, no longer a *ḥaṭâf*.

The imperative: אֱסֹף, אִסְפִי, אִסְפוּ, אֱסֹפְנָה. The infinitive construct: (לְ)אֱסֹף.

(b) In five verbs (אָכַל "eat," אָמַר "say," אָבַד "perish," אָבָה "be willing," אָפָה "bake") the א quiesces, entailing vowel changes thus:

אֹכַל, תֹּאכַל, תֹּאכְלִי, יֹאכַל, תֹּאכַל, נֹאכַל, תֹּאכְלוּ, תֹּאכַלְנָה, יֹאכְלוּ, תֹּאכַלְנָה.

The imperfect consecutive: וַיֹּאכַל, but וַיֹּאמֶר [in pause (§29) וַיֹּאמַר].

The imperative: אֱכֹל, אִכְלִי, אִכְלוּ, אֱכֹלְנָה.

The infinitive construct: (לְ)אֱכֹל, but לֵאמֹר.

In all else initial א verbs inflect as other initial laryngals (§23).

* * * * * * *

Conjugate in qal *and* nif'al:

יָרֵא, קָרָא

Conjugate in pi'el:

קִנֵּא

Conjugate in hif'il:

יָצָא, קָרָא

Fill in perfect, imperfect, and participle of indicated verbs:

שָׁנֵא: 1. הָאִשָּׁה _____ אֶת הַחַיָּה. 2. אַתְּ _____ כָּל עוֹשֵׂה רָע.
קִנֵּא: 3. אֲנִי _____ בְּךָ. 4. הָאִישׁ _____ בְּאָחִיו.
הֵבִיא: 5. הָרוֹעֶה _____ אֶת צֹאנוֹ אֶל הַשָּׂדֶה. 6. אַתְּ _____ אֶת בְּנֵךְ אֶל הַחֶדֶר.

Change subjects and verbs of the preceding exercise to plural.

Vocalize and translate:

1. אל תאמר לי מה לעשות! 2. אלהים צוה את בני ישראל כי לא ישתחוו לאלהים אחרים. 3. אחי יוסף היו מקנאים בו וכאשר שמעו את דבריו הוסיפו עוד לקנא בו. 4. אם יאמר השר לאסר אתכם, קראו אלי בקול גדול ואבוא אליכם! 5. אם השתחוית לשמש ולירח חטאת לאלהים. 6. אל תשנא את אחיך! 7. מלאו את שקיהם שבר כאשר דבר המושל. 8. תוציאו כל איש מהחדר. 9. הוספתי לקרא אליו והוא לא שמע. 10. יצאתם מן העמק הזה ובאתם אל עמק אחר. 11. רחל היתה מקנאת בלאה. 12. אם נבקש ארץ אחרת טובה מזאת לא נמצא. 13. פרותיכם נמצאו בתוך שדנו.

Translate:

1. The shepherds took (out) bread from their sacks and sought a place in which they could sit and eat. 2. Don't (ms) fear to say to her that she sinned. 3. You (mpl) were jealous of your brother because your father loved him more than all his sons. 4. Fill (fs) our sack with provisions for the way. 5. If we sit in the field we shall see

the sun coming up (out) in the morning. 6. Now we can prepare the food, for we know who will eat with us. 7. I cannot say whether she will come down or go up. 8. They will take out all the other prisoners, will put you there alone, and no man will know this. 9. Gather (ms) all the wise men of the city and let them say who will be king over them. 10. She is called Rachel.

(*To be followed by Genesis 37:18–27, 28–36.*)

§ 22

INITIAL נ VERBS

22.1 When נ occurs at the end of a syllable within a word it usually assimilates to the following consonant, if that consonant is not a laryngal (cf. *nif'al* imperfect יִנְשָׁמֵר* > יִשָּׁמֵר; שָׁם + מִן = מִשָּׁם).

Such assimilation occurs regularly in initial נ verbs; e.g., *qal* imperfect יִנְפֹּל* > יִפֹּל "he will fall," *nif'al* perfect נִנְגַּשׁ* > נִגַּשׁ "he drew near," throughout *hif'il* הִנְכִּיר* > הִכִּיר "he recognized," and *hŏf'al* הֻנְכַּר* > הֻכַּר "he was recognized."

22.2 Initial נ verbs:

HIF'IL		NIF'AL		QAL		
				a *impf*	o *impf*	
הִכַּרְתִּי	1cs pf	נִגַּשְׁתִּי	1cs pf	אֶגַּשׁ	אֶפֹּל	1cs
הִכַּרְתָּ–תְּ	2m&f	נִגַּשְׁתָּ–תְּ	2m&f	תִּגַּשׁ–גְּשִׁי	תִּפֹּל–פְּלִי	2m&f
הִכִּיר, הִכִּירָה	3m&f	נִגַּשׁ–גְּשָׁה	3m&f	יִגַּשׁ, תִּ־	יִפֹּל, תִּ־	3m&f
הִכַּרְנוּ	1cpl	נִגַּשְׁנוּ	1cpl	נִגַּשׁ	נִפֹּל	1cpl
הִכַּרְתֶּם–ן	2m&f	נִגַּשְׁתֶּם–ן	2m&f	תִּגְּשׁוּ	תִּפְּלוּ	2m
הִכִּירוּ	3c	נִגְּשׁוּ	3c	תִּגְּשְׁנָה	תִּפֹּלְנָה	2&3f
				יִגְּשׁוּ	יִפְּלוּ	3m

HIF'IL		NIF'AL		QAL		
				a *impf*	o *impf*	
אַכִּיר	1cs impf	נִגָּשׁ	ms pt	גַּשׁ	נְפֹל	ms imv
תַּכִּיר, תַּכִּירִי	2m&f	נִגֶּשֶׁת	f	גְּשִׁי	נִפְלִי	f
יַכִּיר, תַּ־	3m&f	נִגְּשִׁים	mpl	גְּשׁוּ	נִפְלוּ	mpl
נַכִּיר	1cpl	נִגְּשׁוֹת	f	גַּשְׁנָה	נִפְלְנָה	f
תַּכִּירוּ	2m					
תַּכֵּרְנָה	2&3f			גֶּשֶׁת,לָגֶשֶׁת	נְפֹל,לִנְפֹל	inf cs
יַכִּירוּ	3m					
הַכֵּר, הַכִּירִי	m&fs imv					
הַכִּירוּ, הַכֵּרְנָה	m&fpl					
(לְ)הַכִּיר	inf cs					
מַכִּיר	ms pt					

(a) Note that in the *qal a* imperfect נ is dropped in the imperative and infinitive construct. The latter is filled out with the feminine ת termination; cf. the infinitive construct of initial י/ו verbs (לָ)לֶדֶת (§ 20.3).

(b) The verb נִגַּשׁ inflects its perfect and participle in *nif'al*, but its imperfect and related forms and infinitive construct in *qal*, as in the above paradigm.

The verbs נָתַן, לָקַח, נָשָׂא, הִכָּה

22.3 The verb נָתַן "he gave" inflects thus:

pf: נָתַתִּי, נָתַתָּ, נָתַתְּ, נָתַן, נָתְנָה, נָתַנּוּ, נְתַתֶּם־ן, נָתְנוּ

impf: אֶתֵּן, תִּתֵּן, תִּתְּנִי, יִתֵּן, תִּתֵּן, נִתֵּן, תִּתְּנוּ, תִּתֵּנָה, יִתְּנוּ, תִּתֵּנָה

imv: תֵּן (תְּנָה), תְּנִי, תְּנוּ, תֵּנָה inf cs: תֵּת, לָתֵת, w suf תִּתִּי

With the ־ֵ of the imperfect compare יֵלֵד. The infinitive construct is formed thus: **tin-t* > תֵּת, hence with suffix **tinti* > תִּתִּי.

22.4 The verb לָקַח "he took" inflects its imperfect, imperative, and infinitive construct as though it were an initial נ verb; this is apparently owing to an analogy with its antonym נָתַן. Its theme vowel is ־ַ because of the laryngal.

impf: אֶקַּח, תִּקַּח, תִּקְּחִי[1], יִקַּח, תִּקַּח, נִקַּח, תִּקְּחוּ[1], תִּקַּחְנָה, יִקְּחוּ[1], תִּקַּחְנָה

imv: קַח, קְחִי, קְחוּ, קַחְנָה

inf cs: (לָ)קַחַת

22.5 The verb נָשָׂא "he carried" inflects with the peculiarities of both initial נ and final א verbs:

impf: אֶשָּׂא, תִּשָּׂא, תִּשְּׂאִי[1], יִשָּׂא, תִּשָּׂא, נִשָּׂא, תִּשְּׂאוּ[1], תִּשֶּׂאנָה, יִשְּׂאוּ[1], תִּשֶּׂאנָה.

imv: שָׂא, שְׂאִי, שְׂאוּ, שֶׂאנָה

inf cs: (לָ)שֵׂאת

22.6 The verb נכה, common in *hif'il* הִכָּה "he smote, struck," inflects with the peculiarities of both initial נ and final ה verbs:

pf: הִכִּיתִי, הִכִּיתָ, הִכִּית, הִכָּה, הִכְּתָה, הִכִּינוּ, הִכִּיתֶם־ן, הִכּוּ

impf: אַכֶּה, תַּכֶּה, תַּכִּי, יַכֶּה, תַּכֶּה, נַכֶּה, תַּכּוּ, תַּכֶּינָה, יַכּוּ, תַּכֶּינָה

apoc: יַךְ

imv: הַכֵּה, הַכִּי, הַכּוּ, הַכֶּינָה

inf cs: (לְ)הַכּוֹת

pt: מַכֶּה, מַכָּה, מַכִּים, מַכּוֹת

Conjugate in qal:

נשק (*a* impf).

Conjugate in nif'al:

נצל ("be saved" in *nif'al*).

---

1 Lengthening is often given up in sibilants (ז, ס, צ, ש), liquids (ל, מ, נ), and ק when they take mobile *šewâ*.

Conjugate in hif'il:

נשג, נגד

Fill in perfect, imperfect, and participle of indicated verbs:

נָשָׂא: 1. הָאֵם _____ אֶת בְּנָהּ הַקָּטֹן. 2. הַחֲמוֹרִים _____ אֶת הַשַּׂקִּים.

נִגַּשׁ: 3. אֲנִי _____ אֶל הַפֶּתַח. 4. אַתֶּם _____ אֵלָיו.

הִצִּיל: 5. אַתָּה _____ אֶת הַצֹּאן מִפִּי הַחַיָּה. 6. אֲנַחְנוּ _____ אֹתוֹ מִן הַבּוֹר.

הִכָּה: 7. אֲנַחְנוּ _____ אֶת הַחֲמוֹר. 8. הַנָּשִׁים _____ אֶת בְּנוֹתֵיהֶן.

Vocalize and translate:

1. שא עיניך אל אלהים! 2. אם תלך במדבר בלילה תפל בבורות אשר בו. 3. אל תסעו ביום פן תכה אתכם השמש! 4. מי יציל את שעיר העזים מן החיה הטורפת? 5. כאשר יפל הבן בדרך ולא יוכל ללכת עוד ישא אתו אביו. 6. משכו את החמור והכו אתו ולא קם מעל הארץ. 7. אין איש יכל לגשת אל המלך כי שומריו נצבים עליו. 8. הצלנו את העזים מחיות השדה. 9. תנו לי לחם לאכל! 10. עברו על פתח ביתם וקראו להם! 11. יסעו בעוד שנים עשר יום. 12. אל תשא את העז לבדך כי כבדה היא! 13. מי זה נצב שם בפתח?

Translate:

1. They told us that they would give much money to the man who

would rescue them from prison. 2. Tell (fs) me to whom I should give the garment. 3. Many days passed and they still could not overtake him. 4. It is better to give than to take. 5. He will not eat flesh even if you (fs) do not give him another thing. 6. Give well-being to the land and rescue us from all who hate us. 7. She came up to the weeping child and struck him on his face. 8. If you (ms) know who the owner (master) of this tunic is, take it and carry it off from before my house. 9. Many will fall before (that) they come out of the wilderness.

(*To be followed by Genesis 42:1–11, 12–20*).

§ 23

INITIAL LARYNGAL VERBS

The peculiarities of laryngals

23.1 Laryngals (א, ה, ח, ע) and ר are not normally lengthened. In positions where lengthening is called for, laryngals and ר remain short (i.e., do not take strong *dâgeš*). By way of compensation, the preceding vowel may be lengthened: ַ > ָ, ִ > ִי, ֶ > ֵ. Compensatory vowel lengthening occurs:

(a) always in *nif'al* imperfect (and related forms): יֵעָצֵב "he will be grieved" ‖[1] יִשָּׁמֵר;

(b) almost always with א and ר in other forms as well: מֵאֵן "he refused" ‖ סִפֵּר, יְמָאֵן ‖ יְסַפֵּר, בֹּרַךְ "he was blessed" ‖ סֻפַּר;

(c) only sporadically in other forms with ע, ח, ה: examples of nonoccurrence are מְהַר "he hastened," נְחֵשׁ "he divined."

---

1 Read: "corresponding to."

23.2 Laryngals in what would normally be syllable-end position prefer to be preceded by ַ. If in a stressed or a final syllable, they *must* be preceded by ַ (or ָ). If the preceding vowel according to the regular pattern is not ַ:

(a) it is replaced by ַ : יִשְׁמֹר ‖ יִשְׁלַח, שִׁלַּח ‖ סִפֵּר, תַּשְׁמַעְנָה ‖ תַּשְׁלִכְנָה;

(b) between it and a final laryngal, furtive *pa̍ṯaḥ* insinuates itself; this always occurs when the vowel in question is the naturally long וֹ, וּ, ־ִי, ־ֵי : הִשְׁמִיעַ ‖ הִשְׁלִיךְ, שָׁמוֹר ‖ שָׁלוֹחַ, שָׁמוּר ‖ שָׁלוּחַ, שׁוֹמֵר ‖ שׁוֹלֵחַ, לִשְׁמֹר ‖ לִשְׁלֹחַ.

23.3 Laryngals often take *ḥaṭåf* in preference to simple *šewå*:

(a) Mobile *šewå* [§ 2.7(b)] is always replaced by *ḥaṭåf*, usually *ḥaṭåf pa̍ṯaḥ*: עֲמֹד ‖ שְׁמֹר, שָׁאֲלוּ ‖ שָׁמְרוּ;

(b) Quiescent *šewå* [§ 2.7(a)] in a stressed syllable never becomes *ḥaṭåf*: שָׁלַחְנוּ, תִּשְׁלַחְנָה;

(c) In an unstressed syllable quiescent *šewå* may or may not become *ḥaṭåf*. When it does, the *ḥaṭåf* is colored by the preceding vowel, resulting in the patterns ַ ֲ (יַעֲמֹד), ֶ ֱ (אֶעֱמֹד), ָ ֳ (יָעֳמַד);

(d) When in the course of inflection the vowel following the *ḥaṭåf* is reduced to *šewå*, the *ḥaṭåf* becomes a full vowel: יַעַמְדוּ, נֶעֱצְבוּ, יָעָמְדוּ (*yŏʿŏmēdu*).

23.4 In certain forms, ִ before a syllable-ending laryngal is changed to ֶ (נִשְׁמַר ‖ נֶעֱצַב, הִשְׁלִיךְ ‖ הֶאֱמִין, יִכְבַּד ‖ יֶחֱרַד) and ֶ to *qåmeṣ ḥåṭuf* (מֶשְׁלָךְ ‖ מָעֳמָד).

23.5 See paradigms of initial laryngal verbs. *Note*: Initial **א** verbs that depart from the regular laryngal pattern have been treated above (§ 21).

Remarks on the paradigm. The different preformative vowels of the two *qal* imperfects (active יַעֲמֹד, stative יֶחֱרַד) reflect original distinctions that have been lost in the sound verb. The original preformatives were active *ya-* stative *yi-*. The tendency of *a* to become *i* in closed, unstressed syllables caused the two to merge in the sound verb (יִכְבַּד, יִשְׁמֹר). But *ya-* still appears in the hollow verbs (יָשׁוּב) and with initial laryngals (in accordance with § 23.2). Original *yi-* became *ye-* before laryngals (in accordance with § 23.4).

Initial laryngal verbs עָמַד "he stood," חָרַד "he trembled," נֶעֱצַב "he was grieved," הֶאֱמִין "he believed":

HIF'IL	NIF'AL	QAL		
		stative	*active*	
הֶאֱמַנְתִּי	נֶעֱצַבְתִּי	חָרַדְתִּי	עָמַדְתִּי	1cs pf
הֶאֱמַנְתָּ–תְּ	נֶעֱצַבְתָּ–תְּ	חָרַדְתָּ–תְּ	עָמַדְתָּ–תְּ	2m&f
הֶאֱמִין	נֶעֱצַב	חָרַד	עָמַד	3m
הֶאֱמִינָה	נֶעֱצְבָה	חָרְדָה	עָמְדָה	3f
הֶאֱמַנּוּ	נֶעֱצַבְנוּ	חָרַדְנוּ	עָמַדְנוּ	1cpl
הֶאֱמַנְתֶּם–ן	נֶעֱצַבְתֶּם–ן	חֲרַדְתֶּם–ן	עֲמַדְתֶּם–ן	2m&f
הֶאֱמִינוּ	נֶעֱצְבוּ	חָרְדוּ	עָמְדוּ	3c
אַאֲמִין	אֵעָצֵב	אֶחֱרַד	אֶעֱמֹד	1cs impf
תַּאֲמִין	תֵּעָצֵב	תֶּחֱרַד	תַּעֲמֹד	2m
תַּאֲמִינִי	תֵּעָצְבִי	תֶּחֱרְדִי	תַּעַמְדִי	2f
יַאֲמִין	יֵעָצֵב	יֶחֱרַד	יַעֲמֹד	3m
תַּאֲמִין	תֵּעָצֵב	תֶּחֱרַד	תַּעֲמֹד	3f
נַאֲמִין	נֵעָצֵב	נֶחֱרַד	נַעֲמֹד	1cpl
תַּאֲמִינוּ	תֵּעָצְבוּ	תֶּחֱרְדוּ	תַּעַמְדוּ	2m

	QAL *active*	QAL *stative*	NIF'AL	HIF'IL
2&3fpl impf	תַּעֲמֹדְנָה	תֶּחֱרַדְנָה	תֵּעָצַבְנָה	תַּאֲמֵנָה
3m	יַעַמְדוּ	יֶחֱרְדוּ	יֵעָצְבוּ	יַאֲמִינוּ
ms imv	עֲמֹד	חְרַד	הֵעָצֵב	הַאֲמֵן
f	עִמְדִי	חִרְדִי	הֵעָצְבִי	הַאֲמִינִי
mpl	עִמְדוּ	חִרְדוּ	הֵעָצְבוּ	הַאֲמִינוּ
f	עֲמֹדְנָה	חְרַדְנָה	הֵעָצַבְנָה	הַאֲמֵנָה
inf cs	(לַ)עֲמֹד	(לַ)חֲרֹד	(לְ)הֵעָצֵב	(לְ)הַאֲמִין
ms pt	עוֹמֵד	חָרֵד	נֶעֱצָב	מַאֲמִין
f	עוֹמֶדֶת	חֲרֵדָה	נֶעֱצֶבֶת	מַאֲמִינָה
m&fpl	עוֹמְדִים–דוֹת	חֲרֵדִים–דוֹת	נֶעֱצָבִים–בוֹת	מַאֲמִינִים–נוֹת
ms pt pass	הָרוּג "killed"			
f	הֲרוּגָה			
m&fpl	הֲרוּגִים–גוֹת			

* * * * * * *

Give corresponding forms of verbs as indicated:

Of עָבַר, אָשַׁם, עָשָׂה corresponding to: לִשְׁמֹר, שִׁמְרוּ!, שְׁמֹר!, יִשְׁמְרוּ, יִשְׁמֹר, תִּשְׁמְרִי, אֶשְׁמֹר, שְׁמַרְתֶּם

Of הָרַג corresponding to: לְהִשָּׁמֵר, נִשְׁמֶרֶת, יִשָּׁמְרוּ, אֶשָּׁמֵר, נִשְׁמַר, נִשְׁמְרָה

Of עָבַר, חָטָא, עָלָה corresponding to: לְהַשְׁלִיךְ, מַשְׁלִיכִים הִשְׁלַכְתִּי, הִשְׁלִיכָה, יַשְׁלִיךְ, תַּשְׁלֵכְנָה, הַשְׁלֵךְ!

Vocalize and translate:

1. ארץ! אל תכסי את דם הנהרגים אשר נשפך עליך! 2. האיש

אחד יחטא ובכל העם יחרה אפך? 3. אנשי העיר מנער עד זקן נאספו מרחוק ומקרוב לראות בבוא המלך. 4. תעברנה הפרות לפנינו ונראה מי הטובות בהן. 5. כאשר תעברו את הבית ראו היש בו איש אם ריק הוא? 6. חטאתם והחטאתם את הרבים. 7. אם יהרגו את הילד יחטאו לאלהים ויאשמו. 8. תוכל להאמין לדבריו כי איש אמת הוא. 9. החכם ידע לפתר כל חלום אשר יחלמו. 10. אחר אשר תהרג החיה הרעה לא נירא לצאת אל השדה. 11. נאסרנו ולא עשיתם דבר להציל אתנו. 12. תקחו את הילד ותשאו אתו אל אמו.

Translate:

1. We shall sin if we kill them. 2. Won't he answer if you talk to him? 3. She saw that they would pass the empty house. 4. The three who were imprisoned will come and stand before him. 5. The garment will be made as you requested. 6. The slain covered the face of the earth. 7. You (mpl) may not eat the flesh that you find in the field. 8. We didn't believe that he could bring the cow up from the pit. 9. Why do they tremble? Because they are guilty in the eyes of God. 10. We are bringing into the house all the sheaves that were not yet gathered from the midst of the field. 11. Put your (ms) hand in mine and we shall carry this old man.

(*To be followed by Genesis 42:21–28, 29–38.*)

§ 24

MIDDLE AND FINAL LARYNGAL VERBS

24.1 Middle laryngal verbs שָׁאַל "he asked," מֵאֵן "he refused," מִהַר "he hurried":

PI'EL			NIF'AL	QAL	
מִהַרְתִּי	מֵאַנְתִּי	1cs pf	נִשְׁאֲלָה	שָׁאֲלָה	3fs pf
מִהַרְתָּ־תְּ	מֵאַנְתָּ־תְּ	2m&f	נִשְׁאֲלוּ	שָׁאֲלוּ	3cpl
מִהַר	מֵאֵן	3m			
מִהֲרָה	מֵאֲנָה	3f		אֶשְׁאַל	1cs impf
מִהַרְנוּ	מֵאַנּוּ	1cpl		תִּשְׁאַל	2m
מִהַרְתֶּם־ן	מֵאַנְתֶּם־ן	2m&f	תִּשָּׁאֲלִי	תִּשְׁאֲלִי	2f
מִהֲרוּ	מֵאֲנוּ	3c		יִשְׁאַל	3m
				תִּשְׁאַל	3f
אֲמַהֵר	אֲמָאֵן	1cs impf		נִשְׁאַל	1cpl
תְּמַהֵר	תְּמָאֵן	2m	תִּשָּׁאֲלוּ	תִּשְׁאֲלוּ	2m
תְּמַהֲרִי	תְּמָאֲנִי	2f		תִּשְׁאַלְנָה	2&3f
יְמַהֵר	יְמָאֵן	3m	יִשָּׁאֲלוּ	יִשְׁאֲלוּ	3m
תְּמַהֵר	תְּמָאֵן	3f			
נְמַהֵר	נְמָאֵן	1cpl		שְׁאַל	ms imv

PI ʿEL			NIF ʿAL	QAL	
תְּמַהֲרוּ	תְּמָאֲנוּ	2mpl impf	הִשָּׁאֲלִי	שַׁאֲלִי	fs imv
תְּמַהַרְנָה	תְּמָאֵנָה	2&3f	הִשָּׁאֲלוּ	שַׁאֲלוּ	mpl
יְמַהֲרוּ	יְמָאֲנוּ	3m		שְׁאַלְנָה	f
מַהֵר	מָאֵן	ms imv		(לְ)שְׁאֹל	inf cs
מַהֲרִי	מָאֲנִי	f		שׁוֹאֲלִים	mpl pt
מַהֲרוּ	מָאֲנוּ	mpl		שׁוֹאֲלוֹת	f
מַהַרְנָה	מָאֵנָה	f			
(לְ)מַהֵר	(לְ)מָאֵן	inf cs			
מְמַהֵר	מְמָאֵן	ms pt			
מְמַהֶרֶת	מְמָאֶנֶת	f			
מְמַהֲרִים	מְמָאֲנִים	mpl			
מְמַהֲרוֹת	מְמָאֲנוֹת	f			

(a) In *qal* and *nif ʿal* the deviations from the normal pattern are those described in § 23.3. *Qal* imperfect usually has ־ָ as its theme vowel.

(b) For the two inflectional patterns of *piʿel*, cf. § 23.1.

24.2 Final laryngal verbs שָׁלַח "he sent," שִׁלַּח "he released," הִשְׁמִיעַ "he caused to hear":

PI ʿEL	NIF ʿAL	QAL	
שִׁלַּחְתִּי	נִשְׁלַחְתִּי	שָׁלַחְתִּי	1cs pf
שִׁלַּחְתָּ, שִׁלַּחַתְּ	נִשְׁלַחְתָּ, נִשְׁלַחַתְּ	שָׁלַחְתָּ, שָׁלַחַתְּ	2m&f
שִׁלַּח־לְהָה	נִשְׁלַח־לְהָה	שָׁלַח־לְהָה	3m&f
שִׁלַּחְנוּ	נִשְׁלַחְנוּ	שָׁלַחְנוּ	1cpl
שִׁלַּחְתֶּם־ן	נִשְׁלַחְתֶּם־ן	שְׁלַחְתֶּם־ן	2m&f
שִׁלְּחוּ	נִשְׁלְחוּ	שָׁלְחוּ	3c
אֲשַׁלַּח	אֶשָּׁלַח	אֶשְׁלַח	1cs impf
תְּשַׁלַּח־לְחִי	תִּשָּׁלַח־לְחִי	תִּשְׁלַח־לְחִי	2m&f
יְשַׁלַּח, תְּ־	יִשָּׁלַח, תִּ־	יִשְׁלַח, תִּ־	3m&f

	QAL	NIF ʿAL	PI ʿEL
1cpl impf	נִשְׁלַח	נִשָּׁלַח	נְשַׁלַּח
2m	תִּשְׁלְחוּ	תִּשָּׁלְחוּ	תְּשַׁלְּחוּ
2&3f	תִּשְׁלַחְנָה	תִּשָּׁלַחְנָה	תְּשַׁלַּחְנָה
3m	יִשְׁלְחוּ	יִשָּׁלְחוּ	יְשַׁלְּחוּ
m&f imv	שְׁלַח, שִׁלְחִי	הִשָּׁלַח, הִשָּׁלְחִי	שַׁלַּח, שַׁלְּחִי
m&fpl	שִׁלְחוּ, שְׁלַחְנָה	הִשָּׁלְחוּ, הִשָּׁלַחְנָה	שַׁלְּחוּ, שַׁלַּחְנָה
inf abs	שָׁלוֹחַ	נִשְׁלוֹחַ, הִשָּׁלֵחַ	שַׁלֵּחַ
inf cs	(לְ)שִׁלֹּחַ	(לְ)הִשָּׁלַח	(לְ)שַׁלֵּחַ,(לְשַׁלֵּחַ)
m&fs pt	שׁוֹלֵחַ, שׁוֹלַחַת	נִשְׁלָח, נִשְׁלַחַת	מְשַׁלֵּחַ, מְשַׁלַּחַת
m&fpl	שׁוֹלְחִים־וֹת	נִשְׁלָחִים־וֹת	מְשַׁלְּחִים־וֹת
m&fs pt pass	שָׁלוּחַ, שְׁלוּחָה		
m&fpl	שְׁלוּחִים־וֹת		

HITPAʿEL

"he made himself known"	הִתְוַדַּע	3m pf
	יִתְוַדַּע	3m impf
	(לְ)הִתְוַדַּע	inf cs
	מִתְוַדַּע	ms pt

	HIF ʿIL	HIF ʿIL
1cs pf		הִשְׁמַעְתִּי
2m&f		הִשְׁמַעְתָּ, הִשְׁמַעַתְּ
3m&f		הִשְׁמִיעַ, הִשְׁמִיעָה
1cpl		הִשְׁמַעְנוּ
2m&f		הִשְׁמַעְתֶּם־ן
3c		הִשְׁמִיעוּ
1cs impf		אַשְׁמִיעַ
2m&f		תַּשְׁמִיעַ, תַּשְׁמִיעִי
3m&f		יַשְׁמִיעַ, תַּ־
1cpl		נַשְׁמִיעַ
2mpl impf	תַּשְׁמִיעוּ	
2&3f	תַּשְׁמַעְנָה	
3m	יַשְׁמִיעוּ	
juss	יַשְׁמַע	
m&f imv	הַשְׁמַע, הַשְׁמִיעִי	
m&fpl	הַשְׁמִיעוּ, הַשְׁמַעְנָה	
inf abs	הַשְׁמֵעַ	
inf cs	(לְ)הַשְׁמִיעַ	
m&fs pt	מַשְׁמִיעַ, מַשְׁמַעַת	
m&fpl	מַשְׁמִיעִים־וֹת	

(a) In the pf 2fs an auxiliary ַ breaks the consonant cluster at the end of the form: *šalaḥt* > *šalaḥat* שָׁלַחַתְּ. Because this vowel is secondary it does not cause spirantization of the ת.

(b) Owing to the laryngal the pt fs ends in תַ־, in contrast to the תָ־ of the sound verb.

(c) Where the laryngal is at the end of the word, preceding vowels become ַ except in the following cases: *hif'il* forms with long ִי־, infinitive absolute, *qal* (and an alternative *pi'el*) infinitive construct, participle masculine singular.

* * * * * * *

Give corresponding forms of verbs as indicated :

Of פָּתַח, נָסַע, שָׁחַט corresponding to: שָׁמַרְתְּ, שָׁמְרָה, יִשְׁמֹר, תִּשְׁמְרוּ, שְׁמֹר! שִׁמְרוּ! שׁוֹמֵר, שׁוֹמֶרֶת, שׁוֹמְרִים, לִשְׁמֹר

Of שָׁמַע, בָּחַן corresponding to: נִשְׁמַרְתְּ, נִשְׁמְרָה, יִשָּׁמֵר, יִשָּׁמְרוּ, הִשָּׁמֵר! הִשָּׁמְרִי! נִשְׁמֶרֶת, לְהִשָּׁמֵר,

Of פִּתַּח ("loosen"), בֵּרַךְ ("bless"), נִחַם corresponding to: סִפַּרְתְּ, סִפֵּר, סִפְּרָה, יְסַפֵּר, מְסַפֵּר, תְּסַפְּרוּ, מְסַפֶּרֶת, לְסַפֵּר

Of תָּמַהּ, יָדַע corresponding to: הִשְׁלַכְתְּ, הִשְׁלִיךְ, הִשְׁלִיכָה, אַשְׁלִיךְ, תַּשְׁלֵכְנָה, מַשְׁלִיךְ, מַשְׁלֶכֶת

Vocalize and translate :

1. העבד ישא את צרורנו עד אשר נעבר את העמק. 2. לא תדע אם להאמין לה עד אשר יבחנו דבריה. 3. השליט ממאן לשלח את הסוחרים מבית האסורים. 4. ימיתו השומרים את אשר יבקש לשלח יד בנפש המלך. 5. אם תמשכי את שמלתי היא תקרע. 6. עוד לא

אדע מה לקחת עמי כאשר אצא לדרך. 7. פרתי תעתה בשדה.
8. הבנים יראו פן ילקח אביהם מאתם. 9. השמיעיני את קולך.

Translate:

1. He will answer if you (fpl) ask him. 2. Food is being collected to be sent to lands in which there is famine. 3. When the word that you brought back will be heard, the king will tear his clothes and weep. 4. You may tell the owner of that house that we refuse to sell our sheep to him. 5. Let her open her mouth and say what she fears. 6. You (ms) will be astonished to hear that I am taking them with me. 7. The man (who was) sent to me is not honest. 8. She ordered that I fill the vessel (with) water and carry it to her, that she might wash (רַחַץ) her face.

(*To be followed by Genesis 43:1–10, 11–23.*)

§ 25

VOWEL CHANGES IN NOUN INFLECTION

25.1 Vowel changes occur in a word owing to a shift in the position of the stress. The occasions of stress shifts in nouns are (a) the addition of the plural, dual, or feminine termination (§ 4.5); (b) entrance into the construct state (§ 6.1);[1] (c) the addition of possessive suffixes (§ 14.1). On these occasions the stress moves forward, and vowels that are subject to change will change, being either shortened or slurred to mobile *šewå*.

Unchangeable vowels

25.2 Not all vowels, however, are subject to change. The following classes of vowels are unchangeable:

(a) Naturally long vowels: namely, vowels written with a vowel letter in full writing (ֵי, ִי, וֹ, וּ) and certain others. Example:

---

1 The segolate nouns (e.g., כֶּסֶף, עֶבֶד, מֶלֶךְ) are a notable exception: their penultimate stress is retained in the construct state; מֶלֶךְ מִצְרַיִם "king of Egypt." The peculiar inflection of segolates is treated in the next section.

the וֹ of חָמוֹר does not change, regardless of the forward movement of the stress: חֲמוֹרִים, חֲמוֹרֵיהֶם.

(b) Vowels in closed, nonfinal syllables. Syllables are closed by a consonant with quiescent *šewå* (מִשְׁ–גֶּה, מַט–מוֹן, מַנְ–חָה) or by a long (i.e., doubled) consonant (טַבְ–בָּח = טַבָּח, תִּחְלָ–לָה = תִּחְלָה). The first vowel of each of the above examples is unchangeable.

If in place of quiescent *šewå* a *ḥaṭåf* appears (under a laryngal), the preceding vowel is still unchangeable, though now no longer in a closed syllable: מַעֲשֶׂה ‖ מִשְׁגֶּה. The basic form is that with quiescent *šewå*; the peculiar phonetics of laryngals are not enough to upset the stability of the vowel pattern.

(c) Vowels that have arisen by compensatory lengthening. The first *qåmeṣ* of פָּרָה is a compensatorily lengthened *pa̱ṯaḥ*, the basic form being **parrå* from the root פרר; hence it never changes, no matter how far ahead of it the stress falls: פָּרָתִי, פָּרוֹתֵיהֶם (contrast the first *qåmeṣ* of דָּבָר, which is changeable: דְּבָרִי).

Changeable vowels

25.3 Changeable vowels depend for their length and quality on the stress. Their primary form is short ַ, ִ, ֻ. In the stress or near it, these generally lengthen and undergo a qualitative change, becoming, respectively, ָ, ֵ, ֹ. When removed from the stress, these stress-lengthened vowels revert to their original short form in closed syllables and may be slurred to mobile *šewå* in open syllables.

25.4 A closed syllable is one ending in a consonant, as defined above [§ 25.2(b)]. An open syllable is one ending in a vowel: מָ־קוֹם, שָׁ־נָה, דִּבָּ־רִים.

25.5 The tables below give a simplified account of the changeable vowels in the regular noun (the noun stressed on the final syllable).

(a) Primary vowel ַ

	SYLLABLE		
stress	*prestress*	*ante-prestress*	
	ַ	ַ	*open*
ָ[1]	ַ[2]		*closed*

[1] Commonly ָ in monosyllables whose final consonant is latently long (i.e., long, for etymological reasons, wherever it is nonfinal); e.g., רַב (but רַבִּים, from רבב); אַף (but אַפַּיִם, from אנף).

[2] Often becomes ָ, as in בַּת (< בנת•) with suffix בִּתִּי.

Examples:

w suf	*s cs*	*s abs*	
דְּבָרִי	דְּבַר־	דָּבָר	**dabar* "thing"
שְׁנָתִי	שְׁנַת־	שָׁנָה	**šanat* "year"

(b) Primary vowel ִ

	SYLLABLE		
stress	*prestress*	*ante-prestress*	
	ִ[1]	ִ	*open*
ִ	ִ[2] , ִ		*closed*

[1] Many exceptions, of which a common one is the final vowel of *qal* and *pi'el* active participles, which is slurred to ִ in an open prestress: שׁוֹמְרִים (s שׁוֹמֵר); מְסַפְּרִים (s מְסַפֵּר). Contrast the behavior of the final vowel of the stative participle, s כָּבֵד, pl כְּבֵדִים.

[2] Usually ִ before a long consonant (אִתְּכֶם), ִ before a short (אֶתְכֶם).

Examples:

w suf	*s cs*	*s abs*	
שְׂעָרִי	שְׂעַר־	שֵׂעָר	**śi'ar* "hair"
לִבִּי	לֵב־	לֵב	**libb* "heart"

(c) Primary vowel ◌ֶ

SYLLABLE

stress	*unstressed*	
◌ָ	◌ִ	*open*
	◌ֶ, ◌ַ[1] (*ŏ*)	*closed*

[1] Usually ◌ֶ before a long consonant (כֻּלִּי), ◌ַ before a short (כָּל־).

Examples:

w suf	*s cs*	*s abs*	
see § 25.6		שְׁמֹר	**šumur* "guarding" (inf)
כֻּלִּי	כָּל־	כֹּל	**kull* "all"

25.6 If in the course of inflection two consecutive vowels are reduced to ◌ָ◌ְ, the first is restored, though original ◌ֶ usually becomes ◌ָ◌ְ [§ 25.5(a), note 2], except when in contact with a larnygal.

Examples:

pl דְּבָרִים, pl cs (דְּבָרֵי־ <דְּבָרֵי־) דִּבְרֵי־

pl חֲכָמִים, pl cs (חֲכָמֵי־ <חֲכָמֵי־) חַכְמֵי־

**ṣadaqat* "righteousness": s צְדָקָה, s cs (צְדָקַת־ <צְדָקַת־) צִדְקַת־

**ṣa'aqat* "cry": s צְעָקָה, s cs (צְעָקַת־ <צְעָקַת־) צַעֲקַת־

**šumur* "guarding" (inf): שְׁמֹר, w suf (שְׁמָרִי־ <שְׁמָרִי־) שָׁמְרִי־ (*šŏm-*)

25.7 *Paradigms* דָּבָר "thing," צְדָקָה "righteousness":

FEMININE		MASCULINE		
pl	*s*	*pl*	*s*	
צְדָקוֹת	צְדָקָה	דְּבָרִים	דָּבָר	abs
צִדְקוֹת־	צִדְקַת־	דִּבְרֵי־	דְּבַר	cs
צִדְקוֹתַי	צִדְקָתִי	דְּבָרַי	דְּבָרִי	1cs suf
צִדְקוֹתֶיךָ	צִדְקָתְךָ	דְּבָרֶיךָ	דְּבָרְךָ	2m
צִדְקוֹתַיִךְ	צִדְקָתֵךְ	דְּבָרַיִךְ	דְּבָרֵךְ	2f
צִדְקוֹתָיו	צִדְקָתוֹ	דְּבָרָיו	דְּבָרוֹ	3m
צִדְקוֹתֶיהָ	צִדְקָתָהּ	דְּבָרֶיהָ	דְּבָרָהּ	3f
צִדְקוֹתֵינוּ	צִדְקָתֵנוּ	דְּבָרֵינוּ	דְּבָרֵנוּ	1cpl
צִדְקוֹתֵיכֶם־ן	צִדְקַתְכֶם־ן	דִּבְרֵיכֶם־ן	דְּבַרְכֶם־ן	2m&f
צִדְקוֹתֵיהֶם־ן	צִדְקָתָם־ן	דִּבְרֵיהֶם־ן	דְּבָרָם־ן	3m&f

Note on דָּבָר: With heavy suffixes (הֶם־ן, כֶם־ן) the base is the construct form.

25.8 In the inflection of the verb the changeable vowels behave much as they do in nouns; cf. שָׁמַר–שְׁמַרְתֶּם, קָטָן–קִטְנָתֶם, תָּסַב–תְּסֻבֵּינָה, יָשַׁב–יֵשֵׁב, וַיֵּשֶׁב. The chief differences are: (a) ַ does not change to ָ in a closed stressed syllable: שָׁמַר (contrast דָּבָר), יִכְבַּד (contrast מִדְּבָר)[1] (b) Vowels in an open prestress generally are slurred to ְ: **yikbadu* > יִכְבְּדוּ (contrast מִדְּבָרוֹ), **liku* > לְכוּ (contrast **śi'ar* > שֵׂעָר), **šamarat* > שָׁמְרָה (contrast **ṣadaqat* > צְדָקָה).

* * * * * * *

Be able to account for every vowel change in the examples and the two paradigms.

---

[1] Hence the ַ of *nif'al* perfect נִשְׁמַר, a verb form, in contrast with the ָ of the participle נִשְׁמָר, a noun form.

Inflect the following nouns in these forms : of the singular, the cs, and with suf 1cs, 2mpl ; of the plural, the abs, cs, and with suf 1cs, 3mpl :

זָקֵן (זִקְנ־), בָּשָׂר, גָּבִיעַ, שָׁלוֹם, אָדוֹן, רְעָבוֹן, כּוֹכָב, יָרֵחַ, מִדְבָּר, תּוֹעֵבָה, שָׁנָה, עֵז (*'inz*)

Translate :

1. We remained in our lodging place all (the) night. 2. Your (mpl) men will pass by before our men, and we shall see who are the more numerous (many). 3. She remembers how (what) hard the years of famine were, and she weeps. 4. Let us raise our hands to the king and plead with him in order to save our sons and daughters. 5. Their fathers scolded them, but they continued to do evil. 6. Shedders of blood will not be able to cover up the blood on their hands. 7. Do not tremble (fs), for your star is ascending (going up) and your year will be good. 8. Fearers of God, tremble before him. 9. His mother carried him by herself to her father's house and left him in charge of her brothers. 10. Your (fpl) gray hair testifies (answers) that you are among the old women of your people. 11. Her grief is bringing her down to Sheol. 12. Let them slaughter their goats as provisions for the way. 13. Inquire about their welfare and the welfare of their wives.

(*To be followed by Genesis 43 : 24–34, 44 : 1–10.*)

§ 26

SEGOLATE NOUNS

26.1 Masculine nouns stressed on their first syllable and having (normally) *sɛ̱gol* as their second vowel are called segolates. There are three forms, exemplified by מֶ֫לֶךְ "king," סֵ֫פֶר "book," בֹּ֫קֶר "morning," evolved from the monosyllables **malk*, **sifr*, **buqr*, respectively.

The consonant cluster was broken by inserting ־ֶ as a helping vowel before the last consonant (cf. §19.2) — i.e., the monosyllable was *segolated*. Stressed *i* > ־ֵ and stressed *u* > ־ֹ [§25.5(b),(c)], yielding סֵ֫פֶר and בֹּ֫קֶר. The *a* of **malk* assimilated to the *sɛ̱gol*, whence מֶ֫לֶךְ.

The segolated form is generally retained in the construct. Possessive suffixes are attached to the monosyllabic base thus:

26.2 *Singular segolates*:

	בֹּ֫קֶר		סֵ֫פֶר		מֶ֫לֶךְ	abs & cs
	s suf	*pl suf*	*s suf*	*pl suf*	*s suf*	
1c	בָּקְרִי	בָּקְרֵנוּ	סִפְרִי	סִפְרֵנוּ	מַלְכִּי	מַלְכֵּנוּ
2m	בָּקְרְךָ	בָּקְרְכֶם	סִפְרְךָ	סִפְרְכֶם	מַלְכְּךָ	מַלְכְּכֶם
2f	בָּקְרֵךְ	בָּקְרְכֶן	סִפְרֵךְ	סִפְרְכֶן	מַלְכֵּךְ	מַלְכְּכֶן
3m	בָּקְרוֹ	בָּקְרָם	סִפְרוֹ	סִפְרָם	מַלְכּוֹ	מַלְכָּם
3f	בָּקְרָהּ	בָּקְרָן	סִפְרָהּ	סִפְרָן	מַלְכָּהּ	מַלְכָּן

Qåmeṣ ḥåṭuf of בָּקְרִי is in accord with §25.5(c) note 1.

26.3 *Plural segolates.* The absolute form of all three types has the pattern ◌ָ ◌ָ ◌ִים; in the construct, the original vowel appears in the first syllable.

abs	מְלָכִים	סְפָרִים
cs	מַלְכֵי־	סִפְרֵי־

	s suf	*pl suf*	*s suf*	*pl suf*
1c	מְלָכַי	מְלָכֵינוּ	סְפָרַי	סְפָרֵינוּ
2m&f	מְלָכֶיךָ־כַיִךְ	מַלְכֵיכֶם־ן	סְפָרֶיךָ־רַיִךְ	סִפְרֵיכֶם־ן
3m&f	מְלָכָיו־כֶיהָ	מַלְכֵיהֶם־ן	סְפָרָיו־רֶיהָ	סִפְרֵיהֶם־ן

abs	בְּקָרִים
cs	בְּקָרֵי־

	s suf	*pl suf*
1c	בְּקָרַי	בְּקָרֵינוּ
2m&f	בְּקָרֶיךָ־רַיִךְ	בְּקָרֵיכֶם־ן
3m&f	בְּקָרָיו־רֶיהָ	בְּקָרֵיהֶם־ן

Note that the heavy suffixes are attached to the construct base.

26.4 Dual segolates keep their original first vowel in inflection: רֶגֶל (< **ragl*): רַגְלַיִם, רַגְלֵי־, רַגְלַי; אֹזֶן (< **'uzn*): אָזְנַיִם, אָזְנֵי־, אָזְנַי.

26.5 Corresponding to these masculines are three feminine forms: מַלְכָּה (< **malkat*) "queen," מִנְחָה (< **minḥat*) "present," טֻמְאָה (< **ṭum'at*) "impurity." They inflect normally in the singular (§15). In the plural they follow the segolate pattern: the absolute is ◌ָ ◌ָ־וֹת for all three; in the construct and with suffixes the original vowel appears in the first syllable.

Skeleton paradigms:

s abs	מַלְכָּה	מִנְחָה	טֻמְאָה	pl abs	מְלָכוֹת	מְנָחוֹת	טֻמָּאוֹת
s cs	מַלְכַּת־	מִנְחַת־	טֻמְאַת־	pl cs	מַלְכוֹת־	מִנְחוֹת־	טֻמְאוֹת־
1cs suf	מַלְכָּתִי	מִנְחָתִי	טֻמְאָתִי	1cs suf	מַלְכוֹתַי	מִנְחוֹתַי	טֻמְאוֹתַי
2mpl	מַלְכַּתְכֶם	מִנְחַתְכֶם	טֻמְאַתְכֶם				

26.6 Many segolates of the מֶלֶךְ-type inflect with *i* instead of the original *a* in the first syllable [cf. §25.5(a) note 2]: בֶּגֶד, בִּגְדִי; שֶׁבֶר, שִׁבְרִי.

26.7 Laryngals and weak consonants affect the segolate pattern as follows:

(a) initial laryngal:

סֵפֶר־type: חֵלֶב, חֶלְבִּי, חֲלָבִים, חֶלְבֵי־

בֹּקֶר־type: אֹכֶל אֳכָלִים

(b) middle laryngal:

מֶלֶךְ־type: בַּעַל, בַּעֲלִי, בַּעֲלָךְ, בְּעָלִים, בַּעֲלֵי־;

פַּעַם, פַּעֲמַיִם (du); לֶחֶם, לַחְמִי

בֹּקֶר־type: צֹהַר, צָהֳרַיִם (du); אֹהֶל tent

(c) final laryngal:

מֶלֶךְ־type: פֶּתַח, פִּתְחֶךָ

(d) middle *wâw* and *yoḏ*:

מֶלֶךְ־type: תָּוֶךְ, תּוֹךְ־; עַיִן, עֵין־

* * * * * * *

Inflect the following nouns in these forms: of the singular, with suf 1cs, 2ms, 2mpl; of the plural, pl, cs, with suf 1cs, 2mpl.

שֶׁבֶר (שִׁ־), עֶבֶד, אֶרֶץ (ארצות pl), נַעַר, אֹזֶן (du.), חֶדֶר, נֶפֶשׁ (נפשות pl), יַלְדָּה, שִׂמְלָה.

Vocalize and translate :

1. בגדו נקרע. 2. כאשר הגידו לעבדים כי יבוא מלכם בצהרי היום ההוא מהרו להכין לו את חדריו. 3. תן פיך אל אזני ולא ישמע איש מה תדבר אלי. 4. זה פעמים הציל מלכנו את ארצכם מיד השונא. 5. דרכי עוברת על פתחכם. 6. מתו כל מבקשי נפשך. 7. קשה להוציא מפיו דבר אמת על מקום כספו. 8. הוא נשא את רגליו והלך לדרכו. 9. לולא חפשו ילדינו ומצאו לנו מעט אכל כי עתה מתנו כלנו ברעב. 10. עבדי ישארו בעיר ואני אעבר את המדבר לבדי. 11. הוציאו את לחמכם לטף! 12. לולא נתתם לי את בגדיכם כי עתה לא היה לי במה לכסות את בשרי.

Translate :

1. What shall we do when we finish our bread? 2. Take (fs) your money with you and go down to Egypt to your husband. 3. Seven years they gathered grain; but after the famine passed through their land, nothing of it remained. 4. If you (ms) had not been afraid, you might have saved your master's life. 5. Let your (fs) ears hear what your mouth is speaking. 6. All his presents will not stand by (for) him if, indeed, the king has grown angry at him. 7. We answered her according to her words, but she continued to refuse to come out of her room. 8. They were astonished to find their money. 9. Said the youngest to the eldest, "Put a bit of water into my cup that I may drink." 10. Wash your (fs) face and prepare the presents that were given to you to give to our king. 11. May God repay you according to (as) the evil deed that you have done.

(*To be followed by Genesis 44 : 11–23, 24–34 ; 45 : 1–15, 16–28.*)

§ 27
WORD ORDER

27.1 There is a normal, expected word order associated with sentence types; when this order is departed from, a change in emphasis is expressed — the unusually placed element receiving the emphasis.

Noun sentences

27.2 The usual order in a noun sentence (or clause) is subject – predicate: וְהַבּוֹר רֵק (Genesis 37:24) "now the cistern was empty"; וְאָחִיו מֵת (44:20) "and his brother is dead"; אֲנִי יוֹסֵף (45:3) "I am Joseph."

27.3 When inversion occurs and the predicate is first, the predicate receives some emphasis: מְרַגְּלִים אַתֶּם (42:9) "you are spies," בְּנֵי אִישׁ אֶחָד נָחְנוּ כֵּנִים אֲנַחְנוּ (42:11) "we are sons of one man; we are honest men," אֲבָל אֲשֵׁמִים אֲנַחְנוּ (42:21) "ah, we are guilty."

(a) After אִם and כִּי there is normally an emphasis on the predicate, hence inversion usually occurs: כִּי אָחִינוּ בְשָׂרֵנוּ הוּא (37:27) "for he is our brother, our own flesh," כִּי שׁוֹמֵעַ יוֹסֵף (42:23) "that Joseph understood," אִם כֵּנִים אַתֶּם (42:19) "if you are (really) honest men."

If the emphasis remains on the subject, however, the normal order is retained: כִּי אָחִיו מֵת (42:38) "for his brother is dead."

(b) In questions, too, the emphasis is usually on the predicate; hence the interrogative order is usually inverted (cf. English "goest thou?"): הֲכְתֹנֶת בִּנְךָ הִוא (37:32) "is it your son's tunic?"

But when the emphasis is on the subject, or at least is not on the predicate, the normal order is retained: הֲזֶה אֲחִיכֶם הַקָּטֹן (43:29) "is this your youngest brother?" אָנָא אֲנִי בָא (37:30) "where am I to go?"

Verb sentences

27.4 Verbs with *wâw*-consecutive (§16) always stand at the head of their sentence or clause.

When *wâw* is separated from a verb to indicate the lack of consecution, the subject must precede the verb (see examples in §16.2).

27.5 Otherwise the order of subject and verb in a verb sentence is flexible:

(a) Normally the order is subject – verb: אֱלֹהֵיכֶם... נָתַן (43:23) "your God... has put," כַּסְפְּכֶם בָּא אֵלָי (*ibid.*) "your money came to me" (I received your money), אֲדֹנִי שָׁאַל אֶת עֲבָדָיו (44:19) "my lord asked his servants."

(b) But inversion is not uncommon, especially in animated or excited speech or with the report of news: וְהִנֵּה קָמָה אֲלֻמָּתִי, וְהִנֵּה תְסֻבֶּינָה... אֲלֻמֹּתֵיכֶם (37:7) "and lo! my sheaf stood up... then lo! your sheaves came around," טָרֹף טֹרַף יוֹסֵף (37:33) "Joseph must have been torn to pieces," הוּשַׁב כַּסְפִּי (42:28) "my money has been returned," דִּבֶּר הָאִישׁ...קָשׁוֹת (42:30) "the man spoke... harshly," בָּאוּ אֲחֵי יוֹסֵף (45:16) "Joseph's brothers have come."

(c) After כִּי, אִם, לֹא, כֹּה, אֲשֶׁר, כַּאֲשֶׁר inversion usually occurs: כִּי נִכְמְרוּ רַחֲמָיו (43:30) "for his feelings were stirred," לֹא יֵרֵד בְּנִי (42:38) "my son shall not go down," כֹּה אָמַר בִּנְךָ יוֹסֵף (45:9) "thus said your son Joseph," אֲשֶׁר שָׁלַח יוֹסֵף (45:27) "that Joseph had sent," כַּאֲשֶׁר בָּא יוֹסֵף (37:23) "when Joseph came."

But when there is some emphasis on the subject the normal order is retained: לֹא אַתֶּם שְׁלַחְתֶּם אֹתִי (45:8) "it was not you who sent me," כִּי עַבְדְּךָ עָרַב אֶת הַנַּעַר (44:32) "now it was your servant who took the lad on pledge."

The position of objects

27.6 Normally the object follows the verb: הָאֱלֹהִים מָצָא אֶת עֲוֹן עֲבָדֶיךָ (44:16) "God has discovered the iniquity of your servants," אֲדֹנִי שָׁאַל אֶת עֲבָדָיו (44:19) "my lord asked his servants."

27.7 When the object precedes the verb it is emphatic: כִּי אֹתוֹ אָהַב אֲבִיהֶם (37:4) "that it was he whom their father loved," אֹתִי שִׁכַּלְתֶּם (42:36) "it is I whom you have bereaved," כִּי שְׁנַיִם יָלְדָה לִּי אִשְׁתִּי (44:27) "that my wife bore me only two sons," לֹא כִּי עֶרְוַת הָאָרֶץ בָּאתֶם לִרְאוֹת (42:12) "no, it's the secret parts of the land you've come to see" [contrast the place of the unemphasized object (42:9) לִרְאוֹת אֶת עֶרְוַת הָאָרֶץ בָּאתֶם].

27.8 Direct object nouns usually precede indirect object nouns: וַיִּמְכְּרוּ אֶת יוֹסֵף לַיִּשְׁמְעֵאלִים (37:28) "they sold Joseph to the Ishmaelites," וַיִּתֵּן מִסְפּוֹא לַחֲמוֹרֵיהֶם (43:24) "he gave fodder to their donkeys."

(a) But if the indirect object noun is markedly shorter, it comes first: וְהִגַּדְתֶּם לְאָבִי אֶת כָּל כְּבוֹדִי בְּמִצְרַיִם (45:13) "tell my father all about my splendor in Egypt."

(b) Similarly, if either is represented by a pronoun, the pronoun comes first: וְעָשָׂה לוֹ כְּתֹנֶת פַּסִּים (37:3) "he had made for him an ornamented tunic," וַיְסַפֵּר אֹתוֹ לְאֶחָיו (37:9) "he told it to his brothers," לָתֵת לָהֶם צֵדָה (42:25) "to give them provisions."

§ 28

THE ACCENTS

28.1 In printed Hebrew Bibles an accent mark appears on every word that has a stress. Words not so marked are joined by a hyphen (מַקֵּף) to the stress word and are considered with it as one word for stress purposes. The accents appear, with a few exceptions, above or below the first letter of the stressed syllable. If that syllable has a vowel sign that would clash with the accent mark, the accent is placed to the left of the vowel sign. Note the position of the accent marks in the following verse (Genesis 37:15) וַיִּמְצָאֵהוּ אִישׁ וְהִנֵּה תֹעֶה בַּשָּׂדֶה וַיִּשְׁאָלֵהוּ הָאִישׁ לֵאמֹר מַה־תְּבַקֵּשׁ׃. The accents thus mark the stressed syllable(s) of a word, though this, indeed, is not their main purpose.

Certain of the accents are placed either at the extreme right (prepositives) or extreme left (postpositives) of the word, regardless of the stress position. In such cases, only knowledge of the form can indicate where the stress properly falls. In the case of the very common postpositive ֒ פַּשְׁטָא, many printings repeat the mark over the stressed syllable in words not stressed on the final syllable (e.g., תְּסֻבֵּינָהּ Genesis 37:7). (פַּשְׁטָא is to be distinguished from the similar קַדְמָא; the latter appears over the stressed syllable. In 37:2 שָׁנָהּ הָיָה the accent of שָׁנָהּ is פַּשְׁטָא, of הָיָה is קַדְמָא.)

28.2 The accents serve two main purposes: They are guides to the cantillation of the text and are accordingly called נְגִינוֹת "musical notes." At the same time they indicate the breaks and connections between the words of the sentence and are accordingly termed also טְעָמִים "senses."

The accentual system is very intricate. To describe it roughly, it may be said to operate on the "halving" principle: the verse is divided in two, then each part is subdivided until a unit too small for further subdivision is reached. For ordinary purposes of reading, it will be enough to recognize the accents that mark the main breaks in the sentence — the main *disjunctive* accents (distinguished from the *conjunctives*, which connect a word with what follows). In the prose books[1] the main disjunctives are:

(a) סִלּוּק ׀ :׀ (the final sublinear perpendicular bar in a verse[2]) followed by סוֹף פָּסוּק (the colon), marking the verse end.

(b) אֶתְנַחְתָּא ׀ ,׀ marking the chief pause within the verse and dividing it into two (often unequal) parts.

(c) סְגוֹלְתָּא ׀ (postpositive), marking a lesser pause in the first part of the verse.

(d) זָקֵף קָטֹן ׀ and זָקֵף גָּדוֹל ׀ ,׀ marking a lesser pause in either part of the verse (i.e., before or after the אֶתְנַחְתָּא).

---

1 The books of poetry — Psalms, Proverbs, and Job — have a different accentual system.

2 Distinct from מֶתֶג ("bit," "curb"), which is any but the last sublinear perpendicular bar in a verse. The *meteg* marks certain vowels — usually in open, nonfinal syllables — for care in pronunciation. Thus it distinguishes *qāmeṣ* from *qāmeṣ ḥāṭuf* in ambiguous positions: חָכְמָה (*ḥā-ḵᵉmā*) "she was wise"; חָכְמָה (*ḥōḵ-mā*) "wisdom" [*qāmeṣ ḥāṭuf*, being in a closed, unstressed syllable (§2.5)].

(e) ־ טִפְחָא, occuring before סִלּוּק or אֶתְנַחְתָּא; often the principal disjunctive in a verse too short to have אֶתְנַחְתָּא.

(f) ֒ רְבִיעַ, marking a still slighter pause.

In reading the text aloud, the disjunctives ought carefully to be observed. They do not always accord with our notions of where pauses in the flow of thought or speech ought to come. Often, it seems, they indicate no more than a slight emphasis, a nuance suggested by vocal inflection. But the compactness of biblical narrative is so great that we must welcome every hint of significance that tradition offers. The delicate as well as the grosser meanings expressed by the accents make them indispensable aids to the fuller appreciation of this charged text.

§ 29

SOME EFFECTS OF THE STRESS

Pausal forms

29.1 The major disjunctive accents סִלּוּק (־ֽ) and אֶתְנַחְתָּא (־ֽ) regularly, the others sporadically, are accompanied by a particularly long stress that affects the forms of words in the following ways:

(a) ־ַ in the pausal stress becomes ־ָ: כְּנָעַן (Genesis 37:1), חֲלָמְתִּי (37:6), אַרְצָה (37:10).

(b) The original *a* of מָלֵךְ-type segolates (< **malk*) often reappears, stress-lengthened to ־ָ: נֶפֶשׁ (37:21), כֶּסֶף (37:28), לַדֶּרֶךְ (42:25), לֶחֶם (43:25).

(c) Vowels that were slurred before verbal afformatives reappear, bearing the pausal stress and hence stress-lengthened: נִצָּבָה (37:7), תִּבָּחֲנוּ (42:15), וָלֵכוּ (42:33), תִּסְחָרוּ (42:34), וְנֵלְכָה (43:8).

(d) The connecting vowel between the 2ms suf ־ָךָ and the singular noun, which is slurred in context, reappears in the pause as a stressed

segol: בְּעַבְדֶּךָ (44:18). Note also its reappearance, as stress-lengthened ־ָ, in the pausal form of לְךָ, which is לָךְ (45:11) (< **laka*).

(e) Other pausal forms: וַיֹּאמַר (37:30), וַיִּתְאַפַּק (43:31), נִצְטַדָּק (44:16) (the latter two show that in *hitpa'el* impf cons, ־ִ becomes ־ַ in a minor pause, ־ָ in a major one); ־ִ > ־ָ in שָׁכַלְתִּי (43:14) and קָטָן (44:20); ־ֶ > ־ֵ in דִּבֶּר (44:2).

Stress loss and recession

29.2 Hebrew rhythm dislikes the consecution of two main stresses that are not separated by some pause (i.e., a disjunctive accent). The close succession of a word with final stress by a monosyllable or by a word stressed on its first syllable is generally avoided, and that in two ways:

(a) The first word is joined by *maqqef* (§28.1) to the second, making one stress unit of the two and causing the first to lose its stress. Usually only the last word carries an accent mark:[1] וַיִּגְעַר־בּוֹ, וַיַּקְנְאוּ־בוֹ (Genesis 37:10, 11), וַיַּעֲשׂוּ־כֵן (42:20); or, in a three-word series: אַל־תִּשְׁפְּכוּ־דָם (37:22).

Changeable vowels in the word before the *maqqef* shorten in accord with §25.5: לֶךְ־נָא (37:14), לֶאֱכָל־לֶחֶם (37:25), הַכֶּר־נָא (37:32), יֶשׁ־שֶׁבֶר (42:1), לִשְׁבָּר־אֹכֶל (42:10).

(b) Alternatively, the stress of the first word may recede to the penult (this occurs as a rule only when the penult is an open syllable): וְעָשָׂה לוֹ (37:3), יֹאכְלוּ לָחֶם (43:25).

---

1 Occasionally a secondary stress on the word before the *maqqef* is indicated by an accent mark: וַגַּגֵּד־לוֹ (43:7).

§ 30

GEMINATE VERBS

30.1 Geminate ("doubled") verbs are so called because they repeat or lengthen their second root-consonant to fill out the triconsonantal pattern; e.g., סָבַב "he turned about."[1] Repeated (doubled) consonants appear usually in the *qal* active, perfect, 3 person forms and the participle (סָבַב, סָבְבָה; סוֹבֵב), and also in the *pi'el* group — which in geminates also takes the pattern of *polel* (below, §30.4). In the rest of the *qal* paradigm, and in *nif'al*, *hif'il*, and *hof'al* only two root-consonants appear, the second being long except when it is final (יָסֹב, יָסֹבוּ; נָסַב, נָסַבּוּ; הֵסֵב, הֵסֹבּוּ).

30.2 See the paradigms of the geminate verb on p. 219; note the following in the inflection of the *qal:*

(a) The *o* connecting vowel before the pf afformatives [סַבּוֹתִי; cf. the similar case of הֶשִׁיבוֹתִי (§17.3)] may be derived from the *o* of אָנֹכִי; originally proper to the 1 pers only, it invaded the 2 pers forms as well.

(b) The alternative active impf, with a long first root-consonant (יִסֹּב), follows and probably is a reflex of the pattern of geminate verbs in Aramaic.

(c) In postbiblical Hebrew, geminates tend to assimilate their inflection to that of the sound verb: מָדַדְתִּי "I measured," יִמְדֹּד "he will measure."

1 Like hollow verbs, geminates are probably derived from biconsonantal roots.

30.3 The *hifʿil* paradigm may be compared to the *hifʿil* of hollow verbs, §17.3.

(a) Note that where the hollow verb shows long *i*, the geminate shows short *i* (followed by long consonant) in unstressed syllable, *e* (followed by simple consonant) in the stress:

hollow	*geminate*
הֲשִׁיבוֹתִי	הֲסִבּוֹתִי
הֵשִׁיב	הֵסֵב
יָשִׁיב	יָסֵב
מְשִׁיבָה	מְסִבָּה

(b) A simplified form of the pf (comparable to pf type-*b* of the hollow verb paradigm), הֵסַבְתִּי, is found rarely in biblical, more commonly in later Hebrew.

30.4 In the *piʿel* group geminates show two types of inflection: the regular (חִנֵּן, חֵנֵּן, הִתְחַנֵּן) and the by-form *polel*, *polal*, and *hit̲polel* (גּוֹלֵל, גּוֹלַל, הִתְגּוֹלֵל).

(a) The by-forms arose out of the regular form presumably by dissimilation (i.e., the development of dissimilarity between two identical sounds in a word); e.g., **gallel*[2] > *gālel*[3] > *gōlel*[4].

2 The groundform of *piʿel* is believed to have had *a* as its first vowel originally [cf. §25.5(a), note 2].

3 The first syllable *gal* became *gā* by dissimilation; the vowel lengthened compensatorily.

4 The shift of long *a* to long *o* in open, originally stressed syllables (as this was) is widely attested in Hebrew.

READINGS

Reading 1

his brothers	אֶחָיו	Bilhah	בִּלְהָה
no, not	לֹא	Zilpah	זִלְפָּה
he sat, stayed, dwelt	יָשַׁב	he was	הָיָה
he told	הִגִּיד (נגד *hif'il*)	they were	הָיוּ
they told	הִגִּידוּ	Simeon	שִׁמְעוֹן
his father	אָבִיו	shepherding	רוֹעֶה pt
he did, made	עָשָׂה	*sign of a definite direct object (e.g., one having the article, or a proper name); not translated*	אֶת־
they did, made	עָשׂוּ		
thing, matter	דָּבָר		
bad	רָע		
on, about, on account of	עַל	with	עִם

אֵלֶּה נְשֵׁי יַעֲקֹב: רָחֵל וְלֵאָה, בִּלְהָה וְזִלְפָּה. יוֹסֵף וּבִנְיָמִין הָיוּ בְּנֵי רָחֵל; רְאוּבֵן וְשִׁמְעוֹן וִיהוּדָה הָיוּ בְּנֵי לֵאָה.

הָאַחִים הָיוּ רוֹעֵי צֹאן. הַנַּעַר יוֹסֵף הָיָה רוֹעֶה אֶת הַצֹּאן בַּשָּׂדֶה עִם אֶחָיו בְּנֵי בִּלְהָה וּבְנֵי זִלְפָּה.

יַעֲקֹב לֹא הָיָה בַּשָּׂדֶה; הוּא יָשַׁב בַּבַּיִת.

יוֹסֵף הִגִּיד לְאָבִיו מֶה עָשׂוּ אֶחָיו בַּשָּׂדֶה. עָשׂוּ אֶחָיו דָּבָר טוֹב, הִגִּיד יוֹסֵף אֶת הַדָּבָר הַטּוֹב לְאָבִיו. עָשׂוּ אֶחָיו דָּבָר רָע, הִגִּיד יוֹסֵף לְאָבִיו אֶת הַדָּבָר הָרָע. אַחֵי יוֹסֵף לֹא הִגִּידוּ לְיַעֲקֹב דָּבָר עַל יוֹסֵף.

1. מִי נְשֵׁי יַעֲקֹב? 2. מִי בְּנֵי רָחֵל וּמִי בְּנֵי לֵאָה? 3. מֶה הָיוּ הָאַחִים? 4. אֵיפֹה הָיָה יוֹסֵף? 5. מֶה עָשָׂה עִם אֶחָיו? 6. אֵיפֹה יָשַׁב יַעֲקֹב? 7. מַה הִגִּיד יוֹסֵף לְאָבִיו עַל אֶחָיו? 8. מַה הִגִּידוּ הֵם עַל יוֹסֵף?

(*To be followed by Reading 2.*)

Reading 2

to him	לוֹ (ל + 3ms suf וֹ)
ornamented tunic	כְּתֹנֶת פַּסִּים
meaning of פַּסִּים *here uncertain; traditional guesses:* varicolored strip(e)s, palm (*of hand*), sole (*of foot*), *hence* tunic reaching to extremities	
they hated	שָׂנְאוּ (שָׂנֵא)
because	כִּי
why?	לָמָּה (ל + מה "for what")
aged, old	זָקֵן
he loved	אָהַב
they loved	אָהֲבוּ
all (of)	כָּל־ (*kŏl*)
his sons	בָּנָיו
him	אֹתוֹ (את + 3ms suf וֹ)
son of old age (i.e., born to an aged parent)	בֶּן זְקֻנִים
from	מִן, מִ־ [§2.10(b)2]
in comparisons: more than	

יַעֲקֹב הָיָה אִישׁ זָקֵן. הוּא אָהַב אֶת כָּל בָּנָיו. כָּל הַבָּנִים אָהֲבוּ אֶת יַעֲקֹב, וּנְשֵׁי יַעֲקֹב אָהֲבוּ אֹתוֹ.

יוֹסֵף הָיָה בֶּן זְקֻנִים לְיַעֲקֹב: אֶחָיו הָיוּ גְּדוֹלִים וְהוּא הָיָה נַעַר. יַעֲקֹב אָהַב אֶת יוֹסֵף מִכָּל בָּנָיו כִּי בֶן[1] זְקֻנִים הוּא לוֹ. יַעֲקֹב עָשָׂה לְיוֹסֵף כְּתֹנֶת פַּסִּים. הוּא לֹא עָשָׂה כְּתֹנֶת פַּסִּים לִרְאוּבֵן וְלֹא לִיהוּדָה וְלֹא לְכָל הָאַחִים. לְיוֹסֵף עָשָׂה יַעֲקֹב כְּתֹנֶת פַּסִּים כִּי אָהַב אֹתוֹ מִכָּל בָּנָיו.

אֲחֵי יוֹסֵף לֹא אָהֲבוּ אֶת יוֹסֵף. הֵם שָׂנְאוּ אֹתוֹ. שָׂנְאוּ אֹתוֹ כִּי הִגִּיד לְאָבִיו מֶה עָשׂוּ בַּשָּׂדֶה, וְשָׂנְאוּ אֹתוֹ עַל כְּתֹנֶת הַפַּסִּים.

1. מֶה הָיָה יַעֲקֹב? 2. אֶת מִי אָהַב יַעֲקֹב? 3. מִי אָהַב[2] אֹתוֹ? 4. מֶה הָיָה יוֹסֵף לְיַעֲקֹב? 5. אֶת מִי אָהַב יַעֲקֹב מִכָּל בָּנָיו? 6. לָמָּה? 7. מֶה עָשָׂה יַעֲקֹב לְיוֹסֵף? 8. לָמָּה? 9. עַל מָה שָׂנְאוּ אֲחֵי יוֹסֵף אֹתוֹ?

(*To be followed by* §9, *p.* 45.)

---

1 Note the spirantization of the בֶּן, following so closely as it does upon כִּי, which ends in a vowel. In such situations, *begaḏ kefaṯ* (§1.5) are regularly spirantized.

2 מִי is construed as singular, though it may refer to plural subjects.

Reading 3

your sheaves	אֲלֻמֹּתֵיכֶם	he dreamed	חָלַם
he got up	קָם, m קָמָה f (§ 8.2) [קוּם]	dream	חֲלוֹם
(שחוה or חוה[1]) pl הִשְׁתַּחֲווּ, s הִשְׁתַּחֲוָה		his dream	חֲלוֹמוֹ
he prostrated himself		my dream	חֲלוֹמִי
he related	סִפֵּר (*pi'el*)	lo! behold!	הִנֵּה
he said	אָמַר	binding (*pi'el*) pl מְאַלְּמִים, s מְאַלֵּם	
interrogative particle; for vocalization, see below	ה	(*used only with* אֲלֻמָּה)	
		sheaf	אֲלֻמָּה
you (ms) will be king	תִּמְלֹךְ (מָלַךְ)	my sheaf	אֲלֻמָּתִי
		over us	עָלֵינוּ

The normal vocalization of the interrogative particle is הֲ; before laryngals with *qåmeṣ* הֶ (e.g., הֶהָיָה "was he?"); before laryngals with other vowels and before *šewå*, הַ [e.g., הַהִשְׁתַּחֲווּ "did they prostrate themselves?" הַשְׁמַרְתֶּם "did you (mpl) guard?"].

יוֹסֵף חָלַם חֲלוֹם.

בַּחֲלוֹמוֹ, הִנֵּה הוּא בַּשָּׂדֶה עִם אֶחָיו. הָאַחִים הָיוּ מְאַלְּמִים אֲלֻמּוֹת בַּשָּׂדֶה, וְיוֹסֵף הָיָה מְאַלֵּם אֲלֻמּוֹת. וְהִנֵּה קָמָה אֲלֻמַּת יוֹסֵף, וַאֲלֻמּוֹת הָאַחִים הִשְׁתַּחֲווּ לַאֲלֻמַּת יוֹסֵף.

סִפֵּר יוֹסֵף אֶת חֲלוֹמוֹ לְאֶחָיו. אָמַר יוֹסֵף: חָלַמְתִּי חֲלוֹם! בַּחֲלוֹמִי, הִנֵּה אֲנַחְנוּ מְאַלְּמִים אֲלֻמּוֹת בַּשָּׂדֶה. וְהִנֵּה קָמָה אֲלֻמָּתִי, וַאֲלֻמּוֹתֵיכֶם הִשְׁתַּחֲווּ לַאֲלֻמָּתִי!

אָמְרוּ לוֹ אֶחָיו: הֲתִמְלֹךְ עָלֵינוּ?!

אֲחֵי יוֹסֵף שָׂנְאוּ אֹתוֹ עַל הַחֲלוֹם הַזֶּה. שָׂנְאוּ אֹתוֹ כִּי הִגִּיד לְאָבִיו מֶה עָשׂוּ בַּשָּׂדֶה, שָׂנְאוּ אֹתוֹ עַל כְּתֹנֶת הַפַּסִּים וְעַל הַחֲלוֹם.

---

1 Traditionally derived from שָׁחָה (< שחו*) "bow," with doubling of the final root consonant (שחוו* > שחוה*); the verb pattern is הִתְפַּעֵל. Some now take it as a הִשְׁתַּפְעֵל (reflexive causative) of a root חוה*, meaning "coil" in Arabic.

1. אֵיפֹה הָיוּ הָאַחִים בַּחֲלוֹם יוֹסֵף? 2. מֶה הָיוּ עוֹשִׂים (doing)? 3. מֶה עָשׂוּ אֲלֻמּוֹת הָאַחִים? 4. מַה סִּפֵּר יוֹסֵף לְאֶחָיו? 5. מָה אָמְרוּ לוֹ עַל חֲלוֹמוֹ? 6. עַל מָה שָׂנְאוּ אֲחֵי יוֹסֵף אֹתוֹ?

(*To be followed by Reading 4.*)

Reading 4

to you (ms)	לְךָ
that, which, who	אֲשֶׁר
we shall come	נָבוֹא (בּוֹא)
your (ms) mother	אִמְּךָ (אֵם)
your (ms) brothers	אַחֶיךָ
to prostrate oneself	לְהִשְׁתַּחֲוֹות
to the ground	אַרְצָה[1]
he watched, guarded, kept an eye on	שָׁמַר
still, yet, more; *before a noun*, another (besides the aforementioned)	עוֹד
sun	שֶׁמֶשׁ
moon	יָרֵחַ
eleven (lit., one-teen) m	אַחַד־עָשָׂר
star	כּוֹכָב
prostrating oneself s, pl	מִשְׁתַּחֲוֶה, מִשְׁתַּחֲוִים
to me	לִי

יוֹסֵף חָלַם עוֹד חֲלוֹם.

בַּחֲלוֹמוֹ, וְהִנֵּה הַשֶּׁמֶשׁ וְהַיָּרֵחַ וְאַחַד־עָשָׂר כּוֹכָבִים מִשְׁתַּחֲוִים לוֹ.

סִפֵּר יוֹסֵף אֶת הַחֲלוֹם אֲשֶׁר חָלַם לְאֶחָיו. אָמַר: הִנֵּה חָלַמְתִּי עוֹד חֲלוֹם! בַּחֲלוֹמִי וְהִנֵּה הַשֶּׁמֶשׁ וְהַיָּרֵחַ וְאַחַד־עָשָׂר כּוֹכָבִים מִשְׁתַּחֲוִים לִי.

לֹא אָמְרוּ לוֹ אֶחָיו דָּבָר עַל חֲלוֹמוֹ.

סִפֵּר יוֹסֵף אֶת הַחֲלוֹם לְאָבִיו. אָמַר לוֹ יַעֲקֹב: מָה הַחֲלוֹם הַזֶּה אֲשֶׁר חָלַמְתָּ! הֲנָבוֹא אֲנִי וְאִמְּךָ וְאַחַד־עָשָׂר אַחֶיךָ לְהִשְׁתַּחֲוֹות לְךָ אַרְצָה!?

הָאַחִים שָׂנְאוּ אֶת יוֹסֵף עַל הַחֲלוֹמוֹת, וְאָבִיו שָׁמַר אֶת הַדָּבָר.

1. מִי הָיָה מִשְׁתַּחֲוֶה לְיוֹסֵף בַּחֲלוֹם הַזֶּה? 2. לְמִי סִפֵּר יוֹסֵף אֶת חֲלוֹמוֹ? 3. מָה אָמַר? 4. מָה אָמְרוּ לוֹ אֶחָיו? 5. לָמָּה סִפֵּר אֶת הַחֲלוֹם הַזֶּה לְאָבִיו? 6. מָה אָמַר לוֹ יַעֲקֹב? 7. מִי הֵם הַשֶּׁמֶשׁ, הַיָּרֵחַ, וְאַחַד־עָשָׂר הַכּוֹכָבִים?

(*To be followed by § 10, p. 49.*)

---

1 A noun expressing the termination point of a motion often (though not necessarily) bears the *terminative* ־ָה ending. Note that it is *unstressed*, in contrast to the stressed feminine ־ָה ending.

Reading 5

	to call attention to a statement, like English "he's big, isn't he?"
קוּם!	get up!
רָאָה	he saw
רְאֵה!	see!
לִרְאוֹת	to see
שָׁלוֹם (שְׁלוֹם־)	welfare, well-being
כַּאֲשֶׁר (כְּ + אֲשֶׁר)	as
בָּא (בּוֹא)	he came
שָׁם	there
בִּקֵּשׁ (*pi'el*)	he sought
אָנָה (אָן + ־ָה term)	(to) where?
עֵמֶק	valley
חֶבְרוֹן	Hebron
יוֹם	day
אֶחָד m	one
הָלַךְ	he went
לֵךְ!	go!
אֶל	to
בְּנוֹ	his son
שְׁכֶם	Shechem
שְׁכֶמָה (שְׁכֶם + ־ָה term)	to Shechem
הֲלֹא (הֲ + לֹא)	is/are not...? *invites an affirmative answer; used*

יַעֲקֹב וּבֵיתוֹ יָשְׁבוּ בְּעֵמֶק חֶבְרוֹן בְּאֶרֶץ כְּנַעַן. יוֹם אֶחָד קָמוּ אֲחֵי יוֹסֵף וְהָלְכוּ עִם הַצֹּאן שְׁכֶמָה. יוֹסֵף לֹא הָלַךְ עִם אֶחָיו; הוּא יָשַׁב עִם אָבִיו בְּעֵמֶק חֶבְרוֹן.

יוֹם אֶחָד אָמַר יַעֲקֹב אֶל בְּנוֹ יוֹסֵף: הֲלֹא אַחֶיךָ רוֹעִים בִּשְׁכֶם? קוּם לֵךְ שְׁכֶמָה וּרְאֵה אֶת שְׁלוֹם אַחֶיךָ וְאֶת שְׁלוֹם הַצֹּאן.

עָשָׂה יוֹסֵף כַּאֲשֶׁר אָמַר לוֹ אָבִיו. קָם וְהָלַךְ שְׁכֶמָה לִרְאוֹת אֶת שְׁלוֹם אֶחָיו וְאֶת שְׁלוֹם הַצֹּאן.

בָּא יוֹסֵף שְׁכֶמָה, וְהִנֵּה לֹא רָאָה אֶת אֶחָיו שָׁם. בִּקֵּשׁ יוֹסֵף אֶת אֶחָיו בַּשָּׂדֶה; הֵם לֹא הָיוּ שָׁם.

1. אֵיפֹה יָשְׁבוּ יַעֲקֹב וּבֵיתוֹ? 2. אָנָה הָלְכוּ אֲחֵי יוֹסֵף יוֹם אֶחָד? 3. מֶה עָשָׂה יוֹסֵף? 4. לָמָּה הָלַךְ יוֹסֵף שְׁכֶמָה? 5. אֵיפֹה בִּקֵּשׁ אֶת אֶחָיו? 6. הֲהָיוּ שָׁם?

(*To be followed by Reading 6.*)

Reading 6

let's go	גֵּלְכָה coh (הָלַךְ)	he found	מָצָא
Dothan	דוֹתָן	he asked	שָׁאַל
when	כַּאֲשֶׁר	you seek	תְּבַקֵּשׁ impf (*pi'el*)
coming	בָּא pt (בּוֹא)	my brothers	אַחַי
owner, master	בַּעַל	seeking	מְבַקֵּשׁ pt (*pi'el*)
dreamer	בַּעַל חֲלוֹמוֹת	pray tell!	הַגִּידָה־נָּא![1]
he took	לָקַח	he heard	שָׁמַע
pit, cistern	בּוֹר	saying	אוֹמֵר s, אוֹמְרִים pt pl (אָמַר)

he threw הִשְׁלִיךְ (שלך *hif'il*)

אִישׁ אֶחָד מָצָא אֶת יוֹסֵף בַּשָּׂדֶה. שָׁאַל אֹתוֹ הָאִישׁ: מַה תְּבַקֵּשׁ? אָמַר לוֹ יוֹסֵף: אֶת אַחַי אָנֹכִי מְבַקֵּשׁ; הַגִּידָה־נָּא לִי אֵיפֹה הֵם רוֹעִים? אָמַר לוֹ הָאִישׁ: אַחֶיךָ הָלְכוּ מִזֶּה. שָׁמַעְתִּי אֶת אַחֶיךָ אוֹמְרִים: נֵלְכָה אֶל דוֹתָן.

הָלַךְ יוֹסֵף אֶל דוֹתָן. שָׁם מָצָא אֶת אֶחָיו.

כַּאֲשֶׁר רָאוּ הָאַחִים אֶת יוֹסֵף בָּא אָמְרוּ: הִנֵּה בַּעַל הַחֲלוֹמוֹת הַזֶּה בָּא!

כַּאֲשֶׁר בָּא יוֹסֵף לָקְחוּ הָאַחִים אֶת כְּתֹנֶת הַפַּסִּים אֲשֶׁר עָשָׂה לוֹ אָבִיו. רְאוּבֵן מָצָא בּוֹר; לָקְחוּ הָאַחִים אֶת יוֹסֵף וְהִשְׁלִיכוּ אֹתוֹ אֶל הַבּוֹר הַהוּא.

1. מִי מָצָא אֶת יוֹסֵף בַּשָּׂדֶה? 2. מַה שָׁאַל אֹתוֹ הָאִישׁ? 3. מָה אָמַר לוֹ יוֹסֵף? 4. מַה שָׁמַע הָאִישׁ אֶת הָאַחִים אוֹמְרִים? 5. אֵיפֹה מָצָא יוֹסֵף אֶת אֶחָיו? 6. מָה אָמְרוּ אֶחָיו כַּאֲשֶׁר רָאוּ אֹתוֹ בָּא? 7. מֶה עָשׂוּ לוֹ אֶחָיו כַּאֲשֶׁר בָּא? 8. מִי מָצָא אֶת הַבּוֹר?

(*To be followed by § 11, p. 54.*)

---

1 Two words connected by a hyphen (*maqqef*) are considered one, so far as stress is concerned; the main stress falls on נָּא, a secondary stress on הַגִּידָה. The *dāgeš* in the ג is the *conjunctive dāgeš*, which appears in monosyllables or words stressed on their first syllable when they follow closely upon a word ending in ־ָה or ־ֶה not stressed on its last syllable. Whether it signifies lengthening of the consonant (as is generally assumed) or merely that the preceding vowel is somewhat shortened is uncertain.

Reading 7

our hand	יָדֵנוּ	he ate	אָכַל
let (it) not be	אַל תְּהִי juss (הָיָה)	to eat	לֶאֱכֹל
in, on, upon him	בּוֹ	caravan	אֹרְחָה
our brother	אָחִינוּ	Ishmaelite	יִשְׁמְעֵאלִי
words of	דִּבְרֵי־ cs pl (דָּבָר)	to Egypt (term +־ָה)	מִצְרַיְמָה (מִצְרַיִם)
they brought up	הֶעֱלוּ (עָלָה *hif'il*)	go to! come!	לְכוּ! imv pl (הָלַךְ)
midst of, inside of	תּוֹךְ־ (תָּוֶךְ)	he sold	מָכַר
he came/went back	שָׁב (שׁוּב)	let's sell	נִמְכְּרָה (coh)

יָשְׁבוּ הָאַחִים לֶאֱכֹל וְיוֹסֵף בַּבּוֹר. הֵם הָיוּ אוֹכְלִים וְהִנֵּה אֹרְחַת יִשְׁמְעֵאלִים בָּאָה, הוֹלֶכֶת מִצְרַיְמָה.

רָאוּ הָאַחִים אֶת הָאֹרְחָה. קָם יְהוּדָה וְאָמַר אֶל אֶחָיו: לְכוּ וְנִמְכְּרָה אֶת יוֹסֵף לַיִּשְׁמְעֵאלִים, וְיָדֵנוּ אַל תְּהִי בּוֹ[1] כִּי אָחִינוּ הוּא.

דִּבְרֵי יְהוּדָה הָיוּ טוֹבִים בְּעֵינֵי אֶחָיו, וְהֵם שָׁמְעוּ לוֹ. הָלְכוּ אֶל הַבּוֹר אֲשֶׁר בּוֹ הִשְׁלִיכוּ אֶת יוֹסֵף וְהֶעֱלוּ אֶת יוֹסֵף מִתּוֹךְ הַבּוֹר. בָּאוּ אֶל הַיִּשְׁמְעֵאלִים וּמָכְרוּ לָהֶם אֶת יוֹסֵף.

שָׁבוּ הָאַחִים לֶאֱכֹל, וְהַיִּשְׁמְעֵאלִים לָקְחוּ אֶת יוֹסֵף מִצְרַיְמָה.

1. לָמָּה יָשְׁבוּ הָאַחִים? 2. כַּאֲשֶׁר אָכְלוּ אֵיפֹה הָיָה יוֹסֵף? 3. מָה רָאוּ? 4. אָנָה הָלְכָה הָאֹרְחָה? 5. מִי אָמַר לִמְכֹּר אֶת יוֹסֵף? 6. לָמָּה? 7. מִי הֶעֱלָה אֶת יוֹסֵף מִתּוֹךְ הַבּוֹר? 8. מֶה עָשׂוּ אַחֵי יוֹסֵף בּוֹ? 9. כַּאֲשֶׁר הָלְכוּ הַיִּשְׁמְעֵאלִים מֶה עָשׂוּ הָאַחִים? 10. אָנָה לָקְחוּ הַיִּשְׁמְעֵאלִים אֶת יוֹסֵף?

(*To be followed by Reading 8.*)

---

1 On the spirantization of ב see Reading 2 note 1.

Reading 8

if, *in alternatives* or	אִם	he-goat	שָׂעִיר
my son	בְּנִי	he slaughtered	שָׁחַט
animal	חַיָּה	he brought	הֵבִיא (בּוֹא *hif'il*)
he mourned	הִתְאַבֵּל (*hiṯpa'el*)	he gave, put	נָתַן
days	יָמִים (יוֹם s)	her, it (fs di obj)	אֹתָהּ
many, much	רַבִּים (רַב s)	blood	דָּם (דַּם־)
his daughters	בְּנוֹתָיו (בַּת s)	then	אָז
to console, to comfort	לְנַחֵם (*pi'el*)	he recognized	הִכִּיר (נכר *hif'il*)
he was consoled, comforted	הִתְנַחֵם (*hiṯpa'el*)	pray look at (it)!	הַכֶּר־נָא!
		your son	בִּנְךָ

לָקְחוּ הָאַחִים שָׂעִיר אֶחָד וְשָׁחֲטוּ אֹתוֹ. הֵבִיאוּ אֶת כְּתֹנֶת יוֹסֵף וְנָתְנוּ אֹתָהּ בְּדַם הַשָּׂעִיר. אָז שָׁבוּ אֶל עֵמֶק חֶבְרוֹן.

הֵבִיאוּ הָאַחִים אֶת כְּתֹנֶת יוֹסֵף אֶל יַעֲקֹב אֲבִיהֶם. אָמְרוּ לוֹ: זֹאת מָצָאנוּ; הַכֶּר־נָא הַכְּתֹנֶת בִּנְךָ הִיא אִם לֹא?

כַּאֲשֶׁר רָאָה יַעֲקֹב אֶת הַכֻּתֹּנֶת הִכִּיר אֹתָהּ וְאָמַר: כְּתֹנֶת בְּנִי! חַיָּה רָעָה אָכְלָה אֶת יוֹסֵף!

יָשַׁב יַעֲקֹב עַל הָאָרֶץ וְהִתְאַבֵּל עַל בְּנוֹ יָמִים רַבִּים. קָמוּ כָל בָּנָיו וּבְנוֹתָיו לְנַחֵם אֹתוֹ, וְיַעֲקֹב לֹא הִתְנַחֵם.

1. מֶה עָשׂוּ הָאַחִים בַּשָּׂעִיר? 2. מֶה עָשׂוּ בַּכֻּתֹּנֶת? 3. אָנָה שָׁבוּ? 4. אֶל מִי הֵבִיאוּ אֶת הַכֻּתֹּנֶת? 5. מָה אָמְרוּ לְיַעֲקֹב? 6. לָמָּה אָמַר יַעֲקֹב כִּי (that) חַיָּה רָעָה אָכְלָה אֶת יוֹסֵף? 7. מֶה עָשָׂה אָז יַעֲקֹב? 8. מִי בִּקֵּשׁ לְנַחֵם אֹתוֹ? 9. לָמָּה לֹא הִתְנַחֵם?

(*To be followed by* §*12, p. 58.*)

Reading 9

his wife	אִשְׁתּוֹ	Egyptian	מִצְרִי
imprisoned, prisoner	אָסוּר	Potiphar	פּוֹטִיפַר
jail	בֵּית אֲסוּרִים	officer	שַׂר
place	מָקוֹם (מְקוֹם־)	Pharaoh	פַּרְעֹה
after	אַחַר	servant, slave	עֶבֶד
he commited an offense, sinned	חָטָא	he became	הָיָה לְ־
chief butler	שַׂר הַמַּשְׁקִים	——'s anger was kindled against	חָרָה אַף־ בְּ־
chief baker	שַׂר הָאוֹפִים	on account of, because of	עַל דְּבַר־
king	מֶלֶךְ		

הַיִּשְׁמְעֵאלִים הֵבִיאוּ אֶת יוֹסֵף מִצְרַיְמָה. שָׁם מָכְרוּ אֹתוֹ לְאִישׁ מִצְרִי, לְפוֹטִיפַר שַׂר פַּרְעֹה. יָשַׁב יוֹסֵף בְּבֵית פּוֹטִיפַר וְהָיָה לוֹ לְעֶבֶד.

יוֹם אֶחָד חָרָה אַף פּוֹטִיפַר בְּיוֹסֵף עַל דְּבַר אִשְׁתּוֹ, כִּי אָהֲבָה אִשְׁתּוֹ אֶת יוֹסֵף. נָתַן פּוֹטִיפַר אֶת יוֹסֵף בְּבֵית הָאֲסוּרִים, בַּמָּקוֹם אֲשֶׁר שָׁם אֲסוּרֵי הַמֶּלֶךְ אֲסוּרִים.

אַחַר הַדְּבָרִים הָאֵלֶּה חָטְאוּ שַׂר הַמַּשְׁקִים וְשַׂר הָאוֹפִים לְמֶלֶךְ מִצְרַיִם. חָרָה אַף פַּרְעֹה בַּשָּׂרִים, וְנָתַן אֹתָם בְּבֵית הָאֲסוּרִים, בַּמָּקוֹם אֲשֶׁר שָׁם יוֹסֵף אָסוּר.

שַׂר בֵּית הָאֲסוּרִים נָתַן אֶת יוֹסֵף לְשָׂרֵי פַּרְעֹה, וְהוּא הָיָה לָהֶם לְעֶבֶד כָּל הַיָּמִים אֲשֶׁר הָיוּ שָׁם.

1. אָנָה הֵבִיאוּ הַיִּשְׁמְעֵאלִים אֶת יוֹסֵף? 2. לְמִי מָכְרוּ אֹתוֹ? 3. מֶה הָיָה יוֹסֵף לְפוֹטִיפַר? 4. עַל מָה חָרָה אַף פּוֹטִיפַר בְּיוֹסֵף? 5. מֶה עָשָׂה לוֹ? 6. מִי חָטָא לְמֶלֶךְ מִצְרַיִם? 7. מֶה עָשָׂה לָהֶם הַמֶּלֶךְ? 8. מֶה עָשָׂה יוֹסֵף בְּבֵית הָאֲסוּרִים?

(*To be followed by Reading 10.*)

Reading 10

no(t), *negating noun sentences*	אֵין־[1]	night	לַיְלָה m
he interpreted	פָּתַר	each	אִישׁ
God	אֱלֹהִים	he knew	יָדַע
he will return (trans)	יָשִׁיב (שׁוּב *hif'il*)	interpretation	פִּתְרוֹן
		their dreams	חֲלוֹמוֹתֵיהֶם
he returned (trans)	הֵשִׁיב	morning	בֹּקֶר
also, too	גַּם	that (conj)	כִּי
he will put to death	יָמִית (מוּת *hif'il*)	face	פָּנִים (פְּנֵי־)
he put to death	הֵמִית	your faces	פְּנֵיכֶם
just as...so	כַּאֲשֶׁר... כֵּן	today	הַיּוֹם
		how?	אֵיךְ?

לַיְלָה אֶחָד חָלְמוּ שָׂרֵי פַּרְעֹה אִישׁ חֲלוֹמוֹ, וְלֹא יָדְעוּ אֶת פִּתְרוֹן חֲלוֹמוֹתֵיהֶם. בַּבֹּקֶר רָאָה יוֹסֵף כִּי פְּנֵי הַשָּׂרִים רָעִים. שָׁאַל אֹתָם יוֹסֵף: לָמָּה פְּנֵיכֶם רָעִים הַיּוֹם? אָמְרוּ לוֹ: חֲלוֹם חָלַמְנוּ בַּלַּיְלָה, וְאֵין אֲנַחְנוּ יוֹדְעִים אֶת פִּתְרוֹנִים. אָמַר יוֹסֵף: הֲלוֹא לֵאלֹהִים פִּתְרוֹנִים! סַפְּרוּ־נָא לִי.

סִפֵּר שַׂר הַמַּשְׁקִים אֶת חֲלוֹמוֹ; שָׁמַע יוֹסֵף וְאָמַר: זֶה פִּתְרוֹנוֹ: יָשִׁיב אֹתְךָ פַּרְעֹה אֶל בֵּיתְךָ וְאֶל מְקוֹמְךָ.

כַּאֲשֶׁר רָאָה שַׂר הָאוֹפִים כִּי לְטוֹב פָּתַר, סִפֵּר גַּם הוּא אֶת חֲלוֹמוֹ לְיוֹסֵף. שָׁמַע יוֹסֵף וּפָתַר: אֹתְךָ יָמִית פַּרְעֹה.

וְהִנֵּה כַּאֲשֶׁר פָּתַר יוֹסֵף כֵּן הָיָה: אֶת שַׂר הַמַּשְׁקִים הֵשִׁיב מֶלֶךְ מִצְרַיִם אֶל מְקוֹמוֹ וְאֶל בֵּיתוֹ, וְאֶת שַׂר הָאוֹפִים הֵמִית, כַּאֲשֶׁר פָּתַר יוֹסֵף.

וְיוֹסֵף יָשַׁב עוֹד בְּבֵית הָאֲסוּרִים.

---

1 Construct of אַיִן "nought."

1. לָמָּה הָיוּ פְּנֵי הַשָּׂרִים רָעִים? 2. מַה שָּׁאַל אֹתָם יוֹסֵף? 3. מָה אָמְרוּ לוֹ? 4. אֵיךְ יָדַע יוֹסֵף אֶת פִּתְרוֹן חֲלוֹמוֹתֵיהֶם? 5. אֵיךְ פָּתַר אֶת חֲלוֹם שַׂר הַמַּשְׁקִים? 6. לָמָּה סִפֵּר שַׂר הָאוֹפִים אֶת חֲלוֹמוֹ לְיוֹסֵף? 7. אֵיךְ פָּתַר יוֹסֵף אֶת חֲלוֹמוֹ? 8. מֶה עָשָׂה פַּרְעֹה לַשָּׂרִים?

(*To be followed by §13, p. 61.*)

Reading 11

after them (f)	אַחֲרֵיהֶן	he stood	עָמַד
near	קָרוֹב	by	עַל
wise man	חָכָם (חַכְמֵי־ cs pl	the river (Nile)	הַיְאוֹר
he spoke	דִּבֵּר	he came/went up	עָלָה
saying, *introduces*	לֵאמֹר inf	coming up	עוֹלוֹת pt fpl
quotation ; often best left untranslated		seven	שֶׁבַע f
Hebrew	עִבְרִי	appearance, looks	מַרְאֶה
with us	עִמָּנוּ	good-looking	יְפוֹת מַרְאֶה[1] fpl
before, in the	לִפְנֵי (ל + פְּנֵי)	bad-looking	רָעוֹת מַרְאֶה[1] fpl
presence of		he pastured	רָעָה

אַחַר הַדְּבָרִים הָאֵלֶּה חָלַם פַּרְעֹה חֲלוֹם. בַּחֲלוֹמוֹ הוּא עוֹמֵד עַל הַיְאוֹר, וְהִנֵּה מִן הַיְאוֹר עוֹלוֹת שֶׁבַע פָּרוֹת יְפוֹת מַרְאֶה, וְהַפָּרוֹת רָעוּ בַּשָּׂדֶה. אַחֲרֵיהֶן עָלוּ שֶׁבַע פָּרוֹת רָעוֹת מַרְאֶה, וְהֵנָּה עָמְדוּ קָרוֹב אֶל הַפָּרוֹת יְפוֹת הַמַּרְאֶה. אָז אָכְלוּ הַפָּרוֹת רָעוֹת הַמַּרְאֶה אֶת הַפָּרוֹת יְפוֹת הַמַּרְאֶה.

בַּבֹּקֶר סִפֵּר פַּרְעֹה אֶת חֲלוֹמוֹ לְחַכְמֵי מִצְרַיִם, וְלֹא הָיָה אִישׁ בְּכָל חַכְמֵי מִצְרַיִם אֲשֶׁר יָדַע לִפְתֹּר אֹתוֹ לְפַרְעֹה.

אָז דִּבֵּר שַׂר הַמַּשְׁקִים אֶל פַּרְעֹה לֵאמֹר: נַעַר עִבְרִי הָיָה עִמָּנוּ בְּבֵית הָאֲסוּרִים, וְהוּא יָדַע לִפְתֹּר לָנוּ חֲלוֹמוֹת אֲשֶׁר חָלַמְנוּ, וְכַאֲשֶׁר פָּתַר לָנוּ כֵּן הָיָה.

הֵבִיאוּ אֶת יוֹסֵף מִבֵּית הָאֲסוּרִים, וְיוֹסֵף עָמַד לִפְנֵי פַרְעֹה.

1. אֵיפֹה הָיָה פַּרְעֹה עוֹמֵד בַּחֲלוֹמוֹ? 2. מָה רָאָה עוֹלֶה מִן הַיְאוֹר? 3. מֶה עָשׂוּ הַפָּרוֹת? 4. אֶל מִי סִפֵּר פַּרְעֹה אֶת חֲלוֹמוֹ? לָמָּה? 5. מַה סִּפֵּר שַׂר הַמַּשְׁקִים לְפַרְעֹה? 6. לָמָּה הֵבִיאוּ אֶת יוֹסֵף לִפְנֵי פַרְעֹה?

(*To be followed by Reading 12.*)

---

1 Lit., "beautiful/bad (in respect) of appearance." The distinction between the changeable *qâmeṣ* of יָפוֹת, יְפוֹת־ and the unchangeable one of רָעוֹת is explained in § 25.

Reading 12

now	עַתָּה	about you	עָלֶיךָ
let him place, appoint	יִתֵּן (נָתַן) juss	he answered	עָנָה
let him gather	יֶאֱסֹף (אָסַף) juss	year	שָׁנָה (שָׁנִים, שְׁנֵי־)
food	אֹכֶל	they (f) (are)	הֵנָּה
they will die	יָמוּתוּ (מוּת)	plenty, abundance	שָׂבָע
people	עַם	will be (pl)	יִהְיוּ
his servants	עֲבָדָיו (עֶבֶד)	famine	רָעָב
spirit	רוּחַ	(it) will make an end of	יְכַלֶּה (כִּלָּה *pi'el*)
I have appointed	נָתַתִּי (נָתַן)		

אָמַר פַּרְעֹה אֶל יוֹסֵף: חֲלוֹם חָלַמְתִּי, וְאֵין אִישׁ בְּכָל חַכְמֵי מִצְרַיִם יוֹדֵעַ לִפְתֹּר אֹתוֹ לִי; וַאֲנִי שָׁמַעְתִּי עָלֶיךָ כִּי פּוֹתֵר חֲלוֹמוֹת אַתָּה. עָנָה יוֹסֵף: לֵאלֹהִים פִּתְרֹנִים.

סִפֵּר פַּרְעֹה אֶת חֲלוֹמוֹ לְיוֹסֵף. שָׁמַע יוֹסֵף אֶת הַחֲלוֹם וְאָמַר: אֶת אֲשֶׁר אֱלֹהִים עוֹשֶׂה הִגִּיד לְפַרְעֹה: שֶׁבַע הַפָּרוֹת הַטּוֹבוֹת שֶׁבַע שָׁנִים הֵנָּה, וְשֶׁבַע הַפָּרוֹת הָרָעוֹת שֶׁבַע שָׁנִים הֵנָּה. הִנֵּה שֶׁבַע שָׁנִים בָּאוֹת – שָׂבָע גָּדוֹל בְּכָל אֶרֶץ מִצְרַיִם. אַחֲרֵיהֶן יִהְיוּ שֶׁבַע שְׁנֵי רָעָב, וְהָרָעָב יְכַלֶּה אֶת הָאָרֶץ. וְעַתָּה יִתֵּן פַּרְעֹה אִישׁ חָכָם עַל הָאָרֶץ וְיֶאֱסֹף אֶת אֹכֶל הַשָּׁנִים הַטּוֹבוֹת, וְלֹא יָמוּתוּ עַם הָאָרֶץ בָּרָעָב.

דִּבְרֵי יוֹסֵף הָיוּ טוֹבִים בְּעֵינֵי פַּרְעֹה. אָמַר הַמֶּלֶךְ אֶל עֲבָדָיו: הֲנִמְצָא אִישׁ כָּזֶה אֲשֶׁר רוּחַ אֱלֹהִים בּוֹ?

וְאֶל יוֹסֵף אָמַר: רְאֵה נָתַתִּי אֹתְךָ עַל כָּל אֶרֶץ מִצְרַיִם!

1. לָמָּה סִפֵּר פַּרְעֹה אֶת חֲלוֹמוֹ לְיוֹסֵף? 2. מָה אָמַר יוֹסֵף עַל הַחֲלוֹם? 3. מָה אָמַר עַל שֶׁבַע הַפָּרוֹת הַטּוֹבוֹת? 4. עַל שֶׁבַע הַפָּרוֹת הָרָעוֹת? 5. עַל כִּי אָכְלוּ הַפָּרוֹת הָרָעוֹת אֶת הַטּוֹבוֹת? 6. אֵיךְ לֹא יָמוּתוּ עַם הָאָרֶץ? 7. מָה אָמַר פַּרְעֹה אֶל עֲבָדָיו עַל יוֹסֵף? 8. לָמָּה נָתַן פַּרְעֹה אֶת יוֹסֵף עַל הָאָרֶץ?

(*To be followed by §14, p. 64.*)

Reading 13

(to) there (term שָׁמָּה (שָׁם + הָ	city עִיר s, עָרִים fpl
he obtained, procured [rations (שֶׁבֶר)] שָׁבַר	field(s) of שְׂדֵה־ (שָׂדֶה)
we shall live נִחְיֶה (חָיָה)	lands אֲרָצוֹת (אֶרֶץ)
we shall die נָמוּת (מוּת)	bread, food לֶחֶם
ten עֲשָׂרָה m	rations, food supply (in an emergency) שֶׁבֶר
he sent שָׁלַח	you stare at one another (helplessly) תִּתְרָאוּ (*hitpa'el* רָאָה)
lest פֶּן	there is יֵשׁ (opposite of אֵין)
(it) will befall יִקְרֶה (קָרָה)	he went/came down יָרַד
disaster, terrible accident אָסוֹן	go down! רְדוּ!
how many/much? כַּמָּה	

שֶׁבַע שָׁנִים הָיָה שֶׁבָע בָּאָרֶץ, וְיוֹסֵף אָסַף אֶת אֹכֶל הַשָּׁנִים הַטּוֹבוֹת וְנָתַן אֹתוֹ בֶּעָרִים בְּכָל אֶרֶץ מִצְרַיִם: אֹכֶל שְׂדֵה הָעִיר נָתַן בְּתוֹכָהּ. אַחַר הַשָּׁנִים הָאֵלֶּה בָּאוּ שְׁנֵי הָרָעָב, כַּאֲשֶׁר אָמַר יוֹסֵף. בְּכָל הָאֲרָצוֹת הָיָה רָעָב, וּבְאֶרֶץ מִצְרַיִם הָיָה לֶחֶם.

רָאָה יַעֲקֹב כִּי יֵשׁ שֶׁבֶר בְּמִצְרַיִם וְאָמַר לְבָנָיו: לָמָּה תִּתְרָאוּ? הִנֵּה שָׁמַעְתִּי כִּי יֵשׁ שֶׁבֶר בְּמִצְרַיִם; רְדוּ שָׁמָּה וְשִׁבְרוּ לָנוּ מִשָּׁם וְנִחְיֶה וְלֹא נָמוּת!

יָרְדוּ אֲחֵי יוֹסֵף, עֲשָׂרָה, לִשְׁבֹּר מִמִּצְרַיִם. וְאֶת בִּנְיָמִין, אֲחִי יוֹסֵף, לֹא שָׁלַח יַעֲקֹב כִּי אָמַר פֶּן יִקְרֶה אֹתוֹ אָסוֹן.

בָּאוּ בְּנֵי יַעֲקֹב מִצְרַיְמָה בְּתוֹךְ הַבָּאִים, כִּי הָיָה הָרָעָב בְּאֶרֶץ כְּנַעַן.

1. כַּמָּה שְׁנֵי שֶׁבָע הָיוּ? 2. מֶה עָשָׂה יוֹסֵף בַּשָּׁנִים הָאֵלֶּה? 3. מַה נָּתַן בְּתוֹךְ כָּל עִיר? 4. מַה בָּא אַחַר שְׁנֵי הַשָּׁבָע? 5. הֲהָיָה רָעָב בְּמִצְרַיִם? 6. לָמָּה שָׁלַח יַעֲקֹב אֶת בָּנָיו מִצְרַיְמָה? 7. אֶת מִי לֹא שָׁלַח? לָמָּה? 8. מִי עוֹד בָּא מִצְרַיְמָה?

(*To be followed by Reading 14.*)

Reading 14

your words, what you say	דִּבְרֵיכֶם (דָּבָר)	before him	לְפָנָיו
		he remembered	זָכַר
truth	אֱמֶת	spy	מְרַגֵּל, מְרַגְּלִים
whether (or not) you are telling the truth [lit., is truth with you (or not)?]	הַאֱמֶת עִמָּכֶם	to you	אֲלֵיכֶם (אֶל)
		to me	אֵלַי (אֶל)
		my lord	אֲדוֹנִי (אָדוֹן)
die	inf abs מוֹת	your servants	עֲבָדֶיךָ
you shall surely die	מוֹת תָּמוּתוּ	twelve (lit., two-teen)	שְׁנֵים עָשָׂר
let him stay	יֵשֵׁב	with	אֶת־
go back!	שׁוּבוּ!	you will be tested (*nif'al* בָּחַן	תִּבָּחֲנוּ
bring!	הָבִיאוּ!	they will be tested	יִבָּחֲנוּ
when?	מָתַי?	let him come	יָבוֹא

וְיוֹסֵף הוּא הַמּוֹכֵר שֶׁבֶר לְכָל עַם הָאָרֶץ.

בָּאוּ אֲחֵי יוֹסֵף וְהִשְׁתַּחֲווּ לְפָנָיו אַרְצָה. כַּאֲשֶׁר רָאָה יוֹסֵף אֶת אֶחָיו הִכִּיר אֹתָם, וְהֵם לֹא הִכִּירוּ אֹתוֹ. זָכַר יוֹסֵף אֶת חֲלוֹמוֹתָיו אֲשֶׁר חָלַם עֲלֵיהֶם, וְאָמַר אֶל אֶחָיו: מְרַגְּלִים אַתֶּם! לִרְאוֹת אֶת הָאָרֶץ בָּאתֶם!

עָנוּ לוֹ הָאֲנָשִׁים: לֹא אֲדוֹנִי, עֲבָדֶיךָ בָּאוּ לִשְׁבֹּר אֹכֶל! שְׁנֵים עָשָׂר עֲבָדֶיךָ אַחִים אֲנַחְנוּ, בְּנֵי אִישׁ אֶחָד בְּאֶרֶץ כְּנַעַן. הַקָּטֹן אֶת אָבִינוּ הַיּוֹם וְהָאֶחָד אֵינֶנּוּ.

אָמַר לָהֶם יוֹסֵף: הוּא אֲשֶׁר דִּבַּרְתִּי אֲלֵיכֶם לֵאמֹר: מְרַגְּלִים אַתֶּם! בְּזֹאת תִּבָּחֲנוּ: יָבוֹא אֲחִיכֶם הַקָּטֹן אֵלַי, וְיִבָּחֲנוּ דִּבְרֵיכֶם הַאֱמֶת עִמָּכֶם; וְאִם לֹא, מוֹת תָּמוּתוּ! אֲחִיכֶם הָאֶחָד יֵשֵׁב בְּבֵית הָאֲסוּרִים, וְאַתֶּם שׁוּבוּ, הָבִיאוּ שֶׁבֶר לְבָתֵּיכֶם, וְאֶת אֲחִיכֶם הַקָּטֹן הָבִיאוּ אֵלַי וְלֹא תָּמוּתוּ.

1. מֶה עָשׂוּ אֲחֵי יוֹסֵף לְפָנָיו? 2. מִי הִכִּיר אֶת מִי? 3. מָתַי זָכַר יוֹסֵף אֶת חֲלוֹמוֹתָיו? 4. מָה אָמַר יוֹסֵף עַל אֶחָיו? 5. כַּמָּה אַחִים עָמְדוּ

לִפְנֵי יוֹסֵף, וְכַמָּה אָמְרוּ כִּי הָיוּ? 6. מָה אָמְרוּ עַל הָאַחִים אֲשֶׁר לֹא הֵם שָׁם? 7. בַּמֶּה יִבָּחֲנוּ דִּבְרֵי הָאַחִים? 8. הֲיָשׁוּבוּ כָּל הָאַחִים אֶל אֶרֶץ כְּנַעַן?

(*To be followed by* §*15, p. 69.*)

Reading 15

away from them	מֵאִתָּם (מִן + אִתָּם)
he bound, fettered	אָסַר
he filled	מִלֵּא
sack	שַׂק
to return (trans) (*hif'il* שׁוּב)	לְהָשִׁיב
silver, money	כֶּסֶף
their silver, money	כַּסְפָּם
to give	לָתֵת (נָתַן)
way, road	דֶּרֶךְ
he lifted, carried, carried off	נָשָׂא
donkey	חֲמוֹר
guilty	אָשֵׁם, אֲשֵׁמִים
we saw	רָאִינוּ (רָאָה)
distress	צָרָה
life, being, person	נֶפֶשׁ
his mortal distress	צָרַת נַפְשׁוֹ
he pleaded with (*hitpa'el* חנן) אֶל	הִתְחַנֵּן
on account of this, therefore	עַל כֵּן
child	יֶלֶד
interpreter	מֵלִיץ
between them (i.e., between him and them)	בֵּינוֹתָם (בֵּין)

אָמְרוּ הָאֲנָשִׁים אִישׁ אֶל אָחִיו: אֲשֵׁמִים אֲנַחְנוּ עַל יוֹסֵף אָחִינוּ אֲשֶׁר רָאִינוּ אֶת צָרַת נַפְשׁוֹ כַּאֲשֶׁר הִתְחַנֵּן אֵלֵינוּ וְלֹא שָׁמַעְנוּ אֵלָיו. עַל כֵּן בָּאָה אֵלֵינוּ הַצָּרָה הַזֹּאת! עָנָה אוֹתָם רְאוּבֵן לֵאמֹר: הֲלוֹא אָמַרְתִּי אֲלֵיכֶם אַל תֶּחֱטְאוּ בַּיֶּלֶד, וְלֹא שְׁמַעְתֶּם!

וְהֵם לֹא יָדְעוּ כִּי שׁוֹמֵעַ יוֹסֵף כִּי הַמֵּלִיץ בֵּינוֹתָם.

אָז לָקַח יוֹסֵף מֵאִתָּם אֶת שִׁמְעוֹן וְאָסַר אֹתוֹ.

אָמַר יוֹסֵף לַעֲבָדָיו לְמַלֵּא אֶת שַׂקֵּי הָאֲנָשִׁים שֶׁבֶר וּלְהָשִׁיב אֶת כַּסְפָּם, כֶּסֶף אִישׁ אֶל שַׂקּוֹ, וְגַם אֹכֶל לַדֶּרֶךְ אָמַר לָתֵת לָהֶם. וְכֵן עָשׂוּ: מִלְּאוּ אֶת שַׂקֵּיהֶם שֶׁבֶר וְהֵשִׁיבוּ אֶת כַּסְפָּם כֶּסֶף אִישׁ אֶל שַׂקּוֹ וְגַם אֹכֶל לַדֶּרֶךְ נָתְנוּ לָהֶם.

קָמוּ הָאַחִים, נָשְׂאוּ אֶת שִׁבְרָם עַל חֲמוֹרֵיהֶם, וְהָלְכוּ מִשָּׁם אַרְצָה כְּנַעַן.

1. אֵיךְ פָּתְרוּ הָאַחִים אֶת צָרָתָם? 2. מַה זָּכַר רְאוּבֵן? 3. מִי עָמַד בֵּינוֹת הָאַחִים וְיוֹסֵף? 4. מֶה עָשָׂה יוֹסֵף לְשִׁמְעוֹן? 5. מָה אָמַר יוֹסֵף לָתֵת לְאֶחָיו? 6. מֶה עָשׂוּ עֲבָדָיו? 7. אֵיךְ נָשְׂאוּ הָאַחִים אֶת שִׁבְרָם?

(*To be followed by Reading 16.*)

Reading 16

we were/are	הָיִינוּ (הָיָה)	things that	קוֹרוֹת (קָרָה) pt fpl
I shall know	אֵדַע	befell, happenings	
take!	קְחוּ! (לָקַח)	lord of, *cs pl used in sense*	אֲדוֹנֵי־
he opened	פָּתַח	*of s — the so-called pl of majesty*	
mouth	פֶּה (פִּי־)	hard things,	קָשׁוֹת fpl (קָשֶׁה s)
he feared, was afraid	יָרֵא	*used adverbially* — harshly	
you will take	תִּקְחוּ (לָקַח)	regard... as...	נָתַן אֶת... כְּ...
		he will go down	יֵרֵד (יָרַד)

כַּאֲשֶׁר שָׁבוּ הָאַחִים אֶל יַעֲקֹב אֲבִיהֶם הִגִּידוּ לוֹ אֶת כָּל הַקּוֹרוֹת אֹתָם בְּמִצְרַיִם לֵאמֹר: דִּבֶּר הָאִישׁ אֲדוֹנֵי הָאָרֶץ אִתָּנוּ קָשׁוֹת, וְנָתַן אֹתָנוּ כִּמְרַגְּלִים. אָמַרְנוּ אֵלָיו: לֹא הָיִינוּ מְרַגְּלִים! שְׁנֵים עָשָׂר עֲבָדֶיךָ אַחִים אֲנַחְנוּ: הָאֶחָד אֵינֶנּוּ וְהַקָּטֹן הַיּוֹם אֶת אָבִינוּ בְּאֶרֶץ כְּנַעַן. אָמַר אֵלֵינוּ הָאִישׁ אֲדוֹנֵי הָאָרֶץ: בְּזֹאת אֵדַע כִּי אֱמֶת דִּבְרֵיכֶם: אַחִיכֶם הָאֶחָד יֵשֶׁב אִתִּי, וְאֶת שֶׁבֶר רְעַב בָּתֵּיכֶם קְחוּ וּלְכוּ, וְהָבִיאוּ אֶת אֲחִיכֶם הַקָּטֹן אֵלַי וְאֵדַע כִּי לֹא מְרַגְּלִים אַתֶּם.

כַּאֲשֶׁר פָּתְחוּ הָאֲנָשִׁים אֶת שַׂקֵּיהֶם מָצְאוּ אִישׁ אֶת כַּסְפּוֹ בְּפִי שַׂקּוֹ. רָאוּ הֵם וַאֲבִיהֶם אֶת כַּסְפָּם וִיָרְאוּ.

אָז אָמַר אֲלֵיהֶם יַעֲקֹב: יוֹסֵף אֵינֶנּוּ וְשִׁמְעוֹן אֵינֶנּוּ וְאֶת בִּנְיָמִין תִּקְחוּ! עָלַי הָיוּ כָּל אֵלֶּה! לֹא יֵרֵד בְּנִי עִמָּכֶם.

1. מַה סִּפְּרוּ הָאַחִים לְיַעֲקֹב? 2. אֵיךְ דִּבֶּר אֲלֵיהֶם אֲדוֹנֵי הָאָרֶץ? 3. כְּמָה נָתַן אֹתָם? 4. בַּמֶּה יֵדַע הָאִישׁ כִּי אֱמֶת עִמָּהֶם? 5. מַה מָּצְאוּ כַּאֲשֶׁר פָּתְחוּ אֶת שַׂקֵּיהֶם? 6. לָמָּה יָרְאוּ? 7. לָמָּה אָמַר יַעֲקֹב כִּי לֹא יֵרֵד בִּנְיָמִין עִמָּהֶם מִצְרַיְמָה?

(*To be followed by §16, p. 74.*)

Reading 17

I will be responsible for him	אֶעֱרְבֶּנּוּ (עָרַב)	it was, it came to pass	וַיְהִי impf cons (הָיָה)
if (it must be) so	אִם כֵּן	they finished	כִּלּוּ (כִּלָּה *pi'el*)
do!	עֲשׂוּ! (עָשָׂה)	he said	וַיֹּאמֶר impf cons (אָמַר)
your hand	יֶדְכֶם	you will see	תִּרְאוּ (רָאָה)
present	מִנְחָה	releasing, letting go	מְשַׁלֵּחַ (שִׁלַּח *pi'el*)
returned	מוּשָׁב pass pt (שׁוּב *hŏf'al*)	we shall go down	נֵרֵד (יָרַד)
compassion	רַחֲמִים	he inquired about	שָׁאַל לְ־
I am bereaved (of child)	שָׁכֹלְתִּי	living	חַי pt (חָיָה)
(variant at end of verse	שָׁכָלְתִּי)	let's get up	נָקוּמָה coh (קוּם)

וַיְהִי כַּאֲשֶׁר כִּלּוּ לֶאֱכֹל אֶת הַשֶּׁבֶר אֲשֶׁר הֵבִיאוּ מִמִּצְרַיִם וַיֹּאמֶר יַעֲקֹב אֶל בָּנָיו: שׁוּבוּ שִׁבְרוּ לָנוּ עוֹד אֹכֶל.

וַיֹּאמֶר אֵלָיו יְהוּדָה: הֲלוֹא אָמַר לָנוּ הָאִישׁ: לֹא תִרְאוּ פָנַי אִם אֵין אֲחִיכֶם אִתְּכֶם. אִם מְשַׁלֵּחַ אַתָּה אֶת אַחִינוּ אִתָּנוּ נֵרֵד וְנִשְׁבֹּר לְךָ אֹכֶל; וְאִם אֵינְךָ מְשַׁלֵּחַ אֹתוֹ לֹא נֵרֵד.

וַיֹּאמֶר יַעֲקֹב: לָמָּה הִגַּדְתֶּם לָאִישׁ כִּי עוֹד לָכֶם אָח?

וַיֹּאמְרוּ: שָׁאוֹל שָׁאַל[1] הָאִישׁ לָנוּ וּלְבֵיתֵנוּ לֵאמֹר: הַעוֹד אֲבִיכֶם חַי? הֲיֵשׁ לָכֶם אָח? הֲיָדוֹעַ נֵדַע[1] כִּי יֹאמַר: הָבִיאוּ אֶת אֲחִיכֶם!

וַיֹּאמֶר יְהוּדָה אֶל אָבִיו: שְׁלַח אֶת הַנַּעַר אִתִּי וְנָקוּמָה וְנֵלֵכָה, וְנִחְיֶה וְלֹא נָמוּת. אָנֹכִי אֶעֱרְבֶנּוּ, מִיָּדִי תְּבַקְשֶׁנּוּ!

וַיֹּאמֶר אֲלֵיהֶם יַעֲקֹב: אִם כֵּן זֹאת עֲשׂוּ: קְחוּ בְיֶדְכֶם מִנְחָה לָאִישׁ, וְאֶת הַכֶּסֶף הַמּוּשָׁב בְּפִי שַׂקֵּיכֶם תָּשִׁיבוּ בְיֶדְכֶם. וְאֶת אֲחִיכֶם קְחוּ. וֵאלֹהִים יִתֵּן לָכֶם רַחֲמִים לִפְנֵי הָאִישׁ. וַאֲנִי, כַּאֲשֶׁר שָׁכֹלְתִּי שָׁכָלְתִּי.

---

1 See §11.1.

1. מָתַי אָמַר יַעֲקֹב לְבָנָיו לָשׁוּב מִצְרַיְמָה? 2. לָמָּה אָמַר לָהֶם לָשׁוּב? 3. מַה בִּקֵּשׁ יְהוּדָה מֵאָבִיו? 4. מַה שָׁאַל יַעֲקֹב אֶת בָּנָיו? 5. לָמָּה הִגִּידוּ לָאִישׁ בְּמִצְרַיִם כִּי עוֹד לָהֶם אָח? 6. מָתַי שָׁמַע יַעֲקֹב לְבָנָיו וְנָתַן עַל יָדָם אֶת בִּנְיָמִין? 7. מָה עוֹד אָמַר כִּי יִקְחוּ בְּיָדָם? 8. מַה בִּקֵּשׁ מֵאֱלֹהִים? 9. וְאִם לֹא יָשׁוּב גַּם בִּנְיָמִין?

(*To be followed by Reading 18.*)

Reading 18

opening, doorway	פֶּתַח
please, my lord *asking permission to address a superior*	בִּי אֲדוֹנִי
he put	שָׂם (שִׂים)
it is well with -	שָׁלוֹם לְ־
hidden treasure, windfall	מַטְמוֹן
he brought (*hif'il* בוֹא) impf cons	וַיָּבֵא
water	מַיִם
they (*hif'il* כוּן) impf cons prepared	וַיָּכִינוּ
(when) he saw (רָאָה) impf cons	וַיַּרְא
steward (lit., he who is over the household)	אֲשֶׁר עַל הַבַּיִת
bring! (*hif'il* בוֹא)	הָבֵא!
they will eat (אָכַל)	יֹאכְלוּ
noon (*ṣōho-*)	צָהֳרַיִם
brought (*hōf'al* בוֹא) pass pt	מוּבָא
they were afraid (יָרֵא) impf cons	וַיִּירְאוּ
the first time, at first	בַּתְּחִלָּה
they came up to (נגש) impf cons	וַיִּגְּשׁוּ

וַיִּקְחוּ הָאֲנָשִׁים אֶת הַמִּנְחָה וְאֶת בִּנְיָמִין וַיָּקוּמוּ וַיֵּרְדוּ מִצְרַיְמָה; וַיָּבוֹאוּ וַיַּעַמְדוּ לִפְנֵי יוֹסֵף.

וַיַּרְא יוֹסֵף אֹתָם וַיֹּאמֶר לַאֲשֶׁר עַל בֵּיתוֹ: הָבֵא אֶת הָאֲנָשִׁים הַבַּיְתָה; כִּי אִתִּי יֹאכְלוּ הָאֲנָשִׁים בַּצָּהֳרָיִם.

וַיִּרְאוּ הָאֲנָשִׁים כִּי מוּבָאִים הֵם בֵּיתָה יוֹסֵף וַיִּירְאוּ. וַיֹּאמְרוּ: עַל דְּבַר הַכֶּסֶף הַמּוּשָׁב בְּשַׂקֵּינוּ אֲנַחְנוּ מוּבָאִים. וַיִּגְּשׁוּ אֶל הָאִישׁ אֲשֶׁר עַל בֵּית יוֹסֵף וַיְדַבְּרוּ אֵלָיו בְּפֶתַח הַבַּיִת לֵאמֹר: בִּי אֲדוֹנִי, יָרוֹד יָרַדְנוּ בַּתְּחִלָּה לִשְׁבֹּר אֹכֶל. וַיְהִי כַּאֲשֶׁר פָּתַחְנוּ אֶת שַׂקֵּינוּ וַנִּמְצָא אֶת כַּסְפֵּנוּ כֶּסֶף אִישׁ בְּפִי שַׂקּוֹ! לֹא יָדַעְנוּ מִי שָׂם אֹתוֹ בְּשַׂקֵּנוּ וְהִנֵּה הוּא בְּיָדֵנוּ לַהֲשִׁיבוֹ אֵלֶיךָ.

וַיֹּאמֶר הָאִישׁ: שָׁלוֹם לָכֶם, אַל תִּירְאוּ! אֱלֹהֵיכֶם נָתַן לָכֶם מַטְמוֹן בְּשַׂקֵּיכֶם, כַּסְפְּכֶם בָּא אֵלַי.

וַיָּבֵא הָאִישׁ אֹתָם בֵּיתָה יוֹסֵף וַיִּתֵּן לָהֶם מַיִם, וְאֹכֶל נָתַן לַחֲמוֹרֵיהֶם. וַיָּכִינוּ אֶת הַמִּנְחָה כִּי שָׁמְעוּ כִּי שָׁם יֹאכְלוּ בַּצָּהֳרָיִם.

1. מַה לָּקְחוּ אִתָּם הָאַחִים מִצְּרַיְמָה? 2. לָמָּה אָמַר יוֹסֵף לְהָבִיא אִתָּם הַבַּיְתָה? 3. לָמָּה יָרְאוּ הָאַחִים? 4. אֵיפֹה דִּבְּרוּ אֶל הָאִישׁ אֲשֶׁר עַל הַבַּיִת? 5. מַה סִּפְּרוּ לוֹ? 6. מַה אָמַר הָאִישׁ עַל הַכֶּסֶף אֲשֶׁר הָיָה בְּפִי שַׂקֵּיהֶם? 7. מָה אָמַר עַל הַכֶּסֶף אֲשֶׁר הֵבִיאוּ בַּתְּחִלָּה? 8. מַה נָּתַן לָהֶם וְלַחֲמוֹרֵיהֶם?

(*To be followed by §17, p. 78.*)

Reading 19

he hurried; *often* *adverbial* he quickly, hastily	וַיְמַהֵר (מִהַר)
into the (his) room (term הַ־ + הַחֶדֶר)	הַחַדְרָה (הַחֶדֶר)
alone	לְבַד
by himself	לְבַדּוֹ
by themselves	לְבַדָּם
he came out	וַיֵּצֵא (יָצָא)
they drank	וַיִּשְׁתּוּ (שָׁתָה)
they became drunk	וַיִּשְׁכְּרוּ (שָׁכַר)
he returned	וַיָּשָׁב (שׁוּב)
they prepared	הֵכִינוּ (כּוּן *hif'il*)
he raised his eyes; *here,* he looked about	נָשָׂא אֶת עֵינָיו
he wept	בָּכָה
to weep	לִבְכּוֹת
grew hot	נִכְמַר (כמר *nif'al*)
his feelings were stirred	נִכְמְרוּ רַחֲמָיו

וַיְהִי בַּצָּהֳרַיִם וַיָּשָׁב יוֹסֵף אֶל בֵּיתוֹ לֶאֱכֹל. וַיָּבִיאוּ לוֹ הָאֲנָשִׁים אֶת הַמִּנְחָה אֲשֶׁר הֵכִינוּ וַיִּתְּנוּ אֹתָהּ לְפָנָיו וַיִּקָּחֶהָ מִיָּדָם, וַיִּשְׁתַּחֲווּ לוֹ אַרְצָה. וַיִּשְׁאַל לָהֶם לְשָׁלוֹם וַיֹּאמֶר: הֲשָׁלוֹם לַאֲבִיכֶם הַזָּקֵן, הַעוֹדֶנּוּ חַי? וַיֹּאמְרוּ: שָׁלוֹם לְעַבְדְּךָ לְאָבִינוּ, עוֹדֶנּוּ חַי.

נָשָׂא יוֹסֵף אֶת עֵינָיו וַיַּרְא אֶת בִּנְיָמִין אָחִיו בֶּן אִמּוֹ וַיְבַקֵּשׁ לִבְכּוֹת כִּי נִכְמְרוּ רַחֲמָיו אֶל אָחִיו הַקָּטֹן. וַיְמַהֵר יוֹסֵף וַיָּבֹא הַחַדְרָה. שָׁם בָּכָה לְבַדּוֹ.

וַיֵּצֵא וַיֹּאמֶר לַעֲבָדָיו: שִׂימוּ לֶחֶם וְנֹאכַל! וַיָּשִׂימוּ לוֹ לְבַדּוֹ וּלְאֶחָיו לְבַדָּם וְלַמִּצְרִים הָאוֹכְלִים אִתּוֹ לְבַדָּם. וַיֵּשְׁבוּ אֶחָיו לְפָנָיו וַיֹּאכְלוּ עִמּוֹ, וַיִּשְׁתּוּ וַיִּשְׁכְּרוּ עִמּוֹ.

1. מָתַי שָׁב יוֹסֵף? 2. מֶה עָשׂוּ הָאַחִים בַּמִּנְחָה? 3. לִשְׁלוֹם מִי שָׁאַל יוֹסֵף? 4. מָה הִגִּידוּ לוֹ הָאַחִים עַל אָבִיו? 5. לָמָּה מִהַר יוֹסֵף לָבוֹא הַחַדְרָה? 6. מָה אָמַר לַעֲבָדָיו כַּאֲשֶׁר יָצָא מִן הַחֶדֶר? 7. אֵיךְ שָׂמוּ אֶת הָאֹכֶל? 8. מֶה עָשׂוּ אַחֵי יוֹסֵף עִמּוֹ?

(*To be followed by Reading 20.*)

Reading 20

you will overtake	תַּשִּׂיג (נשג *hif'il*)	he ordered	וַיְצַו (צִוָּה *pi'el*)
he overtook	הִשִּׂיג	they are able	יוּכְלוּ (יָכֹל)
you did	עֲשִׂיתֶם	to carry	לָשֵׂאת (נָשָׂא)
he stole	גָּנַב	(wine) cup	גָּבִיעַ (גְּבִיעַ־)
he divined	נִחֵשׁ	he did	וַיַּעַשׂ (עָשָׂה)
far be it from us to do, God forbid that we do	חָלִילָה לָנוּ מֵעֲשׂוֹת	became light	אוֹר
		they were sent off	שֻׁלְּחוּ (*pu'al*)
it will be found	יִמָּצֵא (*nif'al*)	he pursued	רָדַף אַחֲרֵי

וַיְצַו יוֹסֵף אֶת אֲשֶׁר עַל בֵּיתוֹ לֵאמֹר: מַלֵּא אֶת שַׂקֵּי הָאֲנָשִׁים אֹכֶל כַּאֲשֶׁר יוּכְלוּ לָשֵׂאת, וְשִׂים כֶּסֶף אִישׁ בְּפִי שַׂקּוֹ. וְאֶת גְּבִיעִי, גְּבִיעַ הַכֶּסֶף, תָּשִׂים בְּפִי שַׂק הַקָּטֹן עִם כֶּסֶף שִׁבְרוֹ. וַיַּעַשׂ הָאִישׁ כַּאֲשֶׁר צִוָּה יוֹסֵף.

הַבֹּקֶר אוֹר וְהָאֲנָשִׁים שֻׁלְּחוּ. הֵם יָצְאוּ אֶת הָעִיר וְיוֹסֵף צִוָּה אֶת אֲשֶׁר עַל בֵּיתוֹ לֵאמֹר: קוּם רְדֹף אַחֲרֵי הָאֲנָשִׁים! וְכַאֲשֶׁר תַּשִּׂיג אֹתָם וְאָמַרְתָּ אֲלֵיהֶם: לָמָּה עֲשִׂיתֶם אֶת הַדָּבָר הַזֶּה, לִגְנֹב אֶת גְּבִיעַ אֲדֹנִי! הֲלֹא זֶה אֲשֶׁר יִשְׁתֶּה אֲדֹנִי בּוֹ וְהוּא נַחֵשׁ יְנַחֵשׁ בּוֹ!

וַיֵּצֵא הָאִישׁ וַיִּרְדֹּף אַחֲרֵיהֶם. וַיַּשִּׂיגֵם וַיְדַבֵּר אֲלֵיהֶם אֶת הַדְּבָרִים הָאֵלֶּה. וַיֹּאמְרוּ אֵלָיו: חָלִילָה לָנוּ מֵעֲשׂוֹת כַּדָּבָר הַזֶּה! הִנֵּה הַכֶּסֶף אֲשֶׁר מָצָאנוּ בְּפִי שַׂקֵּינוּ הֱשִׁיבֹנוּ אֵלֶיךָ מֵאֶרֶץ כְּנַעַן, וְאֵיךְ נִגְנֹב מִבֵּית אֲדוֹנֶיךָ דָּבָר! הָאִישׁ אֲשֶׁר יִמָּצֵא אִתּוֹ הַגְּבִיעַ יָמוּת, וְגַם אֲנַחְנוּ נִהְיֶה לַאֲדוֹנִי לַעֲבָדִים!

The following sentences are factually incorrect; rewrite correctly.

1. יוֹסֵף צִוָּה לְמַלֵּא אֶת הַשַּׂקִּים מַיִם וְלָשִׂים אֶת גְּבִיעוֹ בְּשַׂק רְאוּבֵן. 2. הָאֲנָשִׁים שֻׁלְּחוּ בַּלַּיְלָה. 3. עֶבֶד יוֹסֵף דִּבֵּר אֶל הָאַחִים אֶת דִּבְרֵי יוֹסֵף לִפְנֵי אֲשֶׁר יָצְאוּ אֶת הָעִיר. 4. יוֹסֵף אֵינֶנּוּ עוֹשֶׂה דָּבָר בַּגְּבִיעַ. 5. כַּאֲשֶׁר גָּנְבוּ הָאַחִים אֶת הַכֶּסֶף הַשָּׁב בְּשַׂקֵּיהֶם כֵּן גָּנְבוּ אֶת הַגְּבִיעַ. 6. אִם יִמָּצֵא הַגְּבִיעַ עִם הָאַחִים יָמוּתוּ כֻּלָּם.

(*To be followed by §18, p. 84.*)

Reading 21

they fell	וַיִּפְּלוּ (נָפַל)	they (pf הוֹרִיד ; *hif'il* ירד) וַיּוֹרִידוּ	took/brought down
deed	מַעֲשֶׂה	saddlebag	אַמְתַּחַת
like me	כָּמוֹנִי	he searched	חִפֵּשׂ
we shall justify ourselves	נִצְטַדָּק (צדק *hitpa'el*)	he began	הֵחֵל (חלל *hif'il*)
iniquity	עָוֹן (עֲוֹן־)	he finished	כִּלָּה (*pi'el*)
lo! we (are)	הִנֵּנוּ	he tore	קָרַע
it was found	נִמְצָא (*nif'al*)	clothes, garment	שִׂמְלָה

וַיְמַהֲרוּ וַיּוֹרִידוּ אִישׁ אַמְתַּחְתּוֹ אַרְצָה, וַיִּפְתְּחוּ. וַיְחַפֵּשׂ הָאִישׁ: בַּגָּדוֹל הֵחֵל וּבַקָּטֹן כִּלָּה. וַיִּמָּצֵא הַגָּבִיעַ בְּאַמְתַּחַת בִּנְיָמִין.

וַיִּרְאוּ הָאֲנָשִׁים אֶת הַגָּבִיעַ וַיִּקְרְעוּ אֶת שִׂמְלוֹתָם. וַיָּשׁוּבוּ הָעִירָה. וַיָּבוֹא יְהוּדָה וְאֶחָיו בֵּיתָה יוֹסֵף – וְהוּא עוֹדֶנּוּ שָׁם – וַיִּפְּלוּ לְפָנָיו אַרְצָה.

וַיֹּאמֶר אֲלֵיהֶם יוֹסֵף: מָה הַמַּעֲשֶׂה הַזֶּה אֲשֶׁר עֲשִׂיתֶם, לִגְנֹב אֶת גְּבִיעִי! הֲלוֹא יְדַעְתֶּם כִּי נַחֵשׁ יְנַחֵשׁ אִישׁ אֲשֶׁר כָּמוֹנִי? וַיַּעַן יְהוּדָה וַיֹּאמַר: מַה נֹּאמַר לַאדֹנִי? מַה נְּדַבֵּר וּמַה נִּצְטַדָּק? הָאֱלֹהִים מָצָא אֶת עֲוֹן עֲבָדֶיךָ; הִנֵּנוּ עֲבָדִים לַאדֹנִי, גַּם אֲנַחְנוּ גַּם אֲשֶׁר נִמְצָא הַגָּבִיעַ בְּיָדוֹ.

וַיֹּאמֶר יוֹסֵף: חָלִילָה לִי מֵעֲשׂוֹת זֹאת! הָאִישׁ אֲשֶׁר נִמְצָא הַגָּבִיעַ בְּיָדוֹ הוּא לְבַדּוֹ יִהְיֶה לִי עֶבֶד, וְאַתֶּם לְכוּ עֲלוּ בְשָׁלוֹם אֶל אֲבִיכֶם.

1. מֶה עָשׂוּ הָאַחִים בְּאַמְתְּחוֹתֵיהֶם? 2. אֵיךְ חִפֵּשׂ הָאִישׁ? 3. אֵיפֹה נִמְצָא הַגָּבִיעַ? 4. אַחַר זֹאת מֶה עָשׂוּ? 5. עַל פִּי (according to) דִּבְרֵי יוֹסֵף אֵיךְ יָדַע כִּי גָּנְבוּ הֵם אֶת הַגָּבִיעַ? 6. מָה אָמַר יְהוּדָה עַל צָרָתָם? 7. עַל פִּי דִּבְרֵי יְהוּדָה מַה יַּעֲשֶׂה לָהֶם? וְעַל פִּי יוֹסֵף?

(*To be followed by Reading 22.*)

Reading 22

to here, now	הֵנָּה	he came up to, approached	וַיִּגַּשׁ (נגש)
you will bring down	pf cons וְהוֹרַדְתֶּם	don't be angry	אַל יִחַר אַפְּךָ juss (חָרָה)
my gray hair	שֵׂיבָתִי (שֵׂיבָה)	he	וַיִּוָּתֵר (יתר *nif 'al*; pf נוֹתַר)
grief	יָגוֹן	bring him down!	הוֹרִידוּהוּ (ירד *hif 'il*)
to Sheol (the netherworld)	שְׁאוֹלָה (שְׁאוֹל + ָה־)	we went up	עָלִינוּ (עָלָה)
he took...on pledge from..., he was responsible for... to...	עָרַב... מֵעִם...	to go down	לָרֶדֶת (יָרַד)
now	עַתָּה	two	שְׁנַיִם m
let him stay	יֵשֶׁב juss (יָשַׁב)	I've seen him	רְאִיתִיו (רָאִיתִי + ו)
instead of	תַּחַת	until, up to	עַד
		let him go up	יַעַל juss (עָלָה)

וַיִּגַּשׁ אֵלָיו יְהוּדָה וַיֹּאמַר: בִּי אֲדוֹנִי, יְדַבֶּר־נָא עַבְדְּךָ דָּבָר בְּאָזְנֵי אֲדוֹנִי וְאַל יִחַר אַפְּךָ בְּעַבְדְּךָ.

אֲדוֹנִי שָׁאַל אֶת עֲבָדָיו לֵאמֹר: הֲיֵשׁ לָכֶם אָב אוֹ אָח? וַנֹּאמֶר אֶל אֲדוֹנִי: יֵשׁ־לָנוּ אָב זָקֵן וְיֶלֶד זְקֻנִים קָטֹן וְאָחִיו מֵת וַיִּוָּתֵר הוּא לְבַדּוֹ לְאִמּוֹ, וְאָבִיו אָהַב אֹתוֹ. וַתֹּאמֶר אֶל עֲבָדֶיךָ: הוֹרִידוּהוּ אֵלַי וְאָשִׂימָה עֵינִי עָלָיו.

כַּאֲשֶׁר עָלִינוּ אֶל אָבִינוּ וַנַּגֵּד־לוֹ אֶת דִּבְרֵי אֲדוֹנִי.

וַיֹּאמֶר אָבִינוּ: שׁוּבוּ שִׁבְרוּ לָנוּ עוֹד אֹכֶל. וַנֹּאמֶר: לֹא נוּכַל לָרֶדֶת אִם אֵין אָחִינוּ הַקָּטֹן אִתָּנוּ. וַיֹּאמֶר אֵלֵינוּ אָבִינוּ: אַתֶּם יְדַעְתֶּם כִּי שְׁנַיִם יָלְדָה לִי אִשְׁתִּי. וַיֵּצֵא הָאֶחָד מֵאִתִּי וְלֹא רְאִיתִיו עַד הֵנָּה; וּלְקַחְתֶּם גַּם אֶת זֶה מֵעִמִּי וְקָרָהוּ אָסוֹן בַּדֶּרֶךְ, וְהוֹרַדְתֶּם אֶת שֵׂיבָתִי בְּיָגוֹן שְׁאוֹלָה.

עַבְדְּךָ עָרַב אֶת הַנַּעַר מֵעִם אָבִי. וְעַתָּה, יֵשֶׁב־נָא עַבְדְּךָ תַּחַת הַנַּעַר עֶבֶד לַאדֹנִי וְהַנַּעַר יַעַל עִם אֶחָיו. כִּי אֵיךְ אֶעֱלֶה אֶל אָבִי וְהַנַּעַר אֵינֶנּוּ אִתִּי? פֶּן אֶרְאֶה בָרָע אֲשֶׁר יִמְצָא אֶת אָבִי.

1. עַל פִּי דִּבְרֵי יְהוּדָה מַה שָׁאַל יוֹסֵף וּמֶה עָנוּ לוֹ אֶחָיו? 2. מַה בִּקֵּשׁ אָז יוֹסֵף? 3. לָמָּה לֹא יָכְלוּ הָאַחִים לָרֶדֶת אִם אֵין בִּנְיָמִין אִתָּם? 4. לָמָּה יָרֵא יַעֲקֹב לְשַׁלַּח אֶת בִּנְיָמִין? 5. מָתַי שִׁלַּח אֹתוֹ? 6. מַה בִּקֵּשׁ יְהוּדָה מִיּוֹסֵף? 7. לָמָּה לֹא יַעֲלֶה יְהוּדָה אִם אֵין בִּנְיָמִין אִתּוֹ?

(*To be followed by §19, p. 88.*)

Reading 23

don't let it vex you אַל יִחַר בְּעֵינֵיכֶם
(lit., let it not burn in your eyes)
sustenance מִחְיָה
it is two years now זֶה שְׁנָתַיִם
midst קֶרֶב
five f חָמֵשׁ
to keep alive (*hif'il* חיה) לְהַחֲיוֹת
thus כֹּה
come down! (§10.9) (יָרַד) רְדָה!
Goshen גֹּשֶׁן
he sustained כִּלְכֵּל
honor (כְּבוֹד־) כָּבוֹד
neck (צַוָּאר־) צַוָּארֵי
to restrain himself לְהִתְאַפֵּק
he called, cried קָרָא
take out! (*hif'il* יצא) הוֹצִיאוּ!
clear out!
from (attendance) (מִן + עָלַי) מֵעָלַי
upon me
he made (*hitpa'el* ידע) הִתְוַדַּע
himself known
lit., in בְּהִתְוַדַּע יוֹסֵף
the-making-himself-known of
J. = when J. made himself
known
he was terrified (*nif'al*) נִבְהַל
he kissed נִשֵּׁק

וְלֹא יָכֹל יוֹסֵף לְהִתְאַפֵּק עוֹד וַיִּקְרָא: הוֹצִיאוּ כָל אִישׁ מֵעָלַי! וְלֹא עָמַד אִישׁ אִתּוֹ בְּהִתְוַדַּע יוֹסֵף אֶל אֶחָיו.

וַיֹּאמֶר יוֹסֵף אֶל אֶחָיו: אֲנִי יוֹסֵף, הַעוֹד אָבִי חַי?

וְלֹא יָכְלוּ אֶחָיו לַעֲנוֹת אֹתוֹ כִּי נִבְהֲלוּ מִפָּנָיו. וַיֹּאמֶר יוֹסֵף לְאֶחָיו: גְּשׁוּ אֵלַי! וַיִּגְּשׁוּ. וַיֹּאמֶר: אֲנִי יוֹסֵף אֲחִיכֶם אֲשֶׁר מְכַרְתֶּם אֹתִי מִצְרַיְמָה. וְעַתָּה אַל יִחַר בְּעֵינֵיכֶם כִּי מְכַרְתֶּם אֹתִי הֵנָּה כִּי לְמִחְיָה שְׁלָחַנִי אֱלֹהִים לִפְנֵיכֶם. כִּי זֶה שְׁנָתַיִם הָרָעָב בְּקֶרֶב הָאָרֶץ, וְעוֹד חָמֵשׁ שָׁנִים יִהְיֶה רָעָב, וַיִּשְׁלָחֵנִי אֱלֹהִים לִפְנֵיכֶם לְהַחֲיוֹת אֶתְכֶם. וְעַתָּה מַהֲרוּ וַעֲלוּ אֶל אָבִי וַאֲמַרְתֶּם אֵלָיו: כֹּה אָמַר בִּנְךָ יוֹסֵף: שָׂמַנִי אֱלֹהִים לְאָדוֹן לְכָל מִצְרַיִם, רְדָה אֵלַי אַל תַּעֲמֹד, וְיָשַׁבְתָּ בְּאֶרֶץ גֹּשֶׁן וְהָיִיתָ קָרוֹב אֵלַי, וְכִלְכַּלְתִּי אֹתְךָ שָׁם. וְהִגַּדְתֶּם לְאָבִי אֶת כָּל כְּבוֹדִי בְּמִצְרַיִם וְאֶת כָּל אֲשֶׁר רְאִיתֶם, וּמְהַרְתֶּם וְהוֹרַדְתֶּם אֶת אָבִי הֵנָּה!

וַיִּפֹּל עַל צַוְּארֵי בִנְיָמִין וַיֵּבְךְּ, וּבִנְיָמִין בָּכָה עַל צַוָּארָיו. וַיְנַשֵּׁק לְכָל אֶחָיו וַיֵּבְךְּ עֲלֵיהֶם, וְאַחֲרֵי־כֵן דִּבְּרוּ אֶחָיו אִתּוֹ.

1. מַה קָּרָא יוֹסֵף לִפְנֵי הִתְוַדְּעוֹ אֶל אֶחָיו? 2. עַל מִי שָׁאַל יוֹסֵף בְּהִתְוַדְּעוֹ? 3. לָמָּה לֹא יָכְלוּ אֶחָיו לַעֲנוֹתוֹ? 4. מָה אָמַר יוֹסֵף עַל הֱיוֹתוֹ בְּמִצְרַיִם? 5. זֶה כַּמָּה שָׁנִים הָיָה הָרָעָב, וְעוֹד כַּמָּה שָׁנִים יִהְיֶה? 6. מַה בִּקֵּשׁ יוֹסֵף מֵאֶחָיו לַעֲשׂוֹת? 7. מָה אָמַר יוֹסֵף כִּי יַעֲשֶׂה לְאָבִיו? 8. מֶה עָשָׂה יוֹסֵף אַחַר דִּבְּרוֹ אֶל אֶחָיו? 9. מָתַי יָכְלוּ אֶחָיו לְדַבֵּר אִתּוֹ?

(*To be followed by Reading 24.*)

Reading 24

ruling, ruler	מוֹשֵׁל pt	sound, voice, report	קוֹל
it grew numb, failed	וַיָּפָג (פּוּג)	was heard	נִשְׁמַע (שמע *nif'al*)
heart	לֵב (לִבִּי w suf)	it was good, pleasing	וַיִּיטַב (יטב)
he believed	הֶאֱמִין (אמן *hif'il*)	wagon	עֲגָלָה
to carry	לָשֵׂאת (נָשָׂא)	little ones	טַף (טַפִּי w suf)
it revived	וַתְּחִי (חָיָה)	the best of	טוּב
enough	רַב	at the command of	עַל פִּי
before	בְּטֶרֶם	provisions	צֵידָה

וְהַקּוֹל נִשְׁמַע בְּבֵית פַּרְעֹה לֵאמֹר: בָּאוּ אֲחֵי יוֹסֵף! וַיִּיטַב הַדָּבָר בְּעֵינֵי פַרְעֹה וּבְעֵינֵי עֲבָדָיו. וַיֹּאמֶר פַּרְעֹה אֶל יוֹסֵף: אֱמֹר אֶל אַחֶיךָ: זֹאת עֲשׂוּ: קְחוּ לָכֶם מֵאֶרֶץ מִצְרַיִם עֲגָלוֹת לְטַפְּכֶם וְלִנְשֵׁיכֶם, וְעַלִּיתֶם אַרְצָה כְּנַעַן, וּנְשָׂאתֶם אֶת אֲבִיכֶם וְאֶת בָּתֵּיכֶם וּבָאתֶם. הִנֵּה טוּב אֶרֶץ מִצְרַיִם לָכֶם הוּא!

וַיִּתֵּן לָהֶם יוֹסֵף עֲגָלוֹת עַל פִּי פַרְעֹה, וַיִּתֵּן לָהֶם צֵידָה לַדֶּרֶךְ. וַיְשַׁלַּח אֶת אֶחָיו וַיֵּלְכוּ.

וַיַּעֲלוּ מִמִּצְרַיִם וַיָּבוֹאוּ אַרְצָה כְּנַעַן אֶל יַעֲקֹב אֲבִיהֶם. וַיַּגִּידוּ לוֹ לֵאמֹר: עוֹד יוֹסֵף חַי! וְהוּא מוֹשֵׁל בְּכָל אֶרֶץ מִצְרַיִם! וַיָּפָג לִבּוֹ כִּי לֹא הֶאֱמִין לָהֶם. וַיְדַבְּרוּ אֵלָיו אֶת כָּל דִּבְרֵי יוֹסֵף וַיְסַפְּרוּ לוֹ אֶת כָּל כְּבוֹדוֹ, וַיַּרְא אֶת הָעֲגָלוֹת אֲשֶׁר שָׁלַח יוֹסֵף לָשֵׂאת אֹתוֹ וַיַּאֲמֵן לָהֶם, וַתְּחִי רוּחַ יַעֲקֹב אֲבִיהֶם. וַיֹּאמֶר: רַב, עוֹד יוֹסֵף בְּנִי חַי. אֵלְכָה וְאֶרְאֶנּוּ בְּטֶרֶם אָמוּת.

1. מָה הַקּוֹל אֲשֶׁר נִשְׁמַע בְּבֵית פַּרְעֹה? 2. מַה צִּוָּה פַּרְעֹה לָתֵת לָאַחִים? לָמָּה? 3. מַה שָּׂם פַּרְעֹה לִפְנֵי בֵּית יַעֲקֹב? 4. מָה הִגִּידוּ הָאַחִים לְיַעֲקֹב? 5. לָמָּה פָּג לִבּוֹ? 6. מָתַי הֶאֱמִין לָהֶם? 7. מַה בִּקֵּשׁ לַעֲשׂוֹת בְּטֶרֶם יָמוּת?

(*To be followed by §20, p. 93.*)

AIDS TO READING THE BIBLE

ORIENTATION IN THE HEBREW BIBLE

The name

The collection of biblical writings is most often called merely סְפָרִים (s סֵפֶר) "books" in Hebrew literature of antiquity. Greek-speaking Jews mediated this term to the world as *biblia*, "books," whence — through Latin and Old French — our "Bible."

The earliest notice of the tripartition of biblical writings comes from the end of the 2nd century B.C.E. In the preface to the Greek translation of the originally Hebrew "Wisdom of Ben-Sira" the translator praises the author's learning in "the Law, the Prophets, and the rest of the books." This division corresponds to the Hebrew designations תּוֹרָה, נְבִיאִים, וּ(שְׁאָר) כְּתוּבִים "Torah, Prophets, and (the rest of the) Writings." Abbreviated as תנ"ך (*Tanak*, *Tenak*), it is the most common of Hebrew names for the Bible.

The three parts

The Torah ("instruction," but Grecized as "the law," i.e., the constitution of the Jewish commonwealth) comprises the earliest

traditions of Israel. It was considered of Mosaic origin certainly no later than the 5th century B.C.E. Beginning with an account of the Creation, attention is gradually focused on the early history of Israel, which is described from patriarchal times to the death of Moses, on the eve of the people's entry into Canaan.

The various strands of tradition embodying the prose, poetry, and law collections of the Torah reached a form essentially the same as their present one probably during the 5th century B.C.E., at which time the Torah was canonized. Critical examination of these traditions confirms their antiquity and general historical worth.

The Prophets are subdivided into "Former Prophets" נְבִיאִים רִאשׁוֹנִים and "Latter Prophets" נְבִיאִים אַחֲרוֹנִים. The Former Prophets comprise the historical records of Israel from its conquest of Canaan (end of the 13th century) to the Babylonian exile (first deportation, 597; fall of Jerusalem, 586). The varied materials of these books were selected and arranged with a view to providing an understanding of the Divine will at work in Israel's history. Because the viewpoint is to a large extent that of the early prophets, the writing of these anonymous books was early ascribed to them.

The records of prophetic utterances began to be kept about 750 B.C.E., when Amos began his prophetic career. The poetic and prose sermons of the "literary prophets" (Amos to Malachi, middle of the 5th century B.C.E.) comprise the Latter Prophets.

The significance of this literature was heightened by the catastrophic fall of Judah and the ensuing Babylonian exile (586-538 B.C.E.). For the restored community of postexilic times, the Prophets furnished the historic example and the warning of what would befall Israel when it

was disloyal to God. Probably by the end of the 3rd century B.C.E., the Prophets had become canonical.

The (rest of the) Writings comprise a heterogeneous collection of wisdom, poetic, and later historical literature. Here are, for example, Psalms, Proverbs, Job, Song of Songs, as well as Ezra-Nehemiah (the account of the return from Babylonia) and Chronicles (a later edition of the history of pre-exilic Israel). While there is a good deal of early (pre-exilic) material here (e.g., many of the Psalms and Proverbs), much of this literature does not antedate the Restoration (538 B.C.E). Part of the book of Daniel — the latest biblical book — dates to Maccabean times (about 165 B.C.E). During the 1st and 2nd centuries C.E. the canonicity of a few of these works was still in question. A 3rd-century Talmudic list is the first to record the canon of 24 books as we now have it.

The structure of the Torah

Since we shall be reading from the Torah, a closer look at its structure is now in order.

The Torah was divided into fifths (for easy handling when written on the parchment scrolls of antiquity), hence the whole is often called חֲמִשָּׁה חֻמְשֵׁי תּוֹרָה "the five fifths (s חֹמֶשׁ) of the Torah" = Greek *penta* ("five") *teuchos* ("roll" of writing material), whence our "Pentateuch."

Following ancient Near-Eastern custom, each fifth is called in Hebrew by its first (significant) word(s): בְּרֵאשִׁית "In the beginning," שְׁמוֹת (וְאֵלֶּה) "(Now these are) the names of," וַיִּקְרָא "Then [God] called," בְּמִדְבַּר "In the wilderness of," and דְּבָרִים (וְאֵלֶּה הַ) "(Now these are the) words."

But this is not the most anciently attested method. The Alexandrian Jews, who, some time in the 3rd century B.C.E. translated the Torah into Greek (the *Septuagint*), titled each part by a rough characterization of its content: *Genesis* "The beginning [of the world]," *Exodos* "The departure [from Egypt]," *Leuitikon* "Levitical [and priestly] matters," *Arithmoi* "Numbers [of the census of Israel]," and *Deuteronomion* "Second (i.e., repetition by Moses before his death of the) Law." The Latinized forms of these titles have reached us through the Vulgate (made by Jerome at the end of the 4th century), the standard Christian Bible of the Middle Ages.

The Jewish custom of a weekly public reading of the Torah is attested as early as the 1st century, and then it is considered to be a custom of great antiquity. The 1st-century historian Josephus writes:

> For ignorance he [Moses] left no pretext. He appointed the Law to be the most excellent and necessary form of instruction, ordaining, not that it should be heard once for all, or twice, or on several occasions, but that every week men should desert their other occupations and assemble to listen to the Law and to obtain a thorough and accurate knowledge of it, a practice which all other legislators seem to have neglected.[1]

Accordingly the Torah was divided into sections which were read through, either in the course of three years — the old Palestinian custom — or in one year — the Babylonian custom — which now prevails. Each of the 54 sections of the one-year cycle — called in Hebrew פָּרָשָׁה (pl פָּרָשִׁיּוֹת) or סִדְרָה (pl סִדְרוֹת) — is entitled by its first significant word(s). In the runninghead of most printings, the name of the *påråšå* follows that of the book. The weekly Sabbath reading of the *påråšå* is

---

1 *Against Apion* II, 175; translated by H. St. J. Thackeray in the Loeb Classical Library, Cambridge, Mass.: Harvard University Press, n.d.

apportioned among seven readers, each of whom, in early times, read his portion; these portions are marked in some printings by ordinal numbers written small in the text or margin.

The paragraphing is found already in the 1st-century Torah fragments from the Wilderness of Judah. It is formally observed only in Torah scrolls. In printed Bibles the traditional paragraphs are indicated by a letter indicating the size of the space between paragraphs: פ [for פְּתוּחָה "open (section)"] indicating a large space, ס [for סְתוּמָה "closed (section)"] indicating a smaller one.[2]

The verse division (not the numbering) is quite ancient, for the meaning often depends on it. A fixed verse division existed by Mishnaic times (3rd century C.E.), although discrepancies persist among various authorities as to the precise number and disposition of the verses.

The chapter division and the numbering of verses were initiated by Christians. Chapters first appeared in the Vulgate in the 13th century, verse numbers in the 16th. From there both were adopted by printers of Hebrew Bibles in the 16th and 17th centuries.

The genealogy of our texts

Before the discovery in 1947 of the scrolls from the Wilderness of Judah, the earliest fragments of Hebrew Bible manuscripts came from about the 8th-9th centuries. Earlier copies perished, owing to the Jewish law requiring that worn-out copies be withdrawn from use, to be disposed of either by burial or by storage in a synagogue lumber-room. In the latter case, such scrolls as were not consumed by rodents were

---

2 In many printings a triple פפפ or ססס marks the break between the weekly *påråšiyyot*. It is followed by a number [in Arabic and/or Hebrew numerals (Hebrew letters serve as numerals)] indicating which of the 54 the new *påråšå* is.

usually lost when the synagogue itself was abandoned or demolished. Most of the surviving 8th-9th century manuscript fragments come from just this sort of a lumber-room, discovered in a still-used Cairo synagogue by Solomon Schechter at the end of the 19th century.

The lineage of our text, however, ascends to the same scholars of Tiberias who developed the present system of vocalization (§2.4). These scholars, called Massoretes ("text-traditionists" from מַסּוֹרָה "text-tradition"), labored for centuries to produce a standard text of the Bible. Their efforts were crowned in the work of the last members of the Ben Asher family of Tiberias who, in the 9th-10th centuries, created the archetypes of all subsequent texts. Owing chiefly to the lifelong researches of Paul Kahle, several Ben Asher texts scattered over Europe and the Near East have been identified, comprising the entire Hebrew Bible. The best recent editions of the Bible have been based on these texts.

Kahle himself participated in the standard scholarly edition of the Bible, the Kittel-Kahle *Biblia Hebraica* (3rd edition, Stuttgart, 1937). The basis for this text is a Ben Asher manuscript (or rather a copy of such a manuscript) dating to 1008/09, now in Leningrad. In 1957 the British and Foreign Bible Society published an edition edited by Norman Snaith based on other manuscripts that Snaith believes to represent the true Ben Asher text and which is substantially similar to Kahle's.

Most present-day Hebrew Bibles, however, are based on the much later, second Rabbinic Bible (מִקְרָאוֹת גְּדוֹלוֹת), edited by Jacob Ben Hayyim and printed at Venice by Daniel Bomberg in 1524-25. Ben Hayyim worked with the best manuscripts then available; but these were late, and he himself was troubled by their dissensions. Of the successive editions of Ben Hayyim's text, that of Van der Hooght

(Amsterdam & Utrecht, 1705) became the basis of those of today. The edition of Meir Letteris (Vienna, 1852) has been reprinted many times over in the type of the British and Foreign Bible Society (first printing: Berlin, 1866). The Hebrew Publishing Company Bible is such a reprint.

NOTES ON THE HEBREW TEXT OF GENESIS 37, 42-45

Genesis 37

Verse 1. וַיֵּשֶׁב יַעֲקֹב "Jacob, however, settled." As indicated by the impf cons, the verse continues the narrative left off in 36:8.

2. שָׁנָה. Numbered nouns with the numbers 2-10 are usually in the plural (חָמֵשׁ שָׁנִים 45:6, עֲשָׂרָה חֲמוֹרִים 45:23). With the numbers 11-19 they may also be in the plural אַחַד עָשָׂר כּוֹכָבִים 37:9), though if they are items frequently numbered (e.g., אִישׁ, יוֹם, or, as here, שָׁנָה) they appear in the singular.

וְהוּא נַעַר ... אָבִיו. The relation of this clause to the preceding is problematic. Two suggested interpretations are: (1) to take each of its phrases as paralleling corresponding phrases in the first clause: יוֹסֵף בֶּן שְׁבַע עֶשְׂרֵה שָׁנָה ‖ וְהוּא נַעַר; הָיָה רוֹעֶה אֶת אֶחָיו בַּצֹּאן ‖ אֶת בְּנֵי בִלְהָה וְאֶת בְּנֵי זִלְפָּה נְשֵׁי אָבִיו "Joseph, at seventeen years of age, used to tend the flocks with his brothers — being a mere lad — with the sons of B. and the sons of Z., his father's wives"; (2) to give נַעַר

a special sense (which it has elsewhere), "servant," and render: "being a helper with (to) the sons of B., etc."

דִּבָּתָם רָעָה. רָעָה is a predicate of דִּבָּתָם, defining its quality: "the report of them, (it being) bad." Cf. our objective predicate: "I bought the book *bound*." Render: "bad reports about them."

3. וְיִשְׂרָאֵל אָהַב "now Israel loved." The flow of the narrative is interrupted to tell of a background (prior) circumstance; hence the verb reverts to the perfect (see §16.2).

וְעָשָׂה לוֹ [on the stress, see §29.2 (b)] "and he had made." The verb is not conceived of as consequent upon אָהַב (not: "because he loved him he made him"; that would have been expressed by the impf cons וַיַּעַשׂ), but as in an independent clause coordinate with the preceding one.

4. וַיִּרְאוּ אֶחָיו... וַיִּשְׂנְאוּ אֹתוֹ "when his brothers saw... they hated him." Of two coordinate impf cons verbs, the first is frequently subordinate to the second as a temporal clause. So, e.g., vs 10 וַיְסַפֵּר... וַיִּגְעַר בּוֹ "when he told it... (his father) scolded him"; vs 21 וַיִּשְׁמַע רְאוּבֵן וַיַּצִּלֵהוּ "when Reuben heard it he tried to rescue him." Cf. note on vs 25.

דַּבְּרוֹ. An unusual case of the suf representing the indirect, rather than the direct, object (the same usage in הֲשִׁבֵנִי "bring back (word) to me" 37:14).

7. וְהִנֵּה. הִנֵּה makes the narrative graphic and vivid and enables the reader to enter into the surprise or satisfaction of the speaker or actor concerned. It is regularly employed in narrating dreams. The opening clause is usually (as here) participial — setting the scene against which the action takes place.

אֲלֻמִּים "sheaves" in general; אֲלֻמָּה "a particular, single sheaf"; אֲלֻמּוֹת "sheaves" in particular.

תְּסֻבֶּינָה. From סבב; on the impf see §10.2.

וַתִּשְׁתַּחֲוִיֻן. ן defectively written (§2.3) for ־נָה.

8. הֲמָלֹךְ ... אִם מָשֹׁל. See §11.1.

12. אֹתֹ. Dots over letters are an ancient scribal device for calling attention to the dotted matter. Dots were employed to indicate what ought to be struck out or to point to some peculiarity of meaning — which of the two is involved in this case is difficult to say. (A rabbinic comment fancifully suggests that the dots point to the fact that "they really went to tend to *themselves*," i.e., to their own interests, not their father's).

17. שָׁמַעְתִּי אוֹמְרִים "I heard them say"; supply the object as in vs 25, לְהוֹרִיד "to bring them down."

דֹּתָן – דֹּתַיְנָה. ־ָן and ־ַיִן interchange as place-name endings.

20. וְעַתָּה "now then." ו often expresses an informal inference or consequence, especially at the beginning of a speech. So too 44:8 וְאֵיךְ נִגְנֹב "how then could we steal."

21. לֹא נַכֶּנּוּ נָפֶשׁ "we mustn't kill him!" (lit., "we mustn't strike him mortally"). נָפֶשׁ is an objective complement, defining the part of the object (־ֶנּוּ "him") specially affected by the action, namely "life."

22. ... לְמַעַן. A parenthetical aside.

25. לֶאֱכָל־לֶחֶם. See §29.2(a).

וַיִּשְׂאוּ עֵינֵיהֶם וַיִּרְאוּ "lifting up their eyes, they saw." The subordinate temporal clause (see note to vs 4 וַיִּרְאוּ אֶחָיו) may sometimes be rendered more neatly by the English participial construction. So too

vs 30 וַיָּשָׁב אֶל אֶחָיו וַיֹּאמַר "returning to his brothers, he said," vs 33 וַיַּכִּירָהּ וַיֹּאמֶר "recognizing it, he said."

וָלֹט. As a rule the copula is vocalized וָ before a monosyllable or a word stressed on the first syllable when that word has a disjunctive accent. So too 44:31 וָמֵת [pf cons whose *wâw* is vocalized like the copula (§16.6)], and compare Genesis 8:22 וְקֹר וָחֹם וְקַיִץ וָחֹרֶף וְיוֹם וָלַיְלָה "cold and heat, summer and winter, day and night."

28. וַיִּמְשְׁכוּ וַיַּעֲלוּ "they pulled up" (lit., "they pulled and brought up"). The second verb, indicating direction of motion, is used adverbially.

עֶשְׂרִים כֶּסֶף "twenty shekels of silver"; similarly in 45:22 שְׁלֹשׁ מֵאוֹת כֶּסֶף "300 shekels of silver."

30. **אָנָה אֲנִי בָא.** The sense is: "what am I to do now?"

32. **הַכְּתֹנֶת.** That the interrogative ה should be followed by a long consonant is very unusual (for the normal vocalization of the interrogative ה see vocabulary of Reading 3).

33. **טָרֹף טֹרַף יוֹסֵף.** See §11.1.

36. **וְהַמִּדָנִים מָכְרוּ.** See §16.2(b).

Genesis 42

1. **יֵשׁ־.** "There *was*..." in Egypt, in contrast to Canaan.

2. שִׁבְרוּ... וְנִחְיֶה וְלֹא נָמוּת "procure food... that we may live and not die." Result or purpose clauses are expressed by *wâw* before a voluntative verb (cohortative, imperative, jussive); e.g., 42:34 וְהָבִיאוּ... וְאֵדְעָה "bring... that I may know," 42:18 זֹאת עֲשׂוּ וִחְיוּ "do this and so live" (if you do this you will live") 42:16 שִׁלְחוּ... וְיִקַּח... וְיִבָּחֲנוּ "send... to take... that (your words) may be tested."

In many cases, as here, the voluntative verb has no distinctive form; the context (e.g., a preceding imperative) is generally a sufficient indication of a result or purpose clause.

A negative result or purpose clause — such as וְלֹא נָמוּת "that we may not die" — does not of course employ a voluntative verb.

3. עֲשָׂרָה. "Ten (in number)."

6. וְיוֹסֵף הוּא הַשַּׁלִּיט "now it was Joseph who was the ruler...." Generally the predicate of a noun sentence or clause does not have the article (see §5.6); when it does, the emphasis which is thereby added is best rendered by "it was/is... who/which...," etc. [Cf. 45:12 פִּי הַמְדַבֵּר "it is my mouth (and not another's) that is speaking."] Further emphasis is given by הוּא; lit., "Now Joseph (note the disjunctive of וְיוֹסֵף), it was he who was the ruler."

7. קָשׁוֹת "harsh things," here adverbial "harshly." For indefinite or abstract expressions the feminine is commonly used: 42:29 הַקֹּרֹת "the things that happened," 44:4 רָעָה "evil" (noun), טוֹבָה "good" (noun).

10. וַעֲבָדֶיךָ. Opposition is expressed by the *wâw*: "the fact is, rather, that..."

11. לֹא הָיוּ "have never been," §9.3 end.

13. עֲבָדֶיךָ... אֲנַחְנוּ. The change from 3 pers (הָיוּ in vs 11) to 1 pers when using the self-appellation is normal in Hebrew. Cf. the similar changes in 44:7–9. When a superior is respectfully addressed as אֲדֹנִי a similar inconsistency between 3 and 2 pers is found: 44:18ff. יְדַבֶּר נָא עַבְדְּךָ דָבָר בְּאָזְנֵי אֲדֹנִי וְאַל יִחַר אַפְּךָ בְּעַבְדֶּךָ... אֲדֹנִי שָׁאַל אֶת עֲבָדָיו... וַתֹּאמֶר אֶל עֲבָדֶיךָ "Please, my lord, let your servant have a word with my lord, and don't be angry with

your servant.... My lord asked his servants... then you said to your servants...."

14. הוּא אֲשֶׁר דִּבַּרְתִּי אֲלֵיכֶם לֵאמֹר "it is just as I spoke to you, when I said...."

15. חַי פַּרְעֹה אִם תֵּצְאוּ מִזֶּה... הֵנָּה "(I swear) by Pharaoh's life! you shall not leave this place unless your youngest brother comes here." The oath is introduced by אִם and takes the form of an "if" clause; the "then" clause, which contains a self-imprecation, the teeth of the oath, is left unspoken. Literally, then: "If you leave this place except with the coming of your youngest brother here (may I be cursed)!"

16. הֵאָסְרוּ "submit to imprisonment!"

חַי פַּרְעֹה כִּי מְרַגְּלִים אַתֶּם "(I swear) by Pharaoh's life that you are spies!" (Only verb clauses are introduced by אִם, as in vs 15.)

21. אֲשֶׁר רָאִינוּ. It is not clear to what אֲשֶׁר is attached; if to אֲנַחְנוּ, then render "(we) who saw" ("for we saw"); but if to אָחִינוּ, the clause is to be construed אָחִינוּ אֲשֶׁר (אֶת) צָרַת נַפְשׁוֹ בְּהִתְחַנְנוֹ אֵלֵינוּ רָאִינוּ "whose mortal distress when he pleaded with us we saw."

צָרַת נַפְשׁוֹ "his mortal distress." The suffix refers to the whole construction: "his distress-with-regard-to-life." Similarly below, vs 35 צְרוֹר כַּסְפּוֹ "his money-bag," צְרֹרוֹת כַּסְפֵיהֶם "their money-bags," 44:2 כֶּסֶף שִׁבְרוֹ "his ration-money."

22. וְגַם "so now...." גַּם sometimes expresses consequence in the sense of "measure for measure."

23. הַמֵּלִיץ. The article may be used with items which, though as yet not mentioned, are associated so closely with a given situation that the writer assumes their presence there all along to be well known.

הַמֵּלִיץ "the interpreter (who customarily mediated between Joseph and foreigners)." English idiom requires "an interpreter."

25. וַיְצַו... וַיְמַלְאוּ[1]... וּלְהָשִׁיב "he gave orders... to fill... and to give back...." Two ways of expressing the complement of צִוָּה are here combined: וַיְצַו וַיְמַלְאוּ and וַיְצַו לְהָשִׁיב.

וַיַּעַשׂ לָהֶם כֵּן "it was so done for them." The subject is indefinite (the medieval Hebrew grammarians supplied it as הָעוֹשֶׂה "the doer"); "one did so for them," best rendered by English passive.

28. וַיֶּחֶרְדוּ אִישׁ אֶל אָחִיו "they turned trembling to one another." חָרַד cannot normally govern the preposition אֶל since it does not in itself convey an idea of motion *toward* anything. אֶל depends, rather, on some inexplicit verb expressing a movement made by the brothers אִישׁ אֶל אָחִיו — such as turning the head toward or looking at — which was accompanied by trembling. Such a construction as חָרַד אֶל which implies more than the words say explicitly is called a *pregnant construction*. Another pregnant construction is 43:33 וַיִּתְמְהוּ הָאֲנָשִׁים אִישׁ אֶל רֵעֵהוּ "the men looked at one another in astonishment."

31. לֹא הָיִינוּ "we have never been," §9.3 end.

32. שְׁנֵים עָשָׂר אֲנַחְנוּ "we are twelve," "there are twelve of us."

33. שֶׁבֶר רַעֲבוֹן=רַעֲבוֹן as in vs 19.

34. כִּי לֹא מְרַגְּלִים אַתֶּם "that you are not spies (but honest men)." Noun clauses are normally negated by אֵין: 37:29 אֵין יוֹסֵף בַּבּוֹר "Joseph was not in the pit," and the word order אֵין – subject – predicate is preserved even after כִּי: I Kings 21:15 כִּי אֵין נָבוֹת חַי "for Naboth is not alive," Esther 3:5 כִּי אֵין מָרְדְּכַי כֹּרֵעַ "that Mordecai did not kneel." But when, as here, it is desired to negate the

---

1 On the absence of *dāgeš* in the ל (though the verb is *pi'el*) see §22.4, note 1.

predicate forcefully, not only is the word order reversed to predicate–subject, לֹא is employed as the negative particle, its force falling on the immediately following predicate rather than on the whole clause. A rising inflection in the voice on "spies" will render the effect of these changes in English.

36. אֹתִי שִׁכַּלְתֶּם "it is I (not yourselves!) whom you have bereaved"; see §27.7. Hence Reuben's response in vs 37.

כֻּלָּנָה "all these things" i.e., these troubles. The form is that taken by כֻּלָּן in a major pause; for the feminine, see note on vs 7 above.

38. וּקְרָאָהוּ אָסוֹן ...וְהוֹרַדְתֶּם "if disaster befalls him... you will bring down...." Conditions are often expressed by simple juxtaposition of the "if" and the "then" clauses, each preceded by ו (in this case *wâw*-consecutive with the perfect) to bring out the correlation of clauses. Cf. 44:22 וְעָזַב אֶת אָבִיו וָמֵת "if he should leave his father, he will die"; 44:29 וּלְקַחְתֶּם גַּם אֶת זֶה... וְקָרָהוּ אָסוֹן וְהוֹרַדְתֶּם "if you take this one too... and disaster befalls him, you will bring down...."

Genesis 43

3. הָעֵד הֵעִד בָּנוּ "he solemnly/strictly/clearly warned us."

4–5. אִם יֶשְׁךָ מְשַׁלֵּחַ, וְאִם אֵינְךָ מְשַׁלֵּחַ "if you really mean to let our brother go... but if you do not mean to let him go." יֵשׁ and אֵין here express disposition or nondisposition to do something.

7. שָׁאוֹל שָׁאַל, הֲיָדוֹעַ נֵדַע. See §11.1.

8. ... שִׁלְחָה. See §10.9.

9. אִם לֹא הֲבִיאֹתִיו, וְהִצַּגְתִּיו, וְחָטָאתִי. The verbs concern future time but are perfects; hence future perfects: "if (at that time) I shall

not have brought him to you and set him before you, I shall have incurred life-long guilt toward you." Render: "if I do not bring him to you and set him before you, I shall stand guilty before you all my life."

14. יִתֵּן לָכֶם רַחֲמִים לִפְנֵי הָאִישׁ "may He show you compassion (when you are) in the presence of the man," i.e., by inclining the man to be favorable toward you.

אֲחִיכֶם אַחֵר. We expect אֲחִיכֶם הָאַחֵר; has the article been omitted for the sake of euphony (to avoid adding another laryngal)? Cf. 42:19 אֲחִיכֶם אֶחָד as compared with vs 33 אֲחִיכֶם הָאֶחָד [but perhaps there the intent is first "any one of your brothers," but when the brothers narrate the tale, "the one (that Joseph did in fact imprison) of your brothers"].

כַּאֲשֶׁר שָׁכֹלְתִּי שָׁכָלְתִּי "if I am to be bereaved, I must be bereaved." On שָׁכָלְתִּי see §29.1(e).

15. וּמִשְׁנֶה כֶּסֶף. Note that in vs 12 the word order is reversed. Numbers too may precede or follow the noun: שְׁלֹשָׁה יָמִים or יָמִים שְׁלֹשָׁה.

מִצְרַיְמָה = מִצְרַיִם; cf. vs 18 בֵּיתָה יוֹסֵף = בֵּית יוֹסֵף; similarly in vs 19 בְּפֶתַח הַבַּיִת = פֶּתַח הַבַּיִת.

16. טְבֹחַ טֶבַח "slaughter an animal," lit., "slaughter a slaughtering." טֶבַח is a *cognate accusative*, i.e., a direct object noun derived from the verb — a very common usage in Hebrew.

20. יָרֹד יָרַדְנוּ. The force of the inf abs is unclear.

27. הֲשָׁלוֹם אֲבִיכֶם הַזָּקֵן "is your aged father well?" lit., "is your aged father well-being?" The predicate of a nominal sentence need not be wholly applicable in substance to the subject; it is enough

if, as here, something of it is shared in common with the subject. The reply in vs 28 שָׁלוֹם לְעַבְדְּךָ לְאָבִינוּ is of course a different construction: "your servant our father enjoys (is possessed of) well-being."

28. וַיִּקְּדוּ. Root קדד

29. יָחְנְךָ. Root חנן

30. The main clause is וַיְמַהֵר יוֹסֵף ... וַיָּבֹא הַחַדְרָה; כִּי begins the clause giving the reason.

31. וַיִּתְאַפַּק. See §29.1(e).

32. יוּכְלוּן. The ן is an archaic ending attached occasionally to the vowel afformatives of the impf; cf 44:23 תֹּסִפוּן (note final stress).

33. וַיִּתְמְהוּ ... אִישׁ אֶל רֵעֵהוּ. On this pregnant construction see note on 42:28.

34. וַיִּשָּׂא מַשְׂאוֹת "he had portions carried," i.e., at his command. Or render as a passive: "portions were carried"; see note to 42:25 וַיַּעַשׂ לָהֶם כֵּן.

חָמֵשׁ יָדוֹת "by five shares," i.e., it was five times as large.

Genesis 44

3,4. הַבֹּקֶר אוֹר וְהָאֲנָשִׁים שֻׁלְּחוּ "when morning dawned, the men were sent off." הֵם יָצְאוּ אֶת הָעִיר ... וְיוֹסֵף אָמַר "when they had left the city, Joseph said...." וְהִשַּׂגְתֶּם וְאָמַרְתָּ אֲלֵיהֶם "and when you overtake them, say to them...." These are three examples of temporal expressions, in which the temporal and the main clause are merely juxtaposed and linked by ו, the simplest and most elegant manner of expressing such a relation in Hebrew. Cf. note to 37:4 וַיִּרְאוּ אֶחָיו.

לֹא הִרְחִיקוּ "without/not having gone very far": a circumstantial verb clause, qualifying יָצְאוּ; it is identifiable by being set off from

the main clause without וְ. Another such circumstantial verb clause appears in vs 12: וַיְחַפֵּשׂ בַּגָּדוֹל הֵחֵל וּבַקָּטֹן כִּלָּה "he searched them, beginning with the eldest and ending with the youngest."

5. וְהוּא נַחֵשׁ יְנַחֵשׁ בּוֹ "by which in fact he usually divines"; or "about which he'd certainly divine" (cf. vs 15).

הֲרֵעֹתֶם. Root רעע. הֲרֵעֹתֶם אֲשֶׁר עֲשִׂיתֶם lit., "you did evil (in that) which you did"; render: "you did evil in so doing."

8. וְאֵיךְ נִגְנֹב "how then could we steal"; see note to 37:20 and §10.3.

9. וְגַם אֲנַחְנוּ "moreover the rest of us." Similarly וְאַתֶּם in vss 10 and 17 is "the rest of you"; so too in 42:19.

10. גַּם עַתָּה כְּדִבְרֵיכֶם כֵּן הוּא "though what you say is right"; lit., "though now it is right as you say."

14. וַיָּבֹא יְהוּדָה וְאֶחָיו... וַיִּפְּלוּ With a subject composed of two (or more) coordinate nouns, a verb that precedes may agree with only the first noun, but a verb that follows is generally in the plural.

18. בְּאָזְנֵי אֲדֹנִי "in the hearing of my lord." The sense of the whole clause is: "Please permit me to speak, and give what I have to say a favorable hearing." It does not mean, "Let me have a private word with you."

On the changes of person in these verses see note to 42:13.

כָּמוֹךָ כְּפַרְעֹה "you and Pharaoh are alike." The sense of כ...כ is not merely "a is like b," but includes the idea that "b is like a."

20. אֲהֵבוֹ "loves him"; see §9.3 end and note the stative vowel ־ֵ that reappears when אָהַב takes a suffix.

22. וְעָזַב... וָמֵת. See note to 42:38.

26. וְאָחִינוּ הַקָּטֹן אֵינֶנּוּ אִתָּנוּ "unless our youngest brother is with us"; lit., "our youngest brother not being with us." This is a circum-

stantial noun clause, usually linked by ו to the main clause; cf. vs 30 וְהַנַּעַר אֵינֶנּוּ אִתָּנוּ "the lad not being with us" = "without the lad" and similarly in vs 34.

27. אַתֶּם יְדַעְתֶּם. The independent pronoun is used with finite verbs to add emphasis (cf. vs 17 הוּא יִהְיֶה "he *alone* will be"). Here Jacob wishes to recall to his sons what they know full well but seem to have disregarded; אַתֶּם יְדַעְתֶּם almost: "let me remind you."

כִּי שְׁנַיִם "only two sons"; cf. §27.7.

29. ...וּלְקַחְתֶּם. See note to 42:38.

30. וְנַפְשׁוֹ קְשׁוּרָה בְּנַפְשׁוֹ "and his whole being is so bound up with him."

32. כִּי עַבְדְּךָ עָרַב "now it was your servant who took the lad on pledge"; §27.5(c). Here Judah supplies the motive for his princely offer in the next verse.

34. פֶּן "(I could not) lest...."

Genesis 45

1. לְכָל. ל "for" here conveys the idea "as was proper in the presence of."

2. וַיִּתֵּן אֶת קֹלוֹ בִּבְכִי "he wept loud and freely"; the phrase expresses giving vent to pent-up emotion.

4. אֲשֶׁר מְכַרְתֶּם אֹתִי. Note how the retrospective אֹתִי agrees with אֲנִי יוֹסֵף rather than with אֲחִיכֶם — the rule in relative clauses.

6. אֵין חָרִישׁ וְקָצִיר "there will be no yield from tilling." חָרִישׁ and קָצִיר are combined here into one concept; not that there will be no plowing *or* harvesting (even in famine the farmer may plow his field in hope of a return), but that there will be no plowing that produces a harvest.

7. לָשׂוּם לָכֶם שְׁאֵרִית "to establish for you a remnant"; i.e., to insure that you and yours survive.

לְהַחֲיוֹת אֶתְכֶם=וּלְהַחֲיוֹת לָכֶם. The presence of לָכֶם is probably due to the influence of לָשׂוּם לָכֶם.

לִפְלֵיטָה גְּדֹלָה. Unclear; it has been understood either as "to (become) a great band of survivors" — alluding perhaps to the numerous future progeny of these survivors of famine — or "for a great escape" — alluding to the marvelous manner of their deliverance.

12. פִּי הַמְדַבֵּר. See note on 42:6.

19. וְאַתָּה צֻוִּיתָה "you are charged (to bid them)."

23. כְּזֹאת "as follows."

26. וְכִי. Not part of the quotation. It may be understood either as unexpectedly introducing indirect speech, or better, as dependent upon וַיַּגִּדוּ... לֵאמֹר and taking up the direct speech anew.

QUESTIONS FOR REVIEW

GENESIS 37

עֲנֵה:

1. לָמָּה שָׂנְאוּ אֲחֵי יוֹסֵף אֹתוֹ, וְלָמָּה קִנְּאוּ בּוֹ? 2. מַה פִּתְרוֹנֵי חֲלוֹמוֹת יוֹסֵף? 3. לָמָּה שָׁלַח יַעֲקֹב אֶת יוֹסֵף שְׁכֶמָה? 4. אֵיךְ מָצָא יוֹסֵף אֶת אֶחָיו בְּדוֹתָן? 5. אֵיךְ הִצִּיל רְאוּבֵן אֶת יוֹסֵף מִיַּד אֶחָיו? 6. אֵיךְ כִּסּוּ הָאַחִים מִיַּעֲקֹב אֶת אֲשֶׁר עָשׂוּ לְיוֹסֵף? 7. לָמָּה מֵאֵן יַעֲקֹב לְהִתְנַחֵם?

מִי אָמַר אֶל מִי וּמָתַי?

1. אֶת אַחַי אָנֹכִי מְבַקֵּשׁ. 2. הִנֵּה בַּעַל הַחֲלוֹמוֹת הַלָּזֶה בָּא. 3. אַל תִּשְׁפְּכוּ דָם. 4. אָחִינוּ בְשָׂרֵנוּ הוּא.

GENESIS 42

עֲנֵה:

1. לָמָּה לֹא שִׁלַּח יַעֲקֹב אֶת בִּנְיָמִין אֶת אֶחָיו מִצְרַיְמָה? 2. מָה הִגִּידוּ הָאַחִים לְיוֹסֵף? 3. מַה בֵּין דִּבְרֵי יוֹסֵף לְאֶחָיו לִפְנֵי אֲשֶׁר הָיוּ בַּמִּשְׁמָר לִדְבָרָיו אַחֲרֵי אֲשֶׁר הָיוּ שָׁם שְׁלֹשֶׁת יָמִים? 4. אֵיךְ פָּתְרוּ הָאַחִים אֶת דְּבַר צָרָתָם? אֵיךְ פָּתַר אֹתוֹ רְאוּבֵן? 5. מַה מִּכָּל הַקּוֹרוֹת אֹתָם בְּמִצְרַיִם לֹא הִגִּידוּ בְּנֵי יַעֲקֹב לַאֲבִיהֶם? 6. לָמָּה אָמַר רְאוּבֵן: אֶת שְׁנֵי בָנַי תָּמִית?

מִי אָמַר אֶל מִי וּמָתַי?

1. מֵאַיִן בָּאתֶם? 2. וְגַם דָּמוֹ הִנֵּה נִדְרָשׁ. 3. אַחִיכֶם הָאֶחָד הַנִּיחוּ אִתִּי.

GENESIS 43

עֲנֵה:

1. לָמָּה בִּקֵּשׁ יְהוּדָה מִיַּעֲקֹב כִּי יְשַׁלַּח אֶת בִּנְיָמִין? 2. לָמָּה הִגִּידוּ לָאִישׁ כִּי עוֹד לָהֶם אָח? 3. מָה אָמַר יְהוּדָה לְיַעֲקֹב כַּאֲשֶׁר עָרַב אֶת בִּנְיָמִין מִמֶּנּוּ? 4. מַה זִּמְרַת אֶרֶץ כְּנַעַן? 5. כַּמָּה כֶּסֶף הֵשִׁיבוּ הָאַחִים בְּיָדָם? לָמָּה? 6. לָמָּה יָרְאוּ כַּאֲשֶׁר הוּבְאוּ בֵּיתָה יוֹסֵף? 7. אֵיךְ פָּתַר לָהֶם הָאִישׁ אֶת דְּבַר הַכֶּסֶף אֲשֶׁר נִמְצָא בְּשַׂקֵּיהֶם? 8. מֶה עָשָׂה לָהֶם כַּאֲשֶׁר הֵבִיא אֹתָם הַבַּיְתָה? 9. עַל מַה בָּכָה יוֹסֵף? 10. עַל מַה תָּמְהוּ הָאַחִים?

Utilize in a sentence :

רָחַץ. עַד. נִכְמְרוּ רַחֲמָיו. הִתְאַפֵּק. תּוֹעֵבָה. רָבָה.

GENESIS 44

עֲנֵה:

1. מַה צִּוָּה יוֹסֵף לָשִׂים בְּאַמְתְּחוֹת הָאַחִים? 2. מַה יַּעֲשֶׂה יוֹסֵף בַּגָּבִיעַ – עַל פִּי הָאִישׁ אֲשֶׁר עַל בֵּית יוֹסֵף? 3. עַל פִּי דִּבְרֵי הָאַחִים מַה לַּעֲשׂוֹת בָּאִישׁ אֲשֶׁר יִמָּצֵא הַגָּבִיעַ בְּיָדוֹ? וְעַל פִּי דִּבְרֵי יוֹסֵף? 4. לָמָּה לֹא יוּכַל יְהוּדָה לַעֲלוֹת אֶל אָבִיו אִם הַנַּעַר אֵינֶנּוּ אִתּוֹ?

מִי אָמַר אֶל/עַל מִי וּמָתַי?

1. לָמָּה שִׁלַּמְתֶּם רָעָה תַּחַת טוֹבָה? 2. וְאַתֶּם תִּהְיוּ נְקִיִּם. 3. כָּמוֹךָ כְּפַרְעֹה. 4. נַפְשׁוֹ קְשׁוּרָה בְּנַפְשׁוֹ. 5. טָרוֹף טֹרַף.

Utilize in a sentence :

מִלֵּא. רָדַף. שִׁלֵּם. זָהָב. גָּנַב. נָקִי. עָזַב. שְׁנַיִם. יָלַד. עָלָה.

GENESIS 45

עֲנֵה :

1. לָמָּה לֹא יָכֹל יוֹסֵף לְהִתְאַפֵּק עוֹד? 2. אֵיךְ פָּתַר יוֹסֵף אֶת דְּבַר רִדְתּוֹ מִצְרַיְמָה? 3. מָה הָיָה יוֹסֵף בְּמִצְרַיִם? 4. מַה בִּקֵּשׁ לַעֲשׂוֹת לְאָבִיו וּלְבֵיתוֹ? 5. מָתַי יָכְלוּ יוֹסֵף וְאֶחָיו לְדַבֵּר אִישׁ אֶל רֵעֵהוּ? 6. מַה צִוָּה פַּרְעֹה לַעֲשׂוֹת לְבֵית יַעֲקֹב וְלֵאמֹר לָהֶם? 7. מַה נָּתַן יוֹסֵף לְאֶחָיו וּמַה שָׁלַח אֶל אָבִיו? 8. מָתַי הֶאֱמִין יַעֲקֹב כִּי עוֹד יוֹסֵף חַי?

Utilize in a sentence:

הִתְוַדַּע. נִצַּב. קוֹל. נִבְהַל. שְׁנָתַיִם. טַף. חֲלִיפָה. חָס.

* * * * * * *

VOCABULARY REVIEW

Give synonyms :

עָמַד. נָתַן. קָרַב. שְׁאֵרִית. תּוֹךְ. בַּעַל. שַׁלִּיט. עָמַס. חֵלֶב הָאָרֶץ. אֹכֶל. בֶּגֶד. נִשְׁאַר. יָגוֹן. צָרָה. דָּרַשׁ. טָבַח. צָעִיר. מָלַךְ עַל. הָרַג.

Give antonyms :

שָׂבָע. רָחוֹק. לָתֵת. עָנָה. יֵשׁ. בְּכוֹר. טוֹבָה. חַי. הֵרִיק. יָצָא. הֵחֵל. מְעַט. לַעֲלוֹת. מֵאַיִן? אָסַר. לְהָמִית. אָהַב. הֶעֱלָה. עֶבֶד.

Translate :

The numbers : 1, 2, 3, 5, 10, 11, 12, 17, 20, 300; *give a noun with each.*

Parts of the body : (*where possible supply an associated verb*) gray hair, face, eye/s, ear/s, mouth, neck, hips, feet, flesh, blood, heart, hand/s.

Parts of day and concepts of time : day, night, morning, noon, year, two years, one time, twice, afterward.

Verbs of motion: come, go, come/go up, — down, — in, — out, — back; bring up, — down, — out, — back; pass; arise; pursue; overtake.

Family and age: father, mother, son, daughter, brother, little ones, child, lad, firstborn, youngest, old man, family, household.

Utterance: say, tell, speak, narrate, call, weep, scold, ask, answer, order, sound (voice).

Emotion: love, hate, be afraid, be terrified, tremble, be astonished, have feelings stirred, restrain oneself, console, be consoled, have pity (regard) for, be angry at, be wrought up at.

GLOSSARY

GENESIS 37, 42-45

Words are listed in alphabetical order; שׂ precedes שׁ. Verbs are defined in the English infinitive form.

A parenthesis with chapter and verse followed by n refers to the section "Notes on the Hebrew Text."

אָב (§14.5) *father*, in 45:8 *counsellor*

אֲבָל *the truth is, that...*, affirming what one would gladly deny

אָבַל *be in mourning*; *hitpa'el* הִתְאַבֵּל *mourn for* (עַל)

אָדוֹן, suf לַאדֹנִי, אֲדֹנִי *lord, master;* cs pl אֲדֹנֵי־ is used with s meaning

אָהַב, אָהֵב *love*

אוֹ *or*

אוּלַי *perhaps*

אוֹר *become light*

אֹזֶן, du אָזְנַיִם, אָזְנֵי־ f *ear*

אָח (§14.5) *brother;* אִישׁ אֶל אָחִיו *one to the other*

אֶחָד (אַחַד־) m *one;* אַחַד עָשָׂר "*one-teen*" (*eleven*)

אַחֵר (*an*)*other*

אַחַר, אַחֲרֵי־ *after*; אַחֲרֵי כֵן *afterward*

אֵיךְ *how?*

אַיִן (cs of אַיִן *nought;* §15.8) *no, not* negating noun sentence (42:34 n)

אֵיפֹה *where?*

אִישׁ, אֲנָשִׁים, אַנְשֵׁי־ *a man, one, each;* אִישׁ אֶל אָחִיו *one to the other*

אַךְ *surely!*

אָכַל, impf יֹאכַל [§21.4(b)] pf 3fs w suf 3ms אֲכָלָתְהוּ *eat*

אֹכֶל *food*

אַל (*do*) *not* w juss

אֶל (§15.4) *to, into*

אֵל *god;* אֵל שַׁדַּי *El Shadday* (usually rendered *God Almighty*); שַׁדַּי is a

divine epithet of as yet undetermined meaning; אֵל שַׁדַּי is an antique name of God used chiefly in stories of patriarchal times

אֵלֶּה *these*

אֱלֹהִים pl of majesty, *God*

אֲלֻמָּה, אֲלֻמִּים, אֲלֻמּוֹת (37:7n) *sheaf*

אלם, *pi'el* אִלֵּם *bind* (sheaves)

אֵם, suf אִמּוֹ *mother*

אִם *if, or;* introduces an oath (42:15n)

אמן, *nif'al* impf יֵאָמֵן *be verified, proven true*; *hif'il* pf הֶאֱמִין *consider true, believe*

אָמַר, impf יֹאמַר [§21.4(b)] *say, command*; the inf cs לֵאמֹר, usually rendered *saying*, often has no meaning beyond that of our colon or comma with quotation marks marking a direct address

אֱמֶת *truth*

אַמְתַּחַת *saddlebag*

אָנָה *whither?*

אָנֹכִי, אֲנִי *I;* pl אֲנַחְנוּ *we*

אָסוֹן *disaster, terrible accident*

אָסַף [§21.4(a)] *gather*

אָסַר *bind, imprison; nif'al* impf יֵאָסֵר *be imprisoned*

אַף *nose, anger;* חָרָה אַפּוֹ בְּ־ *his anger was kindled against;* אַפַּיִם du *face* (=פָּנִים)

אֵפוֹא particle *then;* אִם כֵּן אֵפוֹא *if so, then....*

אפק, *hitpa'el* הִתְאַפֵּק, וַיִּתְאַפֵּק [§29.1(e)] *restrain oneself*

אֹרְחָה *caravan*

אֶרֶץ w art הָאָרֶץ, w term אַרְצָה f *land, ground*

אִשָּׁה, אֵשֶׁת־, נָשִׁים, נְשֵׁי־ *woman, wife* also used for *concubine*

אָשַׁם *be guilty*

אֲשֶׁר word of relation *that, which, who*

אֵת (§14.6) (*together*) *with* מֵאֵת (*away*) *from*

אֵת (§14.6) the sign of the definite direct object; precedes direct object defined either by (1) the art (2) being in the cs (3) having a pron suf (4) being a proper name

אָתוֹן, אֲתֹנוֹת *she-donkey*

בְּ (§14.6) (1) *in, at, upon.* (2) prefixed to the object of some verbs; e.g., רָעָה, מָשַׁל, נָעַר. (3) *by* בְּזֹאת תִּבָּחֲנוּ *by this will you be tested*

בְּגָדִים, בֶּגֶד *clothing*

בהל, *nif'al* נִבְהַל *be terrified*

בוֹא, pf בָּא (§17.2) *come; hif'il* הֵבִיא (§17.3) *bring*; *hŏf'al* הוּבָא *be brought*

בּוֹר, בּוֹרוֹת *pit, cistern*

בחן, *nif'al* impf יִבָּחֵן *be tested*

בָּטְנִים *pistachios*

בִּי אֲדֹנִי formula craving permission to open a conversation with a superior, *please, my lord*

בֵּין־, בֵּינוֹת־ *between*

בַּיִת, בֵּית־, suf בֵּיתוֹ, pl בָּתִּים, בָּתֵּי־ *house, household*

בָּכָה, impf יִבְכֶּה, יַיבְךְ *weep, bewail*

בְּכוֹר *firstborn, oldest son*

בְּכִי *weeping*

בְּכֹרָה *seniority* (lit., *firstborn status*)

בִּלְהָה *Bilhah*, one of Jacob's concubines, the maid of Rachel

בִּלְתִּי *except, unless*, only with a noun clause

בֵּן, בֵּן־, בָּנִים, בְּנֵי־ (§14.5) *son;* בֵּן שְׁבַע עֶשְׂרֵה שָׁנָה *son of* 17 *years* (17 *years old*)

בִּנְיָמִין *Benjamin*

בְּעִיר collective *beasts*

בַּעַל *owner, master;* בַּעַל חֲלוֹמוֹת *dreamer*

בֶּצַע *gain, profit*

בֹּקֶר *morning*

בָּקָר *cattle*

בקש, *pi'el* בִּקֵּשׁ *seek, want, demand*

בָּר *grain*

בָּשָׂר *flesh*

בַּת, בָּנוֹת (§15.3) *daughter*

גָּבִיעַ־, גְּבִיעֵי־, suf גְּבִיעִי *cup*

גָּדוֹל *big, old* (mature)

גלל, *hitpolel* הִתְגֹּלֵל *find a pretext against* (עַל)

גִּלְעָד *Gilead*

גַּם *also, even*, 44:10 *even though;* גַּם...גַּם *both... and*

גָּמָל, גְּמַלִּים *camel*

גָּנַב *steal*

גָּעַר, impf יִגְעַר *rebuke, scold* (בְּ־)

גֹּשֶׁן *Goshen*, district in NE Egypt

דִּבָּה *report*

דבר, *pi'el* דִּבֵּר *speak*

דָּבָר *thing, matter, word, something said*

דְּבַשׁ *honey*

דָּם *blood*

דֶּרֶךְ f *way*

דָּרַשׁ *require; nif'al* 42:22 דָּמוֹ... נִדְרָשׁ *his blood* (i.e., an accounting for the shedding of his innocent blood) *is being required*

דֹּתָן w term דֹּתָנָה *Dothan*

הֲ (for vocalization see vocabulary to Reading 3) interrogative particle; prefixed to the first word of a statement it makes it a question, הֲמָלֹךְ תִּמְלֹךְ עָלֵינוּ? *Would you indeed be king over us?* in indirect questions *whether*, 42:16 יִבָּחֲנוּ דִבְרֵיכֶם הַאֱמֶת אִתְּכֶם *let your words be tested* (*to see*) *whether you are telling the truth;* 43:6 לְהַגִּיד לָאִישׁ הַעוֹד לָכֶם אָח *telling the man whether you had another brother*

הַ, הָ, הֶ (§5) art *the*, w pt *who, which, that*

הוּא m הוּא (הִיא) f (§7.1) 3s pron *he she, it;* as a demonstrative *that*

הָיָה impf יִהְיֶה, וַיְהִי (§19.4) *be, become*

הַזֶּה = הַלָּזֶה

הָלַךְ, impf יֵלֵךְ, וַיֵּלֶךְ (§20.4) *go;* the

imv לֵךְ (לְכָה) לְכוּ is often used to exhort, *come*!

הֵם, הֵמָּה m הֵנָּה f 3 pl pron *they*

הֵן = הִנֵּה

הֵנָּה *hither;* temporally *now* as in עַד הֵנָּה *until now*

הִנֵּה *lo*! הִנֶּנִּי *lo*! *I* (*here I am*) הִנֵּנוּ *lo*! *we* (*are*)

הָרַג *kill*

וָ, וַ, וּ, וְ (on vocalization see § 4 exercise vocabulary, p. 36, note 1, 37 : 25n) the copula *and;* it may express, according to context, *but, yet, so that, or, while,* and the like

זֶה m זֹאת f (1) *this,* מִזֶּה *from this place* (2) with expressions of time *already, by now,* 43:10 זֶה פַּעֲמַיִם *already twice;* 45:6 זֶה שְׁנָתַיִם *it is two years now*

זָהָב *gold*

זָכַר *remember*

זִלְפָּה *Zilpah,* Leah's maid, a concubine of Jacob

זִמְרָה collective *choice products*

זְקֻנִים *old age;* בֶּן־זְקֻנִים *son of old age*

חֶבְרוֹן *Hebron*

חֶדֶר, w term חַדְרָה *private chamber, room*

חוּס, juss 3fs תָּחֹס *pity, have compassion for* (עַל), 45:20 וְעֵינְכֶם אַל תָּחֹס עַל כְּלֵיכֶם *let your eye not pity* (*never mind about*) *your household stuff*

חָטָא, impf יֶחֱטָא *sin against* (בְּ־); *stand guilty before* (לְ־)

חֵי־ (cs of חַיִּ* appearing otherwise in the pl חַיִּים *life*) in oaths: (*by*) *the life of*... e.g., 42:15 חֵי פַּרְעֹה (*I swear*) *by Pharaoh's life*!

חָיָה, impf יִחְיֶה, impf cons 3fs וַתִּחִי, pt חַי (§19.4) *live, revive; hif'il* inf cs לְהַחֲיוֹת *keep alive, preserve*

חַיָּה *beast;* חַיָּה רָעָה *wild beast*

חֵלֶב *fat,* figuratively used in חֵלֶב הָאָרֶץ *the fat* (*best*) *of the land*

חָלַם *dream*

חֲלוֹם, חֲלוֹמוֹת *a dream*

חָלִילָה in חָלִילָה לִי־ מִ־(מֵ־), e.g., 44:7 חָלִילָה לַעֲבָדֶיךָ מֵעֲשׂוֹת *far be it from your servants to* (*God forbid that we*) *do*

חלל, *hif'il* הֵחֵל *begin*

חֲלִיפָה *change of clothing, suit*

חֲמוֹר *donkey*

חָמֵשׁ f חֲמִשָּׁה m *five*

חָנַן, impf יָחֹן juss, w 2ms suf יָחְנְךָ *be gracious toward; hitpa'el* הִתְחַנֵּן *implore favor for oneself, plead with* (אֶל)

חפשׂ, *pi'el* חִפֵּשׂ *search*

חָרַד, impf יֶחֱרַד *tremble; look trembling at* (אֶל)

חָרָה, juss יִחַר *burn, be kindled.* (אַף anger) *against* (בְּ־), 44:18 אַל יִחַר אַפְּךָ בְּעַבְדֶּךָ *don't be angry with your servant;* 45:5 אַל יִחַר בְּעֵינֵיכֶם *don't let it vex you*

חָרִישׁ *plowing*

טָבַח *slaughter*

טֶבַח *a slaughtering* of animals

טַבָּח in הַטַּבָּחִים (שַׂר) (*captain of*) *the bodyguard*

טָבַל *dip*

טוֹב *good;* f טוֹבָה is used as a noun *good* in 44:4

טוּב *the best* (*of*)

טָעַן *load*

טַף, suf טַפִּי *little ones*

טֶרֶם or בְּטֶרֶם *ere, before* w impf

טָרַף *tear in pieces* (said of wild beasts); pass *qal* pf טֹרַף *was torn in pieces* (§8.3 note 2)

יָגוֹן *grief*

יָד f (1) du יָדַיִם, יְדֵי־ *hand;* עַל יָדִי *into my charge, custody;* בְּיַד־ w לָקַח, הֵשִׁיב, etc. *with.* (2) pl יָדוֹת *share*

יָדַע, impf יֵדַע (§20) *know; hitpa'el* הִתְוַדַּע *make oneself known*

יְהוּדָה *Judah*

יוֹם, יָמִים *day;* הַיּוֹם *now, at present;* כָּל הַיָּמִים *all one's life*

יוֹסֵף *Joseph*

יטב only impf, יִיטַב (§20.8) *be good, pleasing* וַיִּיטַב בְּעֵינֵי פַרְעֹה *it was good in the eyes of Pharaoh* (*Pharaoh was pleased*)

יָכֹל, impf יוּכַל (§20.6,7) *be able*

יָלַד *bear a child*

יֶלֶד *child*

יסף, *hif 'il* הוֹסִיף *do again* or *more* w inf cs (with or without ל), 37:8 וַיֹּסִפוּ עוֹד שְׂנֹא אֹתוֹ *they did yet more* (*of*) *hating him* (*they hated him all the more;*) 44:23 לֹא תֹסִפוּן לִרְאוֹת פָּנָי *you shall not do more* (*of*) *seeing my face* (*you shall not see my face again*)

יַעֲקֹב *Jacob*

יָצָא, impf יֵצֵא (§20.3) *go* or *come out, leave; hif 'il* הוֹצִיא *take* or *bring out*

יָרֵא, impf יִירָא (§20.5) *be afraid*

יָרַד, impf יֵרֵד (§20.3) *go* or *come down hif 'il* הוֹרִיד *bring* or *take down*

יָרֵחַ *moon*

ירש, *nif 'al* impf 2ms תִּוָּרֵשׁ *come to want*

יִשְׂרָאֵל *Israel*, second name of Jacob

יֶשׁ־, יֵשׁ־ (*there*) *is/are*, usually implies some emphasis; with suf it expresses the subj; e.g., 43:4 אִם יֶשְׁךָ מְשַׁלֵּחַ אֶת אָחִינוּ אִתָּנוּ *if you really mean to let our brother go with us*

יָשַׁב, impf יֵשֵׁב (§20.3) *sit, remain, dwell*

יִשְׁמְעֵאלִי *Ishmaelite*

יתר, *nif 'al* impf יִוָּתֵר *be left*

כְּ, suf כָּמֹוךָ, כָּמֹנִי *like, as;* w inf cs *when;* 44:30 כְּבֹאִי *when I come;* 44:31 כִּרְאוֹתוֹ *when he sees*

כַּאֲשֶׁר (כְּ + אֲשֶׁר) *when, as*

כָּבֵד *be heavy, grievous*

כָּבוֹד *honor*

כֹּה *thus*

כּוֹכָב *star*

כּוּן, pt כֵּן *be true, right honest, hif'il;* הֵכִין *make right, ready, put in order*

כִּי (1) conj *that* introducing object clause of verbs of seeing, hearing, knowing, saying, etc. וַיַּרְאוּ... כִּי אֹתוֹ אָהַב *they saw that he loved him.* (2) *for, because.* (3) *when* (= כַּאֲשֶׁר), 43:21 כִּי בָאנוּ *when we came;* 44:24 כִּי עָלִינוּ *when we went up.* (4) *but* (*rather*) 45:8. Combination: כִּי אִם *except;* כִּי עַתָּה expresses strong affirmation; *indeed now* (see לוּלֵא)

כֹּל, כָּל־ suf 1cpl כֻּלָּנוּ, 3 mpl כֻּלָּם, 3fpl כֻּלָּן, כֻּלָּנָה, *all*

כלה, *pi'el* כִּלָּה *finish, make an end of*

כְּלִי, כְּלֵי־, כֵּלִים *vessel,* in pl *household stuff*

כִּלְכֵּל, *pilpel* of כּוּל *sustain, maintain*

כְּמוֹ־ see כְּ־

כמר, *nif'al* נִכְמַר *grow hot, be stirred* said of רַחֲמִים *tender feelings*

(I) כֵּן *thus, so;* אַחֲרֵי כֵן *afterwards*

(II) כֵּן *qal* pt כּוֹן (*up*)*right, honest*

כְּנַעַן Canaan

כסה, *pi'el* כִּסָּה *cover* (*up*)

כֶּסֶף, suf כַּסְפֵּיהֶם, כַּסְפִּי *silver, money*

כְּתֹנֶת, כְּתֹנֶת־ suf כֻּתָּנְתּוֹ *tunic;* כְּתֹנֶת פַּסִּים *ornamented tunic* (but see פַּס)

ל (see §14.6 and §4 exercise vocabulary) (1) *to, toward.* (2) transition *into* a new condition, 44:9 נִהְיֶה לַעֲבָדִים *we shall become slaves;* 45:8 וַיְשִׂימֵנִי לְאָב לְפַרְעֹה *he appointed me counsellor to Ph.* (3) *belonging to,* 45:10 כָּל אֲשֶׁר לְךָ *all that belongs to you.* (4) *in relation to,* 44:17 הוּא יִהְיֶה לִי עָבֶד *he will be a slave in relation to me* (*he will be my slave*). (5) *about,* 43:7 שָׁאוֹל שָׁאַל הָאִישׁ לָנוּ וּלְמוֹלַדְתֵּנוּ *the man inquired closely about us and our family.* (6) *in a manner or condition,* 37:4 דַּבְּרוֹ לְשָׁלֹם *to speak to him in a friendly manner*

לֹא *no, not,* הֲלוֹא *is/are not...? was/were not..? did not...?* invites an affirmative answer

לֵב, suf לִבּוֹ *heart, sense,* 42:28 וַיֵּצֵא לִבָּם *their sense left them* (*they panicked*)

לְבַד (ל + בד) properly, *in a state of separation* לְבַדּוֹ *by himself, he alone;* לְבַדָּם *by themselves*

לוּלֵא (לוּ + לֹא) neg cond particle *had...not;* coordinate with כִּי עַתָּה

לֶחֶם *bread, food*

לֹט *ladanum,* an aromatic resin

לָמָה *why? wherefore?*

לְמַעַן *for the sake of, in order to* + inf.

לָקַח (§22.4) *take*

לִפְנֵי (ל + פְּנֵי) *before, in the presence of*

מֵאָה, מֵאוֹת *hundred*

מֵאַיִן (מִן + אַיִן) *from where?*

מאן, *pi'el* מֵאֵן *refuse*

מְגוּרִים *state of being a sojourner;* אֶרֶץ מְגוּרִים *land where one is a sojourner*

מִדְבָּר *wilderness, plain* (used for pasturage)

מִדְיָנִי *Midianite, of Midian* (an Arab tribe); variant: מִדָנִי

מַה, מָה, מֶה *what?* (§5.3) מַה נִּצְטַדָּק 44:16 *how can we justify ourselves*

מהמה (*pilpel* of מהה) *hitpalpel* הִתְמַהְמַה *tarry, delay*

מהר, *pi'el* מִהֵר *do hastily;* usually best rendered as an adverb *hastily, quickly* with its complementary verb: וַיִּמַהֵר יוֹסֵף... וַיָּבֹא הַחַדְרָה 43:30 *J. hastily went into his private chamber*

מוֹלֶדֶת *family, kin*

מוּת, pf מֵת (§17.2) *die; hif'il* הֵמִית *put to death*

מָזוֹן *food*

מִחְיָה *sustenance*

מַטְמוֹן *a hidden treasure*

מַיִם *water*

מָכַר *sell*

מלא, *pi'el* מִלֵּא (§21.3) *fill*

מָלוֹן *lodging place*

מֵלִיץ *interpreter*

מָלַךְ *be king*

מִן, מִ־, מֵ (§15.8; ן usually assimilated except before the art) *from, of, out of;* expresses the comparative in 37:3 אָהַב אֶת יוֹסֵף מִכָּל בָּנָיו *he loved J. out of all (more than all) his sons;* has the sense *some* or *one* out of many in 42:16 שִׁלְחוּ מִכֶּם אֶחָד *send one of you;* קְחוּ מִזִּמְרַת הָאָרֶץ 43:11 *take some of the choice products of the land.* In combinations: מֵעַל *from off, away from,* מֵעִם = מֵאֵת *(away) from*

מִנְחָה *present* (to a superior)

מִסְפּוֹא *fodder*

מְעַט *a little bit, some*

מַעֲשֶׂה *deed*

מָצָא (§21) *find, come across, come upon; nif'al* impf יִמָּצֵא *be found*

מִצְרִי *Egyptian*

מִצְרַיִם *Egypt*

מְרַגֵּל (*pi'el* pt of רָגֵל) *a spy*

מַשְׂאֵת־, מַשְׂאַת־, מַשְׂאֹת *present* from host to guest

מִשְׁגֶּה *mistake, oversight*

מָשַׁךְ *draw, drag*

מָשַׁל *rule over* (בְּ־)

מִשְׁמָר *jail, guardhouse*

מִשְׁנֶה *double amount, extra*

מִשְׁקָל *weight,* כַּסְפֵּנוּ בְּמִשְׁקָלוֹ *our money in its full weight*

מָתְנַיִם *loins, hips*

נָא particle of entreaty or exhortation; *pray! now*

נגד, *hif'il* הִגִּיד *tell*

נגש, pf נִגַּשׁ, impf יִגַּשׁ [§22.2(b)] *draw near to, come up to* (אֶל)

נוח, *hif'il* הִנִּיחַ imv mpl הַנִּיחוּ *set down, leave*

נחם, *pi'el* נִחֵם *comfort, console; hitpa'el* הִתְנַחֵם *be comforted, consoled*

אֲנַחְנוּ = נַחְנוּ

נחשׁ, *pi'el* נִחֵשׁ (*to*) *divine*

נְכֹאת a spice, possibly *tragacanth gum*

נכה, *hif'il* הִכָּה impf יַכֶּה (§22.6) *smite*

נכל, *hitpa'el* הִתְנַכֵּל *plot against* (אֶת)

נכר, *hif'il* הִכִּיר (§22.2) *recognize, look at closely* to see whether or not one recognizes; *hitpa'el* הִתְנַכֵּר *act as a stranger*

נָסַע *set out, journey*

נַעַר *a youth, lad*

נָפַל, impf יִפֹּל (§22.2) *fall; hitpa'el* הִתְנַפֵּל *attack* (עַל)

נֶפֶשׁ, suf נַפְשׁוֹ *soul, life, being*

נצב, *nif'al* נִצַּב *stand (up); נִצַּב עַל stand in attendance upon* a king or other high official

נצג, *hif'il* הִצִּיג *set down*, more forceful than שִׂים

נצל, *hif'il* הִצִּיל *rescue, save*

נָקִי, נְקִיִּם *clear, innocent*

נָשָׂא, impf יִשָּׂא (§22.5) *lift, carry off, away*

נשג, *hif'il* הִשִּׂיג *overtake*

נָשִׁים see אִשָּׁה

נשק, *pi'el* נִשֵּׁק *kiss*

נָתַן, impf יִתֵּן (§22.3) *put, give;* 42:30 כְּ־ נָתַן אֶת... *regard...as*

סָבַב, impf יִסֹּב, וַיִּסֹּב, 3fpl תְּסֻבֶּינָה *turn about, surround*

סָחַר, impf יִסְחַר *travel about;* pt סוֹחֵר (סֹחֲרִים) *trader.*

ספר, *pi'el* סִפֵּר *relate*

סָרִיס, סְרִיס־ *court official*

עֶבֶד *servant, slave, minister, courtier*

עָבַר *pass by*

עִבְרִי *Hebrew*

עֲגָלָה, עֲגָלוֹת *wagon*

עַד *until*

עוד, *hif'il* הֵעִד *warn* (בְּ־)

עוֹד (§15.8) *still, yet, besides, again*

עָוֹן, עֲוֹן־ *iniquity*

עֵז, עִזִּים f *goat*

עָזַב *leave*

עַיִן, suf עֵינִי, du עֵינַיִם f *eye*

עִיר, עָרִים f *town*

עַל (§15.4) *upon, over, about, on account of.* Combinations: עַל דְּבַר *on account of, because of;* עַל כֵּן *therefore;* עַל פִּי *according to, by the command of*

עָלָה, impf יַעֲלֶה, juss יַעַל *go* or *come up; hif'il* הֶעֱלָה impf cons 3mpl וַיַּעֲלוּ *bring* or *take up*

עַם *people*

עִם (§14.6) *with*

עָמַד *stand, tarry*

עָמַס *load* (object) *upon* (עַל)

עֵמֶק *valley*

עָנָה, impf יַעֲנֶה, וַיַּעַן *answer, speak up*

עצב, *nif'al* יֵעָצֵב *be grieved*

עָרַב *stand surety for, be responsible for, take on pledge from* (מֵעִם)

עֶרְוָה *pudenda* עֶרְוַת הָאָרֶץ *the secret parts of the land*

עָשָׂה, impf וַיַּעַשׂ, יַעֲשֶׂה *do, make*

עָשָׂר m עֶשְׂרֵה f *-teen*

שְׁבַע־עֶשְׂרֵה f *seventeen*

אַחַד־עָשָׂר m "*one-teen*" (*eleven*)

שְׁנֵים־עָשָׂר m "*two-teen*" (*twelve*)

עֶשֶׂר f עֲשָׂרָה m *ten* עֶשְׂרִים *twenty*

עַתָּה *now*

פֶּה, פִּי־, 1cs suf פִּי *mouth;* עַל פִּי see עַל

פּוּג, impf cons וַיָּפָג *grow numb, fail*

פּוֹטִיפַר *Potiphar*, Egyptian official

פְּלֵיטָה *an escape*, or *survivors* escaped from a calamity

פֶּן *lest*

פָּנִים, פְּנֵי־, suf 1cs פָּנַי 3ms פָּנָיו *face, presence;* לִפְנֵי־ *before*

פַּס in כְּתֹנֶת פַּסִּים, meaning uncertain; traditional guesses; *varicolored strip(e)s, palm* of hand, *sole* of foot, hence *tunic reaching to extremities*

פַּעַם f *time;* du פַּעֲמַיִם *twice*

פַּרְעֹה *Pharaoh*, Egyptian royal title ("the great house")

פשט, *hif'il* הִפְשִׁיט *divest* of

פָּתַח impf יִפְתַּח *open*

פֶּתַח, *opening, doorway*

צֹאן *sheep, flock(s)*

צֵדָה *provisions*

צדק, *hitpa'el* הִצְטַדֵּק (§18.5) נִצְטַדָּק [§29.1(e)] *justify oneself*

צָהֳרַיִם *noon*

צַוָּאר, suf צַוָּארָיו, pl cs צַוָּארֵי־ used as s *neck*

צוה, *pi'el* צִוָּה, impf יְצַוֶּה, וַיְצַו *charge, order; pu'al* pf 2ms צֻוִּיתָה *be charged* with a command to others.

צָעִיר *small, young*

צְעִירָה *youth*, "*juniority*"

צָרָה *distress, trouble*

צְרוֹר, צְרֹרוֹת *bundle, pouch* (of money)

צְרִי *balsam* (*balm*)

קדד, impf יִקֹּד *bow the head*

קוֹל *voice, report*

קוּם *arise, get up;* with another verb, *make a move to* and the like, 37:35 וַיָּקוּמוּ ... לְנַחֲמוֹ *they tried to console him*

קָטֹן, קָטָן [§29.1(e)] *small, young*

קנא, *pi'el* קִנֵּא *be wrought up at, jealous of* (בְּ־)

קָצִיר *harvesting*

(I) קָרָא, impf יִקְרָא *call*

(II) קָרָא = קרה pf w suf וְקָרָאָהוּ, impf w suf יִקְרָאֻנוּ *befall, happen to*

קֶרֶב *midst*

קָרַב *be* or *draw near*

קָרוֹב *near*

קָרָה, impf יִקְרֶה *befall, happen to;* pt fpl קֹרֹת (קוֹרוֹת) *happening, things that befall*

קָרַע *tear* (trans)

קָשֶׁה *hard, harsh;* fpl קָשׁוֹת is used adverbially *harshly*

קָשַׁר, pass pt fs קְשׁוּרָה *bind, tie*

רָאָה, impf יִרְאֶה, וַיַּרְא *see, behold* (אֶת, בְּ־); *hitpa'el* impf 2mpl תִּתְרָאוּ *stare at one another* at a loss as to what to do

רְאוּבֵן *Reuben*

רַב, רַבִּים *much, many;* as exclamation *enough* !

רָבָה, impf cons 3fs וַתִּרֶב *be much, great,* 43:34 וַתִּרֶב ... מִ־ ... *was greater than*

רָגַז *be agitated, quarrel*

רֶגֶל, du רַגְלַיִם f *foot*

רָדַף *pursue*

רוּחַ *spirit*

רַחֲמִים suf רַחֲמָיו *compassion, tender feelings*

רָחַץ *wash*

רחק, *hif'il* הִרְחִיק *be* or *go very far*

רָחֹק, *(a)far*

ריק, *hif'il* הֵרִיק *empty out*

רָע *evil*; as a noun (also f רָעָה), *evil, calamity*

רֵעַ, suf רֵעֵהוּ *fellow, companion;* אִישׁ אֶל רֵעֵהוּ *one to the other*

רָעָב *famine*

רְעָבוֹן, רַעֲבוֹן־ *hunger, famine*

רָעָה *pasture, tend* (sheep) (אֶת, בְּ־)

רעע, *hif'il* 2mpl הֲרֵעֹתֶם *do evil, do harm,* 44:5 הֲרֵעֹתֶם אֲשֶׁר עֲשִׂיתֶם *you did evil in so doing*

רֵק, (rt ריק) *empty*

שָׂדֶה *field, countryside*

שִׂים, שׂוּם *set, put, appoint as* (לְ־)

שֵׂיבָה *gray hairs*

שִׂמְלָה, שִׂמְלוֹת־, שְׂמָלוֹת *clothing, garment*

שָׂנֵא *hate*

שָׂעִיר, שְׂעִיר־ *buck* (of goats עִזִּים)

שַׂק, suf שַׂקּוֹ, pl שַׂקִּים *sack, sackcloth* for mourning

שַׂר *chief, official;* שַׂר הַטַּבָּחִים *captain of the bodyguard*

שָׁאַל, impf יִשְׁאַל *ask, inquire after* (לְ־)

שְׁאוֹל *Sheol,* the netherworld abode of the dead

שאר, *nif'al* נִשְׁאַר *remain, be left*

שְׁאֵרִית *remnant*

שֶׁבַע־עֶשְׂרֵה f *seven* שְׁבַע־, שֶׁבַע f *seventeen*

שֶׁבֶר, suf שִׁבְרוֹ *rations, emergency food supply;* properly שֶׁבֶר רְעָבוֹן (42:19) "breakhunger"

שָׁבַר (denominative of שֶׁבֶר) *obtain, procure* food (אֹכֶל, שֶׁבֶר) in an emergency; *hif'il* pt מַשְׁבִּיר *supply* food in an emergency

שָׁדַי see אֵל

שוּב (§17.2) *come* or *go back, return* (intrans); *hif'il* הֵשִׁיב (§17.3) *bring back, return; hŏf'al* הוּשַׁב pt מוּשַׁב (§17.4 note) *given back, returned*

שחוה, *hitpa'lel* הִשְׁתַּחֲוָה (see Reading 3, note) *prostrate oneself*

שָׁחַט *slaughter*

שָׁכֹל *be bereaved of child(ren); pi'el* שִׁכֵּל *cause to be bereaved, make childless*

שְׁכֶם *Shechem*

שָׁכַר *become drunk, carouse*

שָׁלוֹם, שְׁלוֹם־ *welfare, amity, wholeness,* 37:4 לֹא יָכְלוּ דַּבְּרוֹ לְשָׁלֹם *they could not speak to him amicably;* 37:14 רְאֵה אֶת שְׁלוֹם אַחֶיךָ *see how your brothers are faring;* 44:17 עֲלוּ לְשָׁלוֹם *go up intact, safe and sound*

שָׁלַח *send; pi'el* שִׁלַּח *send off, release, let go*

שַׁלִּיט *ruler*

שלך, *hif'il* הִשְׁלִיךְ *throw*

שְׁלִישִׁי *third*

שלם, *pi'el* שִׁלֵּם *(re)pay*

שָׁלֹשׁ, שְׁלֹשׁ־, f שְׁלֹשֶׁת־ שְׁלֹשָׁה־ m *three*

שָׁם *there,* שָׁמָּה *thither*

שָׁמַע, impf יִשְׁמַע *hear, understand; nif'al* נִשְׁמַע *be heard*

שִׁמְעוֹן *Simeon*

שָׁמַר *keep, watch, guard*

שֶׁמֶשׁ *sun*

שָׁנָה, du שְׁנָתַיִם, pl שָׁנִים or שָׁנוֹת *year*

שְׁנַיִם, cs שְׁנֵי־, שְׁנֵים־ m *two;* שְׁנֵים עָשָׂר "*two-teen*" (*twelve*)

שָׁפַךְ *spill, shed* (blood)

שָׁקֵד, שְׁקֵדִים *almond*

שָׁתָה *drink*

תָּוֶךְ, תּוֹךְ־ *midst;* בְּתוֹךְ *in the midst of, amongst*

תּוֹלְדוֹת, תּוֹלְדוֹת־ *begettings, family history*

תּוֹעֵבָה *abomination, taboo*

תְּחִלָּה *first time* בַּתְּחִלָּה *the first time, previously*

תַּחַת *instead of, for*

תָּמַהּ *be astonished; look in astonishment at* (אֶל)

תָּעָה *wander about* (lost)

TABLES OF VERB AND NOUN INFLECTION

	QAL (§ *9–11*)			NIF'AL (§ *18*)	PI'EL (§ *12*)	PU'AL (§ *12.3*)	HIṬPA'EL (§ *18*)	HIF'IL (§ *13*)	HŌF'AL (§ *13.3*)
1cs pf	שָׁמַרְתִּי	כָּבַדְתִּי	קָטַנְתִּי	נִשְׁמַרְתִּי	סִפַּרְתִּי	סֻפַּרְתִּי	הִתְאַפַּקְתִּי	הִשְׁלַכְתִּי	הָשְׁלַכְתִּי
2m	שָׁמַרְתָּ	כָּבַדְתָּ	קָטַנְתָּ	נִשְׁמַרְתָּ	סִפַּרְתָּ	סֻפַּרְתָּ	הִתְאַפַּקְתָּ	הִשְׁלַכְתָּ	הָשְׁלַכְתָּ
2f	שָׁמַרְתְּ	כָּבַדְתְּ	קָטַנְתְּ	נִשְׁמַרְתְּ	סִפַּרְתְּ	סֻפַּרְתְּ	הִתְאַפַּקְתְּ	הִשְׁלַכְתְּ	הָשְׁלַכְתְּ
3m	שָׁמַר	כָּבֵד	קָטֹן	נִשְׁמַר	סִפֵּר	סֻפַּר	הִתְאַפֵּק	הִשְׁלִיךְ	הֻשְׁלַךְ
3f	שָׁמְרָה	כָּבְדָה	קָטְנָה	נִשְׁמְרָה	סִפְּרָה	סֻפְּרָה	הִתְאַפְּקָה	הִשְׁלִיכָה	הֻשְׁלְכָה
1cpl	שָׁמַרְנוּ	כָּבַדְנוּ	קָטַנּוּ	נִשְׁמַרְנוּ	סִפַּרְנוּ	סֻפַּרְנוּ	הִתְאַפַּקְנוּ	הִשְׁלַכְנוּ	הָשְׁלַכְנוּ
2m	שְׁמַרְתֶּם	כְּבַדְתֶּם	קְטַנְתֶּם	נִשְׁמַרְתֶּם	סִפַּרְתֶּם	סֻפַּרְתֶּם	הִתְאַפַּקְתֶּם	הִשְׁלַכְתֶּם	הָשְׁלַכְתֶּם
2f	שְׁמַרְתֶּן	כְּבַדְתֶּן	קְטַנְתֶּן	נִשְׁמַרְתֶּן	סִפַּרְתֶּן	סֻפַּרְתֶּן	הִתְאַפַּקְתֶּן	הִשְׁלַכְתֶּן	הָשְׁלַכְתֶּן
3c	שָׁמְרוּ	כָּבְדוּ	קָטְנוּ	נִשְׁמְרוּ	סִפְּרוּ	סֻפְּרוּ	הִתְאַפְּקוּ	הִשְׁלִיכוּ	הֻשְׁלְכוּ
1cs impf	אֶשְׁמֹר	אֶכְבַּד	אֶקְטַן	אֵשָּׁמֵר	אֲסַפֵּר	אֲסֻפַּר	אֶתְאַפֵּק	אַשְׁלִיךְ	אֻשְׁלַךְ
2m	תִּשְׁמֹר	תִּכְבַּד	תִּקְטַן	תִּשָּׁמֵר	תְּסַפֵּר	תְּסֻפַּר	תִּתְאַפֵּק	תַּשְׁלִיךְ	תֻּשְׁלַךְ
2f	תִּשְׁמְרִי	תִּכְבְּדִי	תִּקְטְנִי	תִּשָּׁמְרִי	תְּסַפְּרִי	תְּסֻפְּרִי	תִּתְאַפְּקִי	תַּשְׁלִיכִי	תֻּשְׁלְכִי
3m	יִשְׁמֹר	יִכְבַּד	יִקְטַן	יִשָּׁמֵר	יְסַפֵּר	יְסֻפַּר	יִתְאַפֵּק	יַשְׁלִיךְ	יֻשְׁלַךְ
3f	תִּשְׁמֹר	תִּכְבַּד	תִּקְטַן	תִּשָּׁמֵר	תְּסַפֵּר	תְּסֻפַּר	תִּתְאַפֵּק	תַּשְׁלִיךְ	תֻּשְׁלַךְ
1cpl	נִשְׁמֹר	נִכְבַּד	נִקְטַן	נִשָּׁמֵר	נְסַפֵּר	נְסֻפַּר	נִתְאַפֵּק	נַשְׁלִיךְ	נֻשְׁלַךְ
2m	תִּשְׁמְרוּ	תִּכְבְּדוּ	תִּקְטְנוּ	תִּשָּׁמְרוּ	תְּסַפְּרוּ	תְּסֻפְּרוּ	תִּתְאַפְּקוּ	תַּשְׁלִיכוּ	תֻּשְׁלְכוּ
2f	תִּשְׁמֹרְנָה	תִּכְבַּדְנָה	תִּקְטַנְנָה	תִּשָּׁמַרְנָה	תְּסַפֵּרְנָה	תְּסֻפַּרְנָה	תִּתְאַפֵּקְנָה	תַּשְׁלֵכְנָה	תֻּשְׁלַכְנָה
3m	יִשְׁמְרוּ	יִכְבְּדוּ	יִקְטְנוּ	יִשָּׁמְרוּ	יְסַפְּרוּ	יְסֻפְּרוּ	יִתְאַפְּקוּ	יַשְׁלִיכוּ	יֻשְׁלְכוּ
3f	תִּשְׁמֹרְנָה	תִּכְבַּדְנָה	תִּקְטַנְנָה	תִּשָּׁמַרְנָה	תְּסַפֵּרְנָה	תְּסֻפַּרְנָה	תִּתְאַפֵּקְנָה	תַּשְׁלֵכְנָה	תֻּשְׁלַכְנָה
coh	אָ/נִשְׁמְרָה	אָ/נִכְבְּדָה	אָ/נִקְטְנָה	א/נִשָּׁמְרָה	א/נְסַפְּרָה		אֶ/נִתְאַפְּקָה	אַ/נַשְׁלִיכָה	
juss *waw*-cons								יַשְׁלֵךְ וַיַּשְׁלֵךְ	
ms imv	שְׁמֹר	כְּבַד		הִשָּׁמֵר	סַפֵּר		הִתְאַפֵּק	הַשְׁלֵךְ	
f	שְׁמְרִי	כִּבְדִי		הִשָּׁמְרִי	סַפְּרִי		הִתְאַפְּקִי	הַשְׁלִיכִי	
mpl	שִׁמְרוּ	כִּבְדוּ		הִשָּׁמְרוּ	סַפְּרוּ		הִתְאַפְּקוּ	הַשְׁלִיכוּ	
f	שְׁמֹרְנָה	כִּבְדְנָה		הִשָּׁמַרְנָה	סַפֵּרְנָה		הִתְאַפֵּקְנָה	הַשְׁלֵכְנָה	
inf abs inf cs	שָׁמוֹר (לְ)שָׁמֹר	כָּבוֹד (לְ)כָבֹד	קָטוֹן (לְ)קָטֹן	נִשְׁמוֹר, הִשָּׁמֵר (לְ)הִשָּׁמֵר	סַפֵּר, סִפֹּר (לְ)סַפֵּר		הִתְאַפֵּק (לְ)הִתְאַפֵּק	הַשְׁלֵךְ (לְ)הַשְׁלִיךְ	
ms pt f mpl f	שׁוֹמֵר שׁוֹמֶרֶת (שׁוֹמְרָה) שׁוֹמְרִים שׁוֹמְרוֹת	כָּבֵד כְּבֵדָה כְּבֵדִים כְּבֵדוֹת	יָכֹל יְכֹלָה יְכֹלִים יְכֹלוֹת	נִשְׁמָר נִשְׁמֶרֶת נִשְׁמָרִים נִשְׁמָרוֹת	מְסַפֵּר מְסַפֶּרֶת מְסַפְּרִים מְסַפְּרוֹת	מְסֻפָּר מְסֻפֶּרֶת מְסֻפָּרִים מְסֻפָּרוֹת	מִתְאַפֵּק מִתְאַפֶּקֶת מִתְאַפְּקִים מִתְאַפְּקוֹת	מַשְׁלִיךְ מַשְׁלֶכֶת (מַשְׁלִיכָה) מַשְׁלִיכִים מַשְׁלִיכוֹת	מֻשְׁלָךְ מֻשְׁלֶכֶת מֻשְׁלָכִים מֻשְׁלָכוֹת
ms pt pass f	שָׁמוּר שְׁמוּרָה								

Hollow Verbs (§ 17)

	HŎF·AL	HIF·IL	HITPOLEL	POLAL	POLEL	NIF·AL	QAL	
1cs pf	הֹפַרְתִּי	הֵפַרְתִּי	הִתְפּוֹלַלְתִּי	הוּפוֹלַלְתִּי	פּוֹלַלְתִּי	נִפְרַתִּי	פָּרַתִּי	
2m	הֹפַרְתָּ	הֵפַרְתָּ	הִתְפּוֹלַלְתָּ	הוּפוֹלַלְתָּ	פּוֹלַלְתָּ	נִפְרַתָּ	פָּרַתָּ	
2f	הֹפַרְתְּ	הֵפַרְתְּ	הִתְפּוֹלַלְתְּ	הוּפוֹלַלְתְּ	פּוֹלַלְתְּ	נִפְרַתְּ	פָּרַתְּ	
2m	הֹפַרְתֶּם	הֵפַרְתֶּם	הִתְפּוֹלַלְתֶּם	הוּפוֹלַלְתֶּם	פּוֹלַלְתֶּם	נִפְרַתֶּם	פָּרַתֶּם	
2f	הֹפַרְתֶּן	הֵפַרְתֶּן	הִתְפּוֹלַלְתֶּן	הוּפוֹלַלְתֶּן	פּוֹלַלְתֶּן	נִפְרַתֶּן	פָּרַתֶּן	
1cpl	הֹפַרְנוּ	הֵפַרְנוּ	הִתְפּוֹלַלְנוּ	הוּפוֹלַלְנוּ	פּוֹלַלְנוּ	נִפְרַנוּ	פָּרַנוּ	
3c	הֹפַרוּ	הֵפַרוּ	הִתְפּוֹלְלוּ	הוּפוֹלְלוּ	פּוֹלְלוּ	נִפְרְתוּ	פָּרְתוּ	
3m	הֹפַר	הֵפֵר	הִתְפּוֹלֵל	הוּפוֹל	פּוֹלֵל	נִפְרַת	פָּרַת	
3f	הֹפְרָה	הֵפֵרָה	הִתְפּוֹלְלָה	הוּפוֹלְלָה	פּוֹלְלָה	נִפְרְתָה	פָּרְתָה	
3m	הֹפַרוּ	הֵפֵרוּ	הִתְפּוֹלְלוּ	הוּפוֹלְלוּ	פּוֹלְלוּ	נִפְרְתוּ	פָּרְתוּ	
3f	הֹפַרְנָה	הֵפֵרְנָה	הִתְפּוֹלַלְנָה	הוּפוֹלַלְנָה	פּוֹלַלְנָה	נִפְרַתְנָה	פָּרַתְנָה	
2 & 3f	הֹפַרְתֶּן	הֵפַרְתֶּן	הִתְפּוֹלַלְתֶּן	הוּפוֹלַלְתֶּן	פּוֹלַלְתֶּן	נִפְרַתֶּן	פָּרַתֶּן	
3m	הֹפַרוּ	הֵפֵרוּ	הִתְפּוֹלְלוּ	הוּפוֹלְלוּ	פּוֹלְלוּ	נִפְרְתוּ	פָּרְתוּ	
coh	אֲהֹפַרְתֵּנוּ	אַפְרֵנוּ	אֶתְפּוֹלֵלְתֵּנוּ	אוּפוֹלַלְתֵּנוּ	אֲפוֹלֵלְתֵּנוּ	אִפָּרְתֵנוּ	אֶפְרְתֵנוּ	
juss	יֹפַר	יַפֵר				יִפָּרֵת	יִפְרַת	
wəw-cons	וַיֹּפַר	וַיַּפֵר				וַיִּפָּרֵת	וַיִּפְרַת	
ms impv	הֹפַר	הֵפֵר	הִתְפּוֹלֵל	הוּפוֹל	פּוֹלֵל	הִפָּרֵת	פְּרַת	
f	הֹפְרִי	הֵפֵרִי	הִתְפּוֹלְלִי	הוּפוֹלְלִי	פּוֹלְלִי	הִפָּרְתִי	פְּרְתִי	
mpl	הֹפְרוּ	הֵפֵרוּ	הִתְפּוֹלְלוּ	הוּפוֹלְלוּ	פּוֹלְלוּ	הִפָּרְתוּ	פְּרְתוּ	
f	הֹפַרְנָה	הֵפֵרְנָה	הִתְפּוֹלַלְנָה	הוּפוֹלַלְנָה	פּוֹלַלְנָה	הִפָּרַתְנָה	פְּרַתְנָה	
ms pt	הָפֹר	מֵפִר	מִתְפּוֹלֵל	מוּפוֹל	מְפוֹלֵל	נִפְרָת	פָּרֵת	
mpl	הֹפְרִים	מֵפִרִים	מִתְפּוֹלְלִים	מוּפוֹלְלִים	מְפוֹלְלִים	נִפְרָתִים	פָּרֵתִים	
f	הֹפְרוֹת	מֵפִרוֹת	מִתְפּוֹלְלוֹת	מוּפוֹלְלוֹת	מְפוֹלְלוֹת	נִפְרָתוֹת	פָּרֵתוֹת	
inf abs	הָפֵר	הָפֵר	הִתְפּוֹלֵל	הוּפוֹל	פּוֹלֵל	נִפְרֹת	פָּרֹת	
inf cs	(לְ)הָפֵר	(לְ)הָפִיר	הִתְפּוֹלֵל	הוּפוֹל	פּוֹלֵל	נִפְרֹת	פָּרֹת	
ms pt	הָפֵר	מֵפִיר	מִתְפּוֹלֵל	מוּפוֹל	מְפוֹלֵל	נִפְרָת	פָּרֵת	
f	הֹפֶרֶת	מֵפִירָה	מִתְפּוֹלֶלֶת	מוּפוֹלֶלֶת	מְפוֹלֶלֶת	נִפְרָתָה	פָּרֵתָה	
mpl	הֹפְרוֹת	מֵפִירוֹת	מִתְפּוֹלְלוֹת	מוּפוֹלְלוֹת	מְפוֹלְלוֹת	נִפְרָתוֹת	פָּרֵתוֹת	
f	הֹפְרוֹת	מֵפִירוֹת	מִתְפּוֹלְלוֹת	מוּפוֹלְלוֹת	מְפוֹלְלוֹת	נִפְרָתוֹת	פָּרֵתוֹת	

	QAL	NIFʿAL	PIʿEL	PUʿAL	HITPAʿEL	HIFʿIL	HÖFʿAL
1cs pf	בָּכִיתִי	נִבְנֵיתִי[1]	צִוִּיתִי (–וִּ–)	צֻוִּיתִי	הִתְרַצִּיתִי[2]	הֶרְבֵּיתִי (–בֵּ–)	הָרְבֵּיתִי
2m	בָּכִית	נִבְנֵית	צִוִּית	צֻוִּית	הִתְרַצִּית	הִרְבֵּית (–בֵּ–)	הָרְבֵּית
2f	בָּכִית	נִבְנִית	צִוִּית	צֻוִּית	הִתְרַצִּית	הִרְבִּית (–בֵּ–)	הָרְבִּית
3m	בָּכָה	נִבְנָה	צִוָּה	צֻוָּה	הִתְרַצָּה	הִרְבָּה	הָרְבָּה
3f	בָּכְתָה	נִבְנְתָה	צִוְּתָה	צֻוְּתָה	הִתְרַצְּתָה	הִרְבְּתָה	הָרְבְּתָה
1cpl	בָּכִינוּ	נִבְנִינוּ	צִוִּינוּ	צֻוִּינוּ	הִתְרַצִּינוּ	הִרְבֵּינוּ	הָרְבֵּינוּ
2m	בְּכִיתֶם	נִבְנִיתֶם	צִוִּיתֶם	צֻוִּיתֶם	הִתְרַצִּיתֶם	הִרְבֵּיתֶם (–בֵּ–)	הָרְבֵּיתֶם
2f	בְּכִיתֶן	נִבְנִיתֶן	צִוִּיתֶן	צֻוִּיתֶן	הִתְרַצִּיתֶן	הִרְבֵּיתֶן (–בֵּ–)	הָרְבֵּיתֶן
3c	בָּכוּ	נִבְנוּ	צִוּוּ	צֻוּוּ	הִתְרַצּוּ	הִרְבּוּ	הָרְבּוּ
1cs impf	אֶבְכֶּה	אֵבָּנֶה	אֲצַוֶּה	אֻצַּוֶּה	אֶתְרַצֶּה	אַרְבֶּה	אָרְבֶּה
2m	תִּבְכֶּה	תִּבָּנֶה	תְּצַוֶּה	תְּצֻוֶּה	תִּתְרַצֶּה	תַּרְבֶּה	תָּרְבֶּה
2f	תִּבְכִּי	תִּבָּנִי	תְּצַוִּי	תְּצֻוִּי	תִּתְרַצִּי	תַּרְבִּי	תָּרְבִּי
3m	יִבְכֶּה	יִבָּנֶה	יְצַוֶּה	יְצֻוֶּה	יִתְרַצֶּה	יַרְבֶּה	יָרְבֶּה
3f	תִּבְכֶּה	תִּבָּנֶה	תְּצַוֶּה	תְּצֻוֶּה	תִּתְרַצֶּה	תַּרְבֶּה	תָּרְבֶּה
1cpl	נִבְכֶּה	נִבָּנֶה	נְצַוֶּה	נְצֻוֶּה	נִתְרַצֶּה	נַרְבֶּה	נָרְבֶּה
2m	תִּבְכּוּ	תִּבָּנוּ	תְּצַוּוּ	תְּצֻוּוּ	תִּתְרַצּוּ	תַּרְבוּ	תָּרְבוּ
2f	תִּבְכֶּינָה	תִּבָּנֶינָה	תְּצַוֶּינָה	תְּצֻוֶּינָה	תִּתְרַצֶּינָה	תַּרְבֶּינָה	תָּרְבֶּינָה
3m	יִבְכּוּ	יִבָּנוּ	יְצַוּוּ	יְצֻוּוּ	יִתְרַצּוּ	יַרְבּוּ	יָרְבּוּ
3f	תִּבְכֶּינָה	תִּבָּנֶינָה	תְּצַוֶּינָה	תְּצֻוֶּינָה	תִּתְרַצֶּינָה	תַּרְבֶּינָה	תָּרְבֶּינָה
apoc	יַבְךְ	יִבֶן	יְצַו		יִתְרַץ	יֶרֶב	
ms imv	בְּכֵה	הִבָּנֵה	צַוֵּה		הִתְרַצֵּה	הַרְבֵּה	
f	בְּכִי	הִבָּנִי	צַוִּי		הִתְרַצִּי	הַרְבִּי	
mpl	בְּכוּ	הִבָּנוּ	צַוּוּ		הִתְרַצּוּ	הַרְבּוּ	
f	בְּכֶינָה	הִבָּנֶינָה	צַוֶּינָה		הִתְרַצֶּינָה	הַרְבֶּינָה	
inf abs	בָּכֹה	נִבְנֹה	צַוֹּה, צַוֵּה		הִתְרַצֵּה	הַרְבֵּה (הַרְבָּה)	
inf cs	(לְ)בָכוֹת	(לְ)הִבָּנוֹת	(לְ)צַוּוֹת		(לְ)הִתְרַצּוֹת	(לְ)הַרְבּוֹת	
ms pt	בּוֹכֶה	נִבְנֶה	מְצַוֶּה	מְצֻוֶּה	מִתְרַצֶּה	מַרְבֶּה	מָרְבֶּה
f	בּוֹכָה	נִבְנָה	מְצַוָּה	מְצֻוָּה	מִתְרַצָּה	מַרְבָּה	מָרְבָּה
mpl	בּוֹכִים	נִבְנִים	מְצַוִּים	מְצֻוִּים	מִתְרַצִּים	מַרְבִּים	מָרְבִּים
f	בּוֹכוֹת	נִבְנוֹת	מְצַוּוֹת	מְצֻוּוֹת	מִתְרַצּוֹת	מַרְבּוֹת	מָרְבּוֹת
ms pt pass	עָשׂוּי						
f	עֲשׂוּיָה						

[1] I was built

	ORIGINALLY INITIAL ו				*ORIGINALLY INITIAL* י			
	QAL				NIF'AL	HIF'IL	HŌF'AL	QAL	HIF'IL
1cs pf	יָלַדְתִּי	יָרֵאתִי	יָכֹלְתִּי		נוֹלַדְתִּי	הוֹלַדְתִּי	הוּלַדְתִּי	(יטב)	הֵיטַבְתִּי
2m					נוֹלַדְתָּ	הוֹלַדְתָּ			הֵיטַבְתָּ
2f					נוֹלַדְתְּ	הוֹלַדְתְּ			הֵיטַבְתְּ
3m					נוֹלַד	הוֹלִיד	הוּלַד		הֵיטִיב
3f					נוֹלְדָה	הוֹלִידָה			הֵיטִיבָה
1cpl					נוֹלַדְנוּ	הוֹלַדְנוּ			הֵיטַבְנוּ
2m					נוֹלַדְתֶּם	הוֹלַדְתֶּם			הֵיטַבְתֶּם
2f					נוֹלַדְתֶּן	הוֹלַדְתֶּן			הֵיטַבְתֶּן
3c					נוֹלְדוּ	הוֹלִידוּ			הֵיטִיבוּ
1cs impf	אֵלֵד	אִירָא	אוּכַל		אִוָּלֵד	אוֹלִיד	אוּלַד	אִיטַב	אֵיטִיב
2m	תֵּלֵד	תִּירָא	תּוּכַל		תִּוָּלֵד	תּוֹלִיד		תִּיטַב	תֵּיטִיב
2f	תֵּלְדִי	תִּירְאִי	תּוּכְלִי		תִּוָּלְדִי	תּוֹלִידִי		תִּיטְבִי	תֵּיטִיבִי
3m	יֵלֵד	יִירָא	יוּכַל		יִוָּלֵד	יוֹלִיד		יִיטַב	יֵיטִיב
3f	תֵּלֵד	תִּירָא	תּוּכַל		תִּוָּלֵד	תּוֹלִיד		תִּיטַב	תֵּיטִיב
1cpl	נֵלֵד	נִירָא	נוּכַל		נִוָּלֵד	נוֹלִיד		נִיטַב	נֵיטִיב
2m	תֵּלְדוּ	תִּירְאוּ	תּוּכְלוּ		תִּוָּלְדוּ	תּוֹלִידוּ		תִּיטְבוּ	תֵּיטִיבוּ
2f	תֵּלַדְנָה	תִּירֶאנָה	תּוּכֹלְנָה		תִּוָּלַדְנָה	תּוֹלַדְנָה		תִּיטַבְנָה	תֵּיטַבְנָה
3m	יֵלְדוּ	יִירְאוּ	יוּכְלוּ		יִוָּלְדוּ	יוֹלִידוּ		יִיטְבוּ	יֵיטִיבוּ
3f	תֵּלַדְנָה	תִּירֶאנָה	תּוּכֹלְנָה		תִּוָּלַדְנָה	תּוֹלַדְנָה		תִּיטַבְנָה	תֵּיטַבְנָה
waw-cons	וַתֵּלֶד	וַיַּרְא	וַיּוּכַל		וַיִּוָּלֶד	וַיּוֹלֶד		וַיִּיטַב	
ms imv	לֵד	יְרָא			הִוָּלֵד	הוֹלֵד		הֵיטַב	
f	לְדִי	יִרְאִי			הִוָּלְדִי	הוֹלִידִי		הֵיטִיבִי	
mpl	לְדוּ	יִרְאוּ			הִוָּלְדוּ	הוֹלִידוּ		הֵיטִיבוּ	
f	לֵדְנָה	יִרְאֶנָה			הִוָּלַדְנָה	הוֹלַדְנָה		הֵיטַבְנָה	
inf abs	יָלוֹד	יָרוֹא			הִוָּלֵד	הוֹלֵד		הֵיטַב	
inf cs	(לְ)לֶדֶת	(לְ)יִרְא			(לְ)הִוָּלֵד	(לְ)הוֹלִיד		(לְ)הֵיטִיב	
ms pt	יוֹלֵד	יָרֵא			נוֹלָד	מוֹלִיד	מוּלָד		מֵיטִיב
f					נוֹלֶדֶת	מוֹלִידָה			מֵיטִיבָה
mpl					נוֹלָדִים	מוֹלִידִים			מֵיטִיבִים
f					נוֹלָדוֹת	מוֹלִידוֹת			מֵיטִיבוֹת

	QAL		NIFʿAL	HIFʿIL	HŎFʿAL
1cs pf	אֹסַפְתִּי	אָסַפְתִּי	נֶאֱסַפְתִּי	הִקְבַּצְתִּי	אֻסַּפְתִּי
2m	אָסַפְתָּ		נֶאֱסַפְתָּ	הִקְבַּצְתָּ	אֻסַּפְתָּ
2f	אָסַפְתְּ		נֶאֱסַפְתְּ	הִקְבַּצְתְּ	אֻסַּפְתְּ
3m	אָסַף		נֶאֱסַף	הִקְבִּיץ	אֻסַּף
3f	אָסְפָה		נֶאֱסְפָה	הִקְבִּיצָה	אֻסְּפָה
1cpl	אָסַפְנוּ		נֶאֱסַפְנוּ	הִקְבַּצְנוּ	אֻסַּפְנוּ
2m	אֲסַפְתֶּם		נֶאֱסַפְתֶּם	הִקְבַּצְתֶּם	אֻסַּפְתֶּם
2f	אֲסַפְתֶּן		נֶאֱסַפְתֶּן	הִקְבַּצְתֶּן	אֻסַּפְתֶּן
3c	אָסְפוּ		נֶאֱסְפוּ	הִקְבִּיצוּ	אֻסְּפוּ
1cs impf	אֶאֱסֹף	אֵיכָה אֶקְבְּצֵנָּה	אֵיכָה אֵאָסֵף	אֶקְבֹּץ	אֵיכָה אֲאֻסַּף
2m	תֶּאֱסֹף	אֵיכָה תְּקַבְּצֵנָּה	אֵיכָה תֵּאָסֵף	תִּקְבֹּץ	תֵּאָסֵף
2f	תֶּאֱסְפִי	אֵיכָה תְּקַבְּצִינָה	אֵיכָה תֵּאָסְפִי	תִּקְבְּצִי	תֵּאָסְפִי
3m	יֶאֱסֹף	אֵיכָה יְקַבְּצֵנָּה	אֵיכָה יֵאָסֵף	יִקְבֹּץ	יֵאָסֵף
3f	תֶּאֱסֹף	אֵיכָה תְּקַבְּצֵנָּה	אֵיכָה תֵּאָסֵף	תִּקְבֹּץ	תֵּאָסֵף
1cpl	נֵאֱסֹף	אֵיכָה נְקַבְּצֵנָּה	אֵיכָה נֵאָסֵף	נִקְבֹּץ	נֵאָסֵף
2m	תֶּאֱסְפוּ	אֵיכָה תְּקַבְּצוּנָה	אֵיכָה תֵּאָסְפוּ	תִּקְבְּצוּ	תֵּאָסְפוּ
2f	תֶּאֱסֹפְנָה	אֵיכָה תְּקַבְּצֹנָה	אֵיכָה תֵּאָסֹפְנָה	תִּקְבֹּצְנָה	תֵּאָסֹפְנָה
3m	יֶאֱסְפוּ	אֵיכָה יְקַבְּצוּנָה	אֵיכָה יֵאָסְפוּ	יִקְבְּצוּ	יֵאָסְפוּ
3f	תֶּאֱסֹפְנָה	אֵיכָה תְּקַבְּצֹנָה	אֵיכָה תֵּאָסֹפְנָה	תִּקְבֹּצְנָה	תֵּאָסֹפְנָה
waw-cons	וָאֶאֱסֹף, וָאֶקְבֹּץ וַיֶּאֱסֹף			וַיַּקְבֵּץ	
ms imv	אֱסֹף	אֶקְבְּצָה	הֵאָסֵף	הַקְבֵּץ	הֻאַסָּף
f	אֲסֹפִי			הַקְבִּיצִי	
mpl	אִסְפוּ	אִקְבְּצוּ		הַקְבִּיצוּ	
f	אִסְפְנָה	אִקְבֹּצְנָה		הַקְבֹּצְנָה	
inf abs	אָסוֹף	קָבוֹץ	נֶאֱסֹף(?)	הַקְבֵּץ(?)	הֻאָסֹף
inf cs	לֶאֱסֹף, אֶסְפָה	קָבְצָה	הֵאָסֵף	הַקְבֵּץ	
ms pt	אוֹסֵף	אוֹסֵף		מַקְבִּיץ	מֻאָסָף
f					
mpl					
f					

HOF'AL	HIF'IL	HITPA'EL	PU'AL	PI'EL	NIF'AL	QAL	
הָמְצֹאתִי	הֵמְצֵאתִי	הִתְמַלֵּאתִי	מֻלֵּאתִי	מִלֵּאתִי	נִמְצֹאתִי	שָׁנֹאתִי	מָצָאתִי	1cs pf
הָמְצֹאתָ	הֵמְצֵאתָ	הִתְמַלֵּאתָ	מֻלֵּאתָ	מִלֵּאתָ	נִמְצֹאתָ	שָׁנֹאתָ	מָצָאתָ	2m
הָמְצֹאת	הֵמְצֵאת	הִתְמַלֵּאת	מֻלֵּאת	מִלֵּאת	נִמְצֵאת	שָׁנֵאת	מָצָאת	2f
הָמְצָא	הֵמְצִיא	הִתְמַלֵּא	מֻלָּא	מִלֵּא	נִמְצָא	שָׂנֵא	מָצָא	3m
הָמְצְאָה	הֵמְצִיאָה	הִתְמַלְּאָה	מֻלְּאָה	מִלְּאָה	נִמְצְאָה	שָׂנְאָה	מָצְאָה	3f
הָמְצֹאנוּ	הֵמְצֵאנוּ	הִתְמַלֵּאנוּ	מֻלֵּאנוּ	מִלֵּאנוּ	נִמְצֹאנוּ	שָׂנֹאנוּ	מָצָאנוּ	1cpl
הָמְצֹאתֶם	הֵמְצֵאתֶם	הִתְמַלֵּאתֶם	מֻלֵּאתֶם	מִלֵּאתֶם	נִמְצֹאתֶם	שִׂנֵאתֶם	מְצָאתֶם	2m
הָמְצֹאתֶן	הֵמְצֵאתֶן	הִתְמַלֵּאתֶן	מֻלֵּאתֶן	מִלֵּאתֶן	נִמְצֵאתֶן	שִׂנֵאתֶן	מְצָאתֶן	3f
הָמְצְאוּ	הֵמְצִיאוּ	הִתְמַלְּאוּ	מֻלְּאוּ	מִלְּאוּ	נִמְצְאוּ	שָׂנְאוּ	מָצְאוּ	3c
אָמְצָא	אַמְצִיא	אֶתְמַלֵּא	אֻמַּלָּא	אֲמַלֵּא	אֵמָּצֵא	אֶשְׂנָא	אֶמְצָא	1cs impf
תָּמְצָא	תַּמְצִיא	תִּתְמַלֵּא	תֻּמַּלָּא	תְּמַלֵּא	תִּמָּצֵא	תִּשְׂנָא	תִּמְצָא	2m
תָּמְצְאִי	תַּמְצִיאִי	תִּתְמַלְּאִי	תֻּמַּלְּאִי	תְּמַלְּאִי	תִּמָּצְאִי	תִּשְׂנְאִי	תִּמְצְאִי	2f
יָמְצָא	יַמְצִיא	יִתְמַלֵּא	יֻמַּלָּא	יְמַלֵּא	יִמָּצֵא	יִשְׂנָא	יִמְצָא	3m
תָּמְצָא	תַּמְצִיא	תִּתְמַלֵּא	תֻּמַּלָּא	תְּמַלֵּא	תִּמָּצֵא	תִּשְׂנָא	תִּמְצָא	3f
נָמְצָא	נַמְצִיא	נִתְמַלֵּא	נֻמַּלָּא	נְמַלֵּא	נִמָּצֵא	נִשְׂנָא	נִמְצָא	1cpl
תָּמְצְאוּ	תַּמְצִיאוּ	תִּתְמַלְּאוּ	תֻּמַּלְּאוּ	תְּמַלְּאוּ	תִּמָּצְאוּ	תִּשְׂנְאוּ	תִּמְצְאוּ	2m
תָּמְצֶאנָה	תַּמְצֵאנָה	תִּתְמַלֶּאנָה	תֻּמַּלֶּאנָה	תְּמַלֶּאנָה	תִּמָּצֶאנָה	תִּשְׂנֶאנָה	תִּמְצְאנָה	2f
יָמְצְאוּ	יַמְצִיאוּ	יִתְמַלְּאוּ	יֻמַּלְּאוּ	יְמַלְּאוּ	יִמָּצְאוּ	יִשְׂנְאוּ	יִמְצְאוּ	3m
תָּמְצֶאנָה	תַּמְצֵאנָה	תִּתְמַלֶּאנָה	תֻּמַּלֶּאנָה	תְּמַלֶּאנָה	תִּמָּצֶאנָה	תִּשְׂנֶאנָה	תִּמְצְאנָה	3f
	יַמְצֵא							juss
	הַמְצֵא	הִתְמַלֵּא		מַלֵּא	הִמָּצֵא	שְׂנָא	מְצָא	ms imv
	הַמְצִיאִי	הִתְמַלְּאִי		מַלְּאִי	הִמָּצְאִי	שְׂנָאִי	מִצְאִי	f
	הַמְצִיאוּ	הִתְמַלְּאוּ		מַלְּאוּ	הִמָּצְאוּ	שְׂנָאוּ	מִצְאוּ	mpl
	הַמְצֵאנָה	הִתְמַלֶּאנָה		מַלֶּאנָה	הִמָּצֶאנָה	שְׂנֶאנָה	מִצְאֶנָה	f
	הַמְצֵא (לְ)הַמְצִיא	הִתְמַלֵּא (לְ)הִתְמַלֵּא		מַלֵּא (לְ)מַלֵּא	נִמְצֹא, הִמָּצֵא (לְ)הִמָּצֵא	שָׂנוֹא (לְ)שָׂנֹא	מָצוֹא (לְ)מְצֹא	inf abs inf cs
מֻמְצָא	מַמְצִיא	מִתְמַלֵּא	מְמֻלָּא	מְמַלֵּא	נִמְצָא	רָצֹא	מוֹצֵא	ms pt
מֻמְצֵאת	מַמְצִאת	מִתְמַלֵּאת	מְמֻלֵּאת	מְמַלֵּאת	נִמְצֵאת	רָצָה	מוֹצֵאת	f
מֻמְצָאִים	מַמְצִיאִים	מִתְמַלְּאִים	מְמֻלָּאִים	מְמַלְּאִים	נִמְצָאִים	רְצֵאִים	מוֹצְאִים	mpl
מֻמְצָאוֹת	מַמְצִיאוֹת	מִתְמַלְּאוֹת	מְמֻלָּאוֹת	מְמַלְּאוֹת	נִמְצָאוֹת	רְצֵאוֹת	מוֹצְאוֹת	f
						מָצוּא		ms pt pass
						מְצוּאָה		f

	HITPA'EL	PU'AL	PI'EL	NIF'AL	QAL	HIF'IL	NIF'AL	QAL
1cs pf	אִתְגַּלֵּיתִי	גֻּלֵּיתִי	גִּלִּיתִי	נִגְלֵיתִי	גָּלִיתִי	הִגְלֵיתִי	נִגְלֵיתִי	גָּלִיתִי
2m	אִתְגַּלִּיתָ	גֻּלִּיתָ	גִּלִּיתָ	נִגְלִיתָ	גָּלִיתָ	הִגְלִיתָ	נִגְלִיתָ	גָּלִיתָ
2f	אִתְגַּלִּית	גֻּלִּית	גִּלִּית	נִגְלִית	גָּלִית	הִגְלִית	נִגְלִית	גָּלִית
3m	אִתְגַּלָּה	גֻּלָּה	גִּלָּה	נִגְלָה	גָּלָה	הִגְלָה	נִגְלָה	גָּלָה
3f	אִתְגַּלְּתָה	גֻּלְּתָה	גִּלְּתָה	נִגְלְתָה	גָּלְתָה	הִגְלְתָה	נִגְלְתָה	גָּלְתָה
1cpl	אִתְגַּלִּינוּ	גֻּלִּינוּ	גִּלִּינוּ	נִגְלִינוּ	גָּלִינוּ	הִגְלִינוּ	נִגְלִינוּ	גָּלִינוּ
2m	אִתְגַּלִּיתֶם	גֻּלִּיתֶם	גִּלִּיתֶם	נִגְלִיתֶם	גָּלִיתֶם	הִגְלִיתֶם	נִגְלִיתֶם	גָּלִיתֶם
2f	אִתְגַּלִּיתֶן	גֻּלִּיתֶן	גִּלִּיתֶן	נִגְלִיתֶן	גָּלִיתֶן	הִגְלִיתֶן	נִגְלִיתֶן	גָּלִיתֶן
3c	אִתְגַּלּוּ	גֻּלּוּ	גִּלּוּ	נִגְלוּ	גָּלוּ	הִגְלוּ	נִגְלוּ	גָּלוּ
1cs impf	אֶתְגַּלֶּה	אֲגֻלֶּה	אֲגַלֶּה	אִגָּלֶה	אֶגְלֶה	אַגְלֶה	אִגָּלֶה	אֶגְלֶה
2m	תִּתְגַּלֶּה	תְּגֻלֶּה	תְּגַלֶּה	תִּגָּלֶה	תִּגְלֶה	תַּגְלֶה	תִּגָּלֶה	תִּגְלֶה
2f	תִּתְגַּלִּי	תְּגֻלִּי	תְּגַלִּי	תִּגָּלִי	תִּגְלִי	תַּגְלִי	תִּגָּלִי	תִּגְלִי
3m	יִתְגַּלֶּה	יְגֻלֶּה	יְגַלֶּה	יִגָּלֶה	יִגְלֶה	יַגְלֶה	יִגָּלֶה	יִגְלֶה
3f	תִּתְגַּלֶּה	תְּגֻלֶּה	תְּגַלֶּה	תִּגָּלֶה	תִּגְלֶה	תַּגְלֶה	תִּגָּלֶה	תִּגְלֶה
1cpl	נִתְגַּלֶּה	נְגֻלֶּה	נְגַלֶּה	נִגָּלֶה	נִגְלֶה	נַגְלֶה	נִגָּלֶה	נִגְלֶה
2m	תִּתְגַּלּוּ	תְּגֻלּוּ	תְּגַלּוּ	תִּגָּלוּ	תִּגְלוּ	תַּגְלוּ	תִּגָּלוּ	תִּגְלוּ
2f	תִּתְגַּלֶּינָה	תְּגֻלֶּינָה	תְּגַלֶּינָה	תִּגָּלֶינָה	תִּגְלֶינָה	תַּגְלֶינָה	תִּגָּלֶינָה	תִּגְלֶינָה
3c	יִתְגַּלּוּ	יְגֻלּוּ	יְגַלּוּ	יִגָּלוּ	יִגְלוּ	יַגְלוּ	יִגָּלוּ	יִגְלוּ
juss						יַגֶל		
ms imv	הִתְגַּלֵּה	גֻּלֵּה	גַּלֵּה	הִגָּלֵה	גְּלֵה	הַגְלֵה	הִגָּלֵה	גְּלֵה
f	הִתְגַּלִּי	גֻּלִּי	גַּלִּי	הִגָּלִי	גְּלִי	הַגְלִי	הִגָּלִי	גְּלִי
mpl	הִתְגַּלּוּ	גֻּלּוּ	גַּלּוּ	הִגָּלוּ	גְּלוּ	הַגְלוּ	הִגָּלוּ	גְּלוּ
f	הִתְגַּלֶּינָה	גֻּלֶּינָה	גַּלֶּינָה	הִגָּלֶינָה	גְּלֶינָה	הַגְלֶינָה	הִגָּלֶינָה	גְּלֶינָה
inf abs .	הִתְגַּלֵּה	גֻּלֵּה	גַּלֵּה	הִגָּלֵה	גָּלֹה	הַגְלֵה	הִגָּלֵה	גָּלֹה
inf cs	הִתְגַּלּוֹת	גֻּלּוֹת	גַּלּוֹת	הִגָּלוֹת	גְּלוֹת	הַגְלוֹת	הִגָּלוֹת	גְּלוֹת
ms pt	מִתְגַּלֶּה	מְגֻלֶּה	מְגַלֶּה	נִגְלֶה	גָּלֶה	מַגְלֶה	נִגְלֶה	גָּלֶה
f	מִתְגַּלָּה	מְגֻלָּה	מְגַלָּה	נִגְלָה	גָּלָה	מַגְלָה	נִגְלָה	גָּלָה
mpl	מִתְגַּלִּים	מְגֻלִּים	מְגַלִּים	נִגְלִים	גָּלִים	מַגְלִים	נִגְלִים	גָּלִים
f	מִתְגַּלּוֹת	מְגֻלּוֹת	מְגַלּוֹת	נִגְלוֹת	גָּלוֹת	מַגְלוֹת	נִגְלוֹת	גָּלוֹת
ms pt pass	מֻתְגָּל							
f	מֻתְגָּלָה							

Final Laryngal Verbs (§24)

	QAL	NIFʿAL	PIʿEL	PUʿAL	HIṮPAʿEL	HIFʿIL	HŎFʿAL
1cs pf	שָׁלַחְתִּי	נִשְׁלַחְתִּי	שִׁלַּחְתִּי	שֻׁלַּחְתִּי	הִתְנַדַּעְתִּי	הִשְׁמַעְתִּי	הָשְׁמַעְתִּי
2m	שָׁלַחְתָּ	נִשְׁלַחְתָּ	שִׁלַּחְתָּ	שֻׁלַּחְתָּ	הִתְנַדַּעְתָּ	הִשְׁמַעְתָּ	הָשְׁמַעְתָּ
2f	שָׁלַחַתְּ	נִשְׁלַחַתְּ	שִׁלַּחַתְּ	שֻׁלַּחַתְּ	הִתְנַדַּעְתְּ	הִשְׁמַעְתְּ	הָשְׁמַעְתְּ
3m	שָׁלַח	נִשְׁלַח	שִׁלַּח	שֻׁלַּח	הִתְנַדַּע	הִשְׁמִיעַ	הָשְׁמַע
3f	שָׁלְחָה	נִשְׁלְחָה	שִׁלְּחָה	שֻׁלְּחָה	הִתְנַדְּעָה	הִשְׁמִיעָה	הָשְׁמְעָה
1cpl	שָׁלַחְנוּ	נִשְׁלַחְנוּ	שִׁלַּחְנוּ	שֻׁלַּחְנוּ	הִתְנַדַּעְנוּ	הִשְׁמַעְנוּ	הָשְׁמְעָנוּ
2m	שָׁלַחְתֶּם	נִשְׁלַחְתֶּם	שִׁלַּחְתֶּם	שֻׁלַּחְתֶּם	הִתְנַדַּעְתֶּם	הִשְׁמַעְתֶּם	הָשְׁמַעְתֶּם
2f	שָׁלַחְתֶּן	נִשְׁלַחְתֶּן	שִׁלַּחְתֶּן	שֻׁלַּחְתֶּן	הִתְנַדַּעְתֶּן	הִשְׁמַעְתֶּן	הָשְׁמַעְתֶּן
3m	שָׁלְחוּ	נִשְׁלְחוּ	שִׁלְּחוּ	שֻׁלְּחוּ	הִתְנַדְּעוּ	הִשְׁמִיעוּ	הָשְׁמְעוּ
1cp impf	אֶשְׁלַח	אִשָּׁלַח	אֲשַׁלֵּח	אֻשַּׁלַּח	אֶתְנַדַּע	אַשְׁמִיעַ	אָשְׁמַע
2m	תִּשְׁלַח	תִּשָּׁלַח	תְּשַׁלֵּח	תֻּשַּׁלַּח	תִּתְנַדַּע	תַּשְׁמִיעַ	תָּשְׁמַע
2f	תִּשְׁלְחִי	תִּשָּׁלְחִי	תְּשַׁלְּחִי	תֻּשַּׁלְּחִי	תִּתְנַדְּעִי	תַּשְׁמִיעִי	תָּשְׁמְעִי
3m	יִשְׁלַח	יִשָּׁלַח	יְשַׁלֵּח	יֻשַּׁלַּח	יִתְנַדַּע	יַשְׁמִיעַ	יָשְׁמַע
3f	תִּשְׁלַח	תִּשָּׁלַח	תְּשַׁלֵּח	תֻּשַּׁלַּח	תִּתְנַדַּע	תַּשְׁמִיעַ	תָּשְׁמַע
1cpl	נִשְׁלַח	נִשָּׁלַח	נְשַׁלֵּח	נֻשַּׁלַּח	נִתְנַדַּע	נַשְׁמִיעַ	נָשְׁמַע
2m	תִּשְׁלְחוּ	תִּשָּׁלְחוּ	תְּשַׁלְּחוּ	תֻּשַּׁלְּחוּ	תִּתְנַדְּעוּ	תַּשְׁמִיעוּ	תָּשְׁמְעוּ
2f	תִּשְׁלַחְנָה	תִּשָּׁלַחְנָה	תְּשַׁלֵּחְנָה	תֻּשַּׁלַּחְנָה	תִּתְנַדַּעְנָה	תַּשְׁמַעְנָה	תָּשְׁמַעְנָה
3m	יִשְׁלְחוּ	יִשָּׁלְחוּ	יְשַׁלְּחוּ	יֻשַּׁלְּחוּ	יִתְנַדְּעוּ	יַשְׁמִיעוּ	יָשְׁמְעוּ
3f	תִּשְׁלַחְנָה	תִּשָּׁלַחְנָה	תְּשַׁלֵּחְנָה	תֻּשַּׁלַּחְנָה	תִּתְנַדַּעְנָה	תַּשְׁמַעְנָה	תָּשְׁמַעְנָה
juss						יַשְׁמַע	
ms imv	שְׁלַח	הִשָּׁלַח	שַׁלֵּח		הִתְנַדַּע	הַשְׁמַע	
f	שִׁלְחִי	הִשָּׁלְחִי	שַׁלְּחִי		הִתְנַדְּעִי	הַשְׁמִיעִי	
mpl	שִׁלְחוּ	הִשָּׁלְחוּ	שַׁלְּחוּ		הִתְנַדְּעוּ	הַשְׁמִיעוּ	
f	שְׁלַחְנָה	הִשָּׁלַחְנָה	שַׁלֵּחְנָה		הִתְנַדַּעְנָה	הַשְׁמַעְנָה	
inf ans	שָׁלוֹחַ	נִשְׁלוֹחַ, הִשָּׁלֵחַ	שַׁלֵּחַ		הִתְנַדֵּעַ	הַשְׁמַע	
inf cs	(לְ)שָׁלֹחַ	(לְ)הִשָּׁלֵחַ	(לְ)שַׁלֵּחַ		(לְ)הִתְנַדֵּעַ	(לְ)הַשְׁמִיעַ	
ms pt	שׁוֹלֵחַ	נִשְׁלָח	מְשַׁלֵּחַ	מֻשְׁלָח	מִתְנַדֵּעַ	מַשְׁמִיעַ	מֻשְׁמָע
f	שׁוֹלַחַת	נִשְׁלַחַת	מְשַׁלַּחַת	מֻשְׁלַחַת	מִתְנַדַּעַת	מַשְׁמַעַת	מֻשְׁמַעַת
mpl	שׁוֹלְחִים	נִשְׁלָחִים	מְשַׁלְּחִים	מֻשְׁלָחִים	מִתְנַדְּעִים	מַשְׁמִיעִים	מֻשְׁמָעִים
f	שׁוֹלְחוֹת	נִשְׁלָחוֹת	מְשַׁלְּחוֹת	מֻשְׁלָחוֹת	מִתְנַדְּעוֹת	מַשְׁמִיעוֹת	מֻשְׁמָעוֹת
ms pt pass	שָׁלוּחַ						

	QAL		NIFʿAL	POLEL	POLAL	HITPOLEL	HIFʿIL	HŌFʿAL
1cs pf	סָבּוֹתִי	קָלּוֹתִי	נְסַבּוֹתִי	גּוֹלַלְתִּי	גּוֹלַלְתִּי	הִתְגּוֹלַלְתִּי	הֵסַבּוֹתִי	הוּסַבּוֹתִי
2m	סַבּוֹת	קָלּוֹתָ	נְסַבּוֹתָ	גּוֹלַלְתָּ		הִתְגּוֹלַלְתָּ	הֵסַבּוֹתָ	
2f	סַבּוֹת	קָלּוֹת	נְסַבּוֹת	גּוֹלַלְתְּ		הִתְגּוֹלַלְתְּ	הֵסַבּוֹת	
3m	סָבַב	קָל	נָסַב	גּוֹלֵל	גּוֹלַל	הִתְגּוֹלֵל	הֵסֵב	הוּסַב
3f	סָבְבָה	קָלָה	נָסְבָה	גּוֹלְלָה		הִתְגּוֹלְלָה	הֵסַבָּה	הוּסַבָּה
1cpl	סַבּוֹנוּ	קָלּוֹנוּ	נְסַבּוֹנוּ	גּוֹלַלְנוּ		הִתְגּוֹלַלְנוּ	הֵסַבּוֹנוּ	
2m	סַבּוֹתֶם	קָלּוֹתֶם	נְסַבּוֹתֶם	גּוֹלַלְתֶּם		הִתְגּוֹלַלְתֶּם	הֵסַבּוֹתֶם	
2f	סַבּוֹתֶן	קָלּוֹתֶן	נְסַבּוֹתֶן	גּוֹלַלְתֶּן		הִתְגּוֹלַלְתֶּן	הֵסַבּוֹתֶן	
3c	סָבְבוּ	קָלוּ	נָסַבּוּ	גּוֹלְלוּ		הִתְגּוֹלְלוּ	הֵסַבּוּ	הוּסַבּוּ
1cs impf	אָסֹב / אֶסֹּב	אֵקַל	אֵסַב	אֲגוֹלֵל	אֲגוֹלַל	אֶתְגּוֹלֵל	אָסֵב (אַסֵּב)	אוּסַב
2m	תָּסֹב / תִּסֹּב	תֵּקַל	תֵּסַב	תְּגוֹלֵל		תִּתְגּוֹלֵל	תָּסֵב	
2f	תָּסֹבִי / תִּסֹּבִי	תְּקַלִּי	תֵּסַבִּי	תְּגוֹלְלִי		תִּתְגּוֹלְלִי	תָּסֵבִי	
3m	יָסֹב / יִסֹּב	יֵקַל	יֵסַב	יְגוֹלֵל		יִתְגּוֹלֵל	יָסֵב	
3f	תָּסֹב / תִּסֹּב	תֵּקַל	תֵּסַב	תְּגוֹלֵל		תִּתְגּוֹלֵל	תָּסֵב	
1cpl	נָסֹב / נִסֹּב	נֵקַל	נִסַּב	נְגוֹלֵל		נִתְגּוֹלֵל	נָסֵב	
2m	תָּסֹבוּ / תִּסֹּבוּ	תִּקַּלּוּ	תִּסַּבּוּ	תְּגוֹלְלוּ		תִּתְגּוֹלְלוּ	תָּסֵבוּ	
2f	תְּסֹבֶּנָה / תִּסֹּבֶּנָה	תִּקְלֶּינָה	תִּסַּבֶּנָה	תְּגוֹלֵלְנָה		תִּתְגּוֹלֵלְנָה	תְּסֵבֶּינָה	
3m	יָסֹבוּ / יִסֹּבוּ	יֵקַלּוּ	יִסַּבּוּ	יְגוֹלְלוּ		יִתְגּוֹלְלוּ	יָסֵבוּ	
3f	תְּסֹבֶּנָה / תִּסֹּבֶּנָה	תִּקְלֶּינָה	תִּסַּבֶּנָה	תְּגוֹלֵלְנָה		תִּתְגּוֹלֵלְנָה	תְּסֵבֶּינָה	
waw-cons	וַיָּסָב							
ms imv	סֹב		הִסָּב	גּוֹלֵל		הִתְגּוֹלֵל	הָסֵב	
f	סֹבִי		הִסָּבִי	גּוֹלְלִי		הִתְגּוֹלְלִי	הָסֵבִי	
mpl	סֹבּוּ		הִסָּבּוּ	גּוֹלְלוּ		הִתְגּוֹלְלוּ	הָסֵבּוּ	
f	סְבֻּבְנָה		הִסָּבֶּנָה	גּוֹלְלֶנָה		הִתְגּוֹלֵלְנָה	הֵסֵבֶּינָה	
inf abs	סָבוֹב		הִסּוֹב	גּוֹלֵל		הִתְגּוֹלֵל	הָסֵב	
inf cs	(לְ)סֹב		(לְ)הִסָּב	(לְ)גוֹלֵל		(לְ)הִתְגּוֹלֵל	(לְ)הָסֵב	
ms pt	סוֹבֵב	קַל	נָסָב	מְגוֹלֵל	מְגוֹלָל	מִתְגּוֹלֵל	מֵסֵב	מוּסָב
f	סוֹבֶבֶת	קַלָּה	נִסֶּבָה	מְגוֹלֶלֶת	מְגוֹלֶלֶת	מִתְגּוֹלֶלֶת	מְסֵבָּה	מוּסַבָּה
mpl	סוֹבְבִים	קַלִּים	נִסָּבִים	מְגוֹלְלִים	מְגוֹלָלִים	מִתְגּוֹלְלִים	מְסֵבִּים	מוּסַבִּים
f	סוֹבְבוֹת	קַלּוֹת	נְסַבּוֹת	מְגוֹלְלוֹת	מְגוֹלָלוֹת	מִתְגּוֹלְלוֹת	מְסֵבּוֹת	מוּסַבּוֹת

| | | |

INDEX

Unless otherwise indicated, all references are to sections. Superscripts refer to footnotes. Chapter and verse followed by *n* refer to matter in the Notes on the Hebrew Text of Genesis 37, 42–45 (pp. 180–192). Hebrew words are indexed in the Glossary (pp. 197–207).

Absolute state, 6.2
Accents, 28
  disjunctive, 28.2
  and stressed syllables, 28.1, 29.2
Adjectives, 5.5–6
  order of attributive and demonstrative, 7.4
Adverbial expressions :
  by adjective, 42 : 7*n*
  by verb, 37 : 28*n*
Afformatives :
  of imperfect, 10.4
  of perfect, 9.4
Agreement :
  of adjectives, 5.5–6
  of verb with compound subject, 44 : 14*n*
Akkadian language, 10.2, *pp.* 1, 2[3]
'Álef :
  pronunciation, 1.3
  quiescence of, 17.2(a), 20.5, 21.1
Alphabet, development of, 1.6
Amarna letters, *p.* 2[3]
Apocopation, apocopated forms, 16.4(b), 19.2
Arabic language, *pp.* 1, 6–7
Aramaic :
  language, 30.2(b), *pp.* 1, 3, 4, 5
  script, 1.7
Article, 5.1–4
  elision of, 5.4
  with familiar items, 42 : 23*n*
  indefinite, 3.1[1]
  omitted in construct state, 6.3
  omitted for euphony, 43 : 14*n*
  vocalization, 2.10(b)3, 5.1–2
Ashkenazic pronunciation of *qâmeṣ*, 2.5
Aspect :
  defined, 9.3[1]
  imperfect, 10.1–3
  perfect, 9.3
Aspirates, 1.4
Assimilation :
  of *a* to *ɛ* in segolates, 26.1
  of consonants, 2.10 (b) 2 (*see also* Lengthening of consonants)
  of *nun*, 2.10(b)2, 18.2, 22
  partial, 18.5

Begaḏ kefaṯ, 1.5, 2.7(c), 2.11, *p.* 140[1]
Bible, *pp.* 173–179
  name, *p.* 173
  parts, *pp.* 173–175
  texts and editions, *pp.* 177–179
Biblical Hebrew, *pp.* 2–3, 7

Canaanite :
  alphabet, 1.6
  language, *pp.* 1, 2[2–3]
Causative :
  defined, 8.4
  hif'il, 13.1
  pi'el, 12.1
  reflexive, *p.* 141[1]
Chapter divisions of Bible, *p.* 177
Circumstantial clause :
  noun, 44 : 26*n*
  verb, 44 : 4*n*
Cognate accusative, 43 : 16*n*
Cohortative, 10.5
  in result or purpose clause, 42 : 2*n*

Commands :
negative, 10.7
positive (*see* Imperative)
Compensatory lengthening of vowels, 5.2(a), 5.3(a), 16.3, 18.2(b), 20.5, 23.1, 25.2(c)
Conditional clause, 42 : 38*n*
Conjugations (*see* Verb patterns)
Consonants, 1 (*see also B^e^gaḏ k^e^faṯ*, Emphatics, Labials, Laryngals, Lengthening of consonants, Liquids, Sibilants)
chief bearers of meaning, 2.1
latently long, 25.5(a)[1]
long, how syllabified, 25.2(b)
weak, 16.4
effect on segolate pattern, 26.7(d)
Construct state, 6
adjective in, *p.* 151[1]
absence of article in, 6.3
stress and vowel changes in, 6.1, 25
Contraction :
a-ha > ־ָה, 14.4(c)
(*a-hu* >) *aw* > *o* (וֹ), 14.4(b), 20.2(a), 20.2(c)
ay > ־ֶה/־ֵי, ־ֶה/־ֵי, 14.3, 19.1(b)
ay-ha > ־ַיִה, 14.4(c)
ayhu > *ayw* > ־ָיו, 14.4(b)
ayi > *e*, 4.5, 6.1
iy > ־ִי, 19.1(b)
אֵת* > אֶת־, 20.3[1], 21.3(c)
Copula *wâw*, *p.* 28, 37 : 25*n*

Dâgeš, 2.10–11
conjunctive, *p.* 145[1]
ḥâzâq, 2.10(b)
qal, 1.5, 2.10(a) (*see also* Spirantization)
Declarative *hif'il*, 13.1
Demonstratives, 7.3–4
Denominative *pi'el*, 12.1
Dotted letters, 37 : 12*n*
Doubling of consonants (*see* Lengthening of consonants)
Dual, 4.3, 6.2(b)

Elative *hif'il*, 13.1
Elision :
of article, 5.4
of ה in *hif'il*, *hitpa'el*, 13.1, 18.4
Emphatics, 1.4
Emphatics (*Cont.*)
partial assimilation to, 18.5
Estimative *hif'il*, 13.1
Ethiopic language, *p.* 1

Feminine gender, 4.1–2
for abstract and indefinite expressions, 42 : 7*n*
double termination in pf 3fs of final ה verbs, 19.1(d)
־ָה-termination, 4.1, 6.2(a), 9.4(c)
ת-termination :
in construct state, 6.2(a)
with infinitives, 20.3, 22.2(b)
with suffixes, 15.1

Geminate verbs, 8.5, 30
Gender, 4.1–2
Glottis, defined, 1.3
Greek(s), 1.7, *p.* 5
Groundform of verb, defined, 9.4

Ḥ^a^ṭâf (*ḥ^a^ṭâf pa̱ṯaḥ*, *ḥ^a^ṭâf segol*, *ḥ^a^ṭâf qâmeṣ*) 2.9, 23.3
before *š^e^wâ*, 23.3(d)
He (*see also* Article) :
with *mappiq*, 2.5(b)[3]
vowel letter, 2.2
Hebrew (*see also* Biblical Hebrew, Modern Hebrew, Rabbinic Hebrew) :
history of language, *pp.* 1–9
meaning of, *p.* 3[5]
Hif'il, 8.4, 13
Ḥîreq, 2.5
as changeable vowel, 2.6, 25.5(b)
for *pa̱ṯaḥ* in closed, unstressed syllable, 23.5, 25.5(a)[2], 25.6, 26.6
Hitpa'el, 18.3–5
Hiṯpolel, 8.5, 30.4
Hŏf'al, 13.3
Ḥôlem, 2.5
as changeable vowel, 2.6, 4.5, 9.4(b), 25.5(c)
position of, 2.6, *p.* 77[1]
Hollow verbs, 8.2, 17
imperfect consecutive of, 16.4
Huf'al (*see Hŏf'al*)

Imperative, 10.8
with paragogic ה, 10.9
in result or purpose clause, 42 : 2*n*
with suffixes, 15.7
Imperfect, 10.1–3
afformatives, 10.4(b)

Imperfect (*Cont.*)
as past, 10.2
preformatives, 10.4(a)
with suffixes, 15.6
Imperfect consecutive, 10.2, 16.1–4
with suffixes, 15.6(b)
Indefinite subject, 42 : 25*n*
Infinitive absolute, 11.1
as imperative, 11.2[1]
Infinitive construct, 11.2
with feminine termination, 20.3, 22.2(a)
with suffixes, 15.7
Intensive *pi'el*, 12.1
Interrogative ה, vocalization, *p.* 141, 37 : 32*n*
Interrogative sentence, word order in, 27.3(b)
Inversion of subject and predicate, 3.2, 27.3, 27.5(b)–(c)

Jussive, 10.6
with suffixes, 15.6(b)

Latin, *p.* 5
Labials, *p.* 28
Laryngals, 1.3, 23.1–4
effect on segolate pattern, 26.7(a)–(c)
effect on vowels :
following, 19.2, 24.1(a), 25.6
preceding, 19.3, 20.3, 23.2, 24.2(b), *p.* 141 (*see also* Compensatory lengthening of vowels)
furtive *pâṯaḥ* with, 2.5(b), 23.2(b)
*ḥ*ᵃ*ṭâf* with, 2.9, 23.3
not normally lengthened, 5.2(a), 16.3, 18.2(b), 23.1
Larynx, defined, 1.3
Lengthening :
of consonants, 2.10(b) (*see also* Assimilation of *nun*)
with article, 5.1
given up, 16.3, *p.* 105[1]
latent, 25.5(a)[1]
with מַה, 5.3
in *nif'al* imperfect, 18.2
in *pi'el* group, 12.2–3, 18.4
with *wâw*-consecutive, 16.3
of vowels :
compensatory (*see* Compensatory lengthening of vowels)
in pause, 29.1
under stress, 2.6, 25.3, 25.5
Letters, 1.1–2 (*see also* Alphabet)

Letters (*Cont.*)
final, 1.2
" square," 1.7
Liquids, *p.* 105[1]

Mappiq, 2.5(b)[3]
Masculine gender, 4.1–2
plural construct, 6.2(b)
Maqqef, 5.3, 28.1, 29.2(a), *p.* 145[1]
Massoretes, *p.* 178
Metathesis, 18.5
Mêṯeg, 28.2[2]
Middle *wâw/yoḏ* nouns in segolate pattern, 26.7(d)
Middle *wâw/yoḏ* verbs, 17.1[1] (*see also* Hollow verbs)
Midrash(im), defined, *p.* 5[6]
Mishnah, defined, *p.* 5[6]
Mishnaic Hebrew (*see* Rabbinic Hebrew)
Modern Hebrew, *pp.* 7–9
*b*ᵉ*gaḏ k*ᵉ*faṯ*, 1.5
emphatics, 1.4
laryngals, 1.3
mobile *š*ᵉ*wâ*, 2.7(c)
ṣêre, 2.5
vowel quantity, 2.6

Negative clauses :
noun, 42 : 34*n*
verb, 27.5(c)
Negative commands, 10.7
Nif'al, 8.3, 18.1–2
Noun structure, 4.1–3
construct state, 6
pronominal suffixes, 14, 15
Noun sentence (clause), 3
הוא as binder in, *p.* 36
negation of, 42 : 34*n*
predicate with article, 42 : 6*n*
word order, 3.2, 27.2–3
Number :
of noun, 4.2–3
of verb with compound subject, 44 : 14*n*
Numerals, syntax of, 37 : 2*n*, 43 : 15*n*
Nun :
archaic verb ending, 43 : 32*n*
assimilation of, 2.10(b)2, 22.1

Oath clause, 42 : 15*n*, 42 : 16*n*
Object :
omitted, 37 : 17*n*
particles, inflection of, 14.6
position, 27.6–8

Object (*Cont.*)
suffixes, 15.5–7, 37 : 4*n*
Objective complement, 37 : 21*n*

Paragogic ה, 10.5, 10.9
Paragraphing in Torah, *p.* 177
Participial clause after הִנֵּה, 37 : 7*n*
Participle, 11.3–5
qal passive, 11.5
with suffixes, 15.7
Particles inflected, 14.6 (*see also* Preposition)
Passive (*see also Hiṯpa'el, Hŏf'al, Nif'al, Pu'al*) :
expressed by 3 pers. indefinite, 42 : 25*n*, 43 : 34*n*
qal, old form, 8.3², 11.1²
Pâṯaḥ, 2.5
becomes *ḥîrεq*, 23.5, 25.5(a)², 25.6, 26.6
as changeable vowel, 2.6, 25.5(a), 25.8(a)
furtive, 2.5(b), 23.2(b)
as helping vowel, 19.2, 24.2(a), 26.7(c)
with laryngals (*see* Laryngals, effect on vowels)
for *ṣére* in *pi'el* pf 3ms, 12.2
for *ṣére* in *hiṯpa'el* impf, 29.1(e)
Pausal forms, 29.1
Pentateuch, *p.* 175 (*see also* Torah)
Perfect, 9.3–4
afformatives, 9.4(b)–(c)
interrupting series of impf cons, 16.2, 37 : 3*n*
with suffixes, 15.5
Perfect consecutive, 16.5–6
Person, change in in address, 42 : 13*n*
Phoenician(s), 1.7, *p.* 2
Pi'el, 8.4, 12.1–2
Pilpel, 8.5
Place-name endings (־ָן, ־ִין), 37 : 17*n*
Plural terminations, 4.2
in construct state, 6.2(b)
־וּ, 9.4(c), 10.4(b)
Polal, polel, 30.4
Postbiblical Hebrew (*see also* Rabbinic Hebrew) :
hif'il pf, 17.3(a)
Preformatives of imperfect, 10.4(a)
original vocalization, 23.5
Predicate :
inversion of (*see* Inversion)
noun, with article, 5.6, 42 : 6*n*
noun instead of adjective, 43 : 27*n*
objective, 37 : 22*n*
Pregnant construction, 42 : 28*n*
Preposition :
article elided after, 5.4
with infinitive construct, 11.2
inflections, 14.6, 15.4, 15.8
Preterit tense, 10.2, 16.1
Pronoun :
demonstrative, 7.3
independent personal, 7.1
for emphasis, 44 : 27*n*
הוּא as binder in noun sentence, *p.* 36
old 2fs אַתִּי*, 10.4(b)
object :
inflection of, 14.6
position, 27.9(b)
Pu'al, as passive of *pi'el*, 12.3
Pu'al, as passive of *qal*, 8.3²
Purpose clause, 42 : 2*n*

Qal, 9–11
defined, 8.3
old passive of, 8.3², 11.1²
Qâmeṣ, 2.5
as changeable vowel, 2.6, 25.5(a)
pronunciation, 2.5
as unchangeable vowel, 25.2
Qâmeṣ ḥâṭuf, 2.5
as changeable vowel, 25.5(c)
distinguished from *qâmeṣ*, 2.5, 28.2²
instead of *qibbuṣ*, 23.4
Qibbuṣ, 2.5
as changeable vowel, 25.5(c)

Rabbinic Hebrew
final א verbs assimilate to final ה, 21.2
literature, *pp.* 5–6
origin, *p.* 4
vowel letters, 2.3
Reciprocal clauses expressed by *hiṯpa'el*, 18.3
Reflexive :
causative, *p.* 141¹
hiṯpa'el, 18.3
nif'al, 18.1
Relative clauses, 42 : 21*n*, 45 : 4*n*
Result clause, 42 : 2*n*
Reš, normally not lengthened, 5.2, 5.3(a), 18.2(b), 23.1
Root, 8.1–2
active and stative, 9.1–2
biconsonantal, 8.2, 8.5, 30.1¹

Sεgol, 2.5
as changeable vowel, 25.5(b)

Segol (*Cont.*)
as helping vowel, 19.2, 26.1
instead of *ḥîrεq*, 23.4
Segolate nouns, 26
Semitic languages, *pp.* 1–2
consonants as chief bearers of meaning in, 2.1
derivation of term, *pp.* 1–2
triconsonantal root in, 8.1
Sentence types (*see* Interrogative sentence, Noun sentence, Verb sentence)
Septuagint, *p.* 176
Ṣére, 2.5
as changeable vowel, 2.6, 25.5(b)
replaced by *páṯaḥ*, in *pi'el* pf, *hiṯpa'el* impf, 12.2, 29.1(e)
Šᵉwâ, 2.7–8
compound (*see Ḥᵃṯáf*)
mobile, 2.7(b)–(c), 25.3, 25.5
bᵉgaḏ kᵉfaṯ spirantized following, 1.5, 2.7(c)
quiescent, 2.7(a), 25.2(b)
with laryngals, 23.3
at word-end, 2.8
Sibilants, 18.5
metathesis in *hiṯpa'el*, 18.5
unlengthened, with mobile *šᵉwâ*, *p.* 105[1]
Spirantization, 1.5, 2.7(c), *p.* 140[1]
Spelling :
defective, 2.3, 11.1[1], 37 : 7*n*
full, 2.3
Stative :
root, 9.2
verb, 9.2–4, 10.4, *p.* 57[1]
Stop, defined, 1.5
Stress :
accents mark position of, 28.1
final, 4.4
exceptions, 4.4
loss in word followed by *maqqef*, 29.2(a)
moves forward :
in noun, 25.1
in perfect consecutive, 16.6
resultant vowel changes, 2.7(b), 4.5, 25.5
in pause, 29.1
in perfect, 9.4(b)
recedes :
to avoid consecution of two main stresses, 29.2(b)
in imperfect consecutive, 16.4(a)
secondary, 6.1, 29.2[1]
stress-lengthened vowels, 25.3
Subject :
compound, construction with verb, 44 : 14*n*
indefinite, 42 : 25*n*
position (*see* Interrogative sentence, Noun sentence, Verb sentence)
Subordination of clauses, 37 : 4*n*, 37 : 25*n*
Substantive :
adjective as, 5.5
participle as, 11.4
Suffixes, pronominal, 7.2, 14, 15
derivation, 14.3–4
with imperative, 15.7(a)
with imperfect, 15.6
for indirect object, 37 : 4*n*
with infinitive, 11.2, 15.7(b)
with noun :
feminine noun, 15.1–3
irregular inflections, 14.5
masculine noun, 14
with participle, 11.4, 15.7(c)
with particles and prepositions, 14.6, 15.4, 15.8
with perfect, 15.5
refers to whole phrase, 42 : 21*n*
Šúrεq, 2.5
naturally long, unchangeable, 23.2(b), 25.2(a)
Syllable :
closed, 2.7(a), 25.2(b)
open, 16.4(a), 25.4

Tanna(im), Tannaitic literature, *p.* 5[5]
Temporal clause, 37 : 4*n*, 44 : 3,4*n*
Tense of noun sentence, 3.1 (*see also* Aspect)
Terminitive ה, *p.* 143[1]
Tiberian vocalization, 2.5–11
Torah :
content, *pp.* 173–174
structure, *pp.* 175–177

Ugarit(ic), 1.6, *pp.* 2[4], 4[5]
Uvula, defined, 1.4

Verb :
patterns, 8.3–5
with pronominal suffixes, 15.5–7
sound, 16.4
stative, 9.2
Verb sentence (clause), word order, 27.4–5
Verse division, *p.* 177
Vocalization :
development of, 2.1–4
Tiberian, 2.5–11

Voiced consonant, defined, 1.3
Vowel letters, 2.2–4
Vowels :
  changeable, 25.3–6
    differences between noun and verb, 25.8
  compensatory lengthening of (*see* Compensatory lengthening of vowels)
  contraction of (*see* Contraction)
  helping, 19.2, 24.2(a), 26.1
  in pause, 29.1
  quantity :
    in Modern Hebrew, 2.6
    naturally long, 23.2(b), 25.2
    short, 25.3
    stress-lengthened, 2.6, 25.3
  signs and pronunciation, 2.5
  unchangeable, 25.2

Wâw :
  copula, vocalization, *p.* 28, 37 : 25*n*
  initial *w* > *y*, 20.2
  as vowel letter, 2.2, 2.5(a)
Wâw-consecutive :
  with imperfect, 16.1–4
  with perfect, 16.5–6
Weak consonants, 16.4
Word order, 27 (*see also* Adjective, Interrogative sentence, Inversion, Noun sentence, Object position, Verb sentence)

Yiddish language, *p.* 7
Yod :
  quiescence, 14.4(b), 19.1
  as vowel letter, 2.2